AMSCO'S

AP Literature and Composition

Preparing for the Advanced Placement Examination

Mary Bevilacqua

Elfie Israel

Rosemary Timoney

AMSCO SCHOOL PUBLICATIONS, INC.
315 Hudson Street, New York, N.Y. 10013

ABOUT THE AUTHORS:

Mary Bevilacqua has taught AP English Literature since 1984 and has been a reader and a Table Leader for the College Board since 1996. With Dr. Israel and Dr. Timoney, she served as co-editor of the Florida *English Journal*. Mrs. Bevilacqua was Florida's English Teacher of the Year for 1991, Western High School's Teacher of the Year three times, and was recently named a Fulbright Memorial Fund Scholar. She has truly followed her life's passion as a teacher. A native New Yorker, Mrs. Bevilacqua and her husband Ralph have lived in Florida since 1973. Her family includes two sons, Greg and Guy, daughter Linda, son-in-law Frank, and grandchildren Alanna and Franklyn O'Rourke.

Elfie Israel has taught AP English Literature and English Language since 1982. An AP reader for eight years, she is currently a College Board AP consultant and vertical team trainer. Dr. Israel was Florida's English Teacher of the Year for 1998 and Nova High School's Teacher of the Year twice. She has received several writing awards from the *English Journal* and from Nova Southeastern University, and was chosen as a Fulbright Memorial Fund Scholar in 1999. An Austrian only by accident of birth, she is a transplanted Barnard graduate and a New Yorker by disposition. Dr. Israel has taught fourth grade through post-graduate level in both private and public schools. She has a daughter, Sharon, and a son, Robert. Dr. Israel and her husband live in Florida.

Rosemary Timoney began teaching AP English Literature and Composition in 1972 in Ft. Lauderdale and helped to introduce the program to numerous other high schools in Florida. She has taught AP classes for a total of 25 years, overlapping with 16 years of teaching at the university level. She also served as a reader for many years. She currently serves as an adjunct professor of English at Florida Atlantic University. Dr. Timoney was selected as Florida's Teacher of the year in Gifted Education for 1987 and as her school's Teacher of the Year a total of eight times. She has studied at Cambridge, Harvard, and Princeton Universities, and she received the Delta Kappa Gamma International Scholarship at the University of Miami for her doctoral dissertation, a study of the impact of Advanced Placement on student achievement and teacher satisfaction. She knows well the truth of the statement that teachers touch the future. Originally from Boston, Dr. Timoney has lived and taught in Florida for 30 years. Her children are Lauren and Jeffrey Upton, and her granddaughter is Alexandra.

REVIEWERS:

Cynthia Baumgartner   Ms. Baumgartner is English Supervisor and an AP English instructor at Howell High School in Farmingdale, New Jersey. Formerly English Department Chairperson at Kearny High School in Kearney, New Jersey, she has taught for 29 years in schools throughout New Jersey and New York City.

John R. Williamson   Mr. Williamson is Assistant Superintendent for Fort Thomas Schools in Ft. Thomas, Kentucky. An AP teacher for six years, he has also served as an AP Literature Reader/Consultant for The College Board. Mr. Williamson is an adjunct faculty member at the University of Kentucky, where he teaches literature, composition, and methods in teaching English.

Tracy Hall   Ms. Hall is a first year AP English teacher at Edison High School in Huntington Beach, California. She has also taught advanced eighth graders, honors freshmen, and college prep juniors in her five years of teaching.

Text and cover design: Howard S. Leiderman
Cartoons: Fred C. Pusterla
Composition: Northeastern Graphics Services, Inc.

When ordering this book, please specify:
either **R 720W** or Amsco's AP Literature and Composition

Please visit our Website at: ***www.amcopub.com***

ISBN: 1-56765-073-2 / NYC Item 56765-073-1

ACKNOWLEDGMENTS

"Lines for a Christmas Card," by Hilaire Belloc. Reprinted by permission of PFD on behalf of Hilaire Belloc. © by Hilaire Belloc.

"Reunion," by John Cheever. From *The Stories of John Cheever* by John Cheever, Copyright © 1978 by John Cheever. Used by permission of Alfred A. Knopf, a division of Random House, Inc.

"Eleven," by Sandra Cisneros. From *Woman Hollering Creek*. Copyright © 1991 by Sandra Cisneros. Published by Vintage Books, a division of Random House, Inc., and originally in hardcover by Random House, Inc. Reprinted by permission of Susan Bergholz Literary Services, New York. All rights reserved.

"l(a," by e.e. cummings. Copyright © 1958, 1986, 1991 by the Trustees for the E.E. Cummings Trust. From *Complete Poems: 1904–1962* by E.E. Cummings, edited by George J. Firmage. Used by permission of Liveright Publishing Corporation.

"A narrow fellow in the grass" (poem 986) and "I like to see it lap the miles" (poem 585), by Emily Dickinson. Reprinted by permission of the publishers and the Trustees of Amherst College from *The Poems of Emily Dickinson*, Thomas H. Johnson, Ed., Cambridge, Mass.: The Belknap Press of Harvard University Press, Copyright © 1951, 1955, 1979 by the President and Fellows of Harvard College.

"Dear John Wayne," from *Jacklight*, by Louise Erdrich, © 1984 by Louise Erdrich. Reprinted by permission of Henry Holt and Company, LLC.

"Punishment," from *Open Ground: Selected Poems 1966–1996* by Seamus Heaney. Copyright © 1998 by Seamus Heaney. Reprinted by permission of Farrar, Straus and Giroux, LLC.

Excerpt from *Obasan*, by Joy Kogawa, copyright © 1991 by Joy Kogawa. Used by permission of Doubleday, a division of Random House, Inc.

Eleanor Rigby, by John Lennon and Paul McCartney. Copyright © 1966 Sony/ATV Tunes LLC. All rights administered by Sony/ATV Music Publishing, 8 Music Square West, Nashville, TN 37203. All rights reserved. Used by permission.

"Aesop Revised by Archy," from *Archy and Mehitabel* by Don Marquis, © 1927 by Doubleday, a division of Bantam, Doubleday, Dell Publishing Group, Inc. Used by permission of Doubleday, a division of Random House, Inc.

Excerpt from *Beloved* by Toni Morrison. Reprinted by permission of International Creative Management, Inc. Copyright © 1987, Toni Morrison.

"Rite of Passage," by Sharon Olds. From *The Dead and the Living* by Sharon Olds, Copyright © 1987 by Sharon Olds. Used by permission of Alfred A. Knopf, a division of Random House, Inc.

Contents

About This Book

It's senior year, you're looking ahead to college, and you've enrolled in an AP English class to prepare for the AP English exam so you can earn college credit. What other tools do you need to succeed? First, make sure you know that there are two different AP courses and exams, and choose the right one for you. The Advanced Placement Language and Composition exam tests your ability to write in various rhetorical modes on a range of topics, as you will be required to do in your college courses and in life. The Advanced Placement English Literature and Composition Test measures your ability to read, analyze, and write insightfully about literature. Amsco's *AP Literature and Composition*, written by seasoned teachers with a combined 70 years of experience, is designed to prepare you for this test. The content you need to know—literary terms, allusions, reading strategies, writing tips, and much more—is presented in a reader-friendly style. Organized into comprehensive units, the book efficiently reviews what you've learned in class so you don't have to re-read your textbook.

This book presents strategies and tips based on the authors' years of experience as AP teachers and readers. Enhance your literary vocabulary and learn to write analyses with precision. Work at your own pace and put extra time into those areas where you need more practice. Understand the rationale behind correct answers on multiple-choice questions, and review scored student essays along with rubrics and reader comments. AP-format questions and two complete practice tests help you develop your test-taking confidence as you hone your skills. This comprehensive review text can also be an excellent resource for those motivated students who opt to take the AP exam without taking the course itself.

Everything you will find in this book has been field-tested by real AP students. As one of these students eloquently puts it, this book is "my life preserver in the infinite sea of literary ignorance. It keeps me above water, that I may see my way to shore."

PART 1
AP Overview

All About Advanced Placement: FAQ

What is the test?

The *Advanced Placement English Literature and Composition Test* is a three-hour examination prepared by Educational Testing Service for the College Board. Its purpose is to evaluate students' proficiency in analyzing and writing about literature. Based on your scores, colleges determine whether you will receive college credit. There are two sections. The first requires you to read passages and answer multiple-choice questions. The second section tests your ability to write a well-structured essay.

The multiple-choice section usually contains 53–60 questions based on four literary pieces—both prose and poetry. It is unlikely that there will be passages from works prior to the 16th century. This portion is worth 45% of the examination. You will have one hour to answer these questions.

The essay section consists of three equally weighted essays. Even though the questions are evaluated and given credit individually, you should pace yourself. That way, you will have time to put as much thought as possible into your essays (see Part 4). One question is based on a prose passage, one is based on a poem, and one is an open question relating to a literary work you select. This section is worth 55% of the examination. You will have two hours to complete it, approximately 40 minutes per question.

AP English Literature and Composition Exam

Section One	Section Two
Multiple Choice	Essay
53–60 Questions	3 Questions
One Hour	Two Hours

Why should I take the test?

If you score a 4 or 5 on the AP, you will automatically earn credit at most colleges and universities. That means you won't have to take the standard first-year English course, which will save you both time and money. In addition, you may find that you can take fewer courses in your freshman year. This will enable you to adjust to college life—and still *have* a life. Or you might decide to take elective courses that would otherwise be unavailable to you. The bottom line is that you will have more freedom to make your own choices. In addition, many colleges look more favorably on students who have taken the test.

Also, by preparing for the AP exam, you will get used to approaching your studies with the seriousness and focus that college success requires. In other words, this process will make the transition to college much smoother. Think of it as college boot camp.

How is the test graded?

The objective (multiple-choice) questions, answered on scanable answer sheets, are graded by computer. The essays, however, are graded by real live human beings, from all fifty states, the protectorates, and American schools abroad, who gather in one location. The graders are college English professors and high school teachers of Advanced Placement English. For six days they lead a semimonastic life, reading your essays.

You may be concerned about a stranger reading your examination—wondering how subjective that person might be. You can put your fears to rest. Readers are advised, cautioned, and *repeatedly* reminded to leave any personal biases at home. They must strictly follow the scoring guide, otherwise known as the *rubric*.

In order to assure that all readers adhere to the rubric, they undergo rigorous training. This training is reinforced daily throughout the reading, which ensures a valid, fair, and reliable evaluation of the essays. Each reader evaluates only one essay question (poetry, prose, or open-ended) and is guided by a question leader who has undergone extensive training and has previously served as a reader.

Each essay you write is read by three different readers. Each reader scores the essay independently, not knowing your scores from the other readers, for that or other essays.

How do they arrive at a score between 1 and 5?

"Raw scores" are converted to total number of points and eventually to a score of 1 to 5. The multiple-choice section is usually about 55 questions. To figure out your raw score, you must add the number of questions you have answered correctly (each correct answer is worth one point) and subtract 1/4 point for each question answered incorrectly. *You are not penalized for leaving a blank response*—but you cannot gain anything with a blank response, either. Working on the assumption that there were 55 multiple-choice questions, and after subtracting 1/4 point for each incorrect answer, you then multiply your raw score by 1.227. Therefore, if you had 34 right out of 55, had 16 wrong, and left 5 blank, your raw score would be 30. Multiply 30 by 1.227 and you have a total of 36.81.

Each essay is scored on a 0–9 scale. This number is then multiplied by 3.055. If you had three perfect essays with a raw score of 9 on each, this would equal 82.5. Now let's add the two together: 82.5 plus 36.81 = 119.31. This score is usually equivalent to an AP score of 5 (although this varies slightly from year to year depending on the distribution of student scores). You are part of the top 10% in the country. In 2000, grades for AP English Literature candidates were distributed as shown on the chart below.

Distribution of Grades for English Literature Candidates, 2000

	Examination Grade	Percentage Earning Grade
Extremely Well Qualified	5	10.6
Well Qualified	4	22.4
Qualified	3	35.8
Possibly Qualified	2	25.1
No Recommendation	1	6.2

Source: The College Board

How can I best study for the exam?

The best way to prepare for the AP English Literature Exam is to take an Advanced Placement Literature and Composition course. In addition, you should carefully read, review, and know at least eight works of literary merit. Develop close-reading skills, become familiar with literary terminology, and practice the skills the test covers. You also need to be a proficient writer. Understanding rhetorical strategies and being able to discuss them in writing is the key to succeeding on the exam. This book will give you essential information to help you practice this.

What if I don't have enough time to take a class?

Ideally, we advise students to take a class. When that is not possible, it's important to keep up with readings in your English classes (and review readings from past English classes), explore vocabulary, practice multiple-choice questions, and practice timed essay writing and revision techniques.

How can I figure out my weaknesses and strengths?

One indicator is your performance on other standardized tests that measure verbal skills, such as the SAT, ACT, or PSAT. You should also meet with your teacher to get his or her input on areas that need attention. Try to analyze what you do well and what you need to work on.

What should I read?

Our eleventh commandment for AP students is this:

Thou shalt not see the movie until thou hast read the book.

Reading means reading the *whole* book, in its original form. It does not mean running out to see the movie, picking up an abridged copy at the local mini-mart, or reading summaries or adolescent literature, no matter how well done. It means close reading, focusing on diction, syntax, and figurative language. A list of recommended titles is found in the appendix of this book.

Except for the open question, the prose and poetry selections will probably be new to you. The College Board, in an effort to be fair to everyone taking the examination, uses new selections each year, typically works that are not found in most high school textbooks. It is therefore to your advantage to analyze many different genres from different time periods. What you learn about analysis in one situation transfers to analysis in another.

When will the scores be released?

The scores are usually sent out in mid-July.

How do different colleges treat the AP score?

You need to contact each university or college, since policies vary and change from one year to the next.

What materials should I take to the exam?

For the essay section, you should have two pens—black or dark blue. These "AP pens" should be comfortable to use and should glide smoothly. You might even find it helpful to use the same type of pen all year. For the multiple-choice section, you should have two sharpened No. 2 pencils. (*Note:* Never use a pencil to write your essays.) You are not permitted to use a highlighter, dictionary, or thesaurus during the exam.

The College Board will provide you with all the paper you need. Scantron sheets are provided for the multiple-choice section; pink or blue books are distributed for essays. Proctors will provide extra paper if it is necessary.

Only students with documented special needs who have received prior permission from the College Board may use special equipment or have other accommodations made.

Does penmanship count?

Not officially. But don't expect to receive points if your essay is illegible.

Should I skip lines when writing my essays?

Yes, you should always skip lines. The reader will no doubt appreciate it, especially if your handwriting is very large or difficult to read.

Is it okay to cross out words/sections in the essay?

Yes. Although you should try to organize your ideas before you begin writing, you may make changes, draw arrows, and do whatever proofing you feel is necessary. The readers are advised to reward what you do well. They recognize that you are writing in a high-pressure situation and that this is a rough draft, not necessarily a finished, elegant product.

How important is grammar?

Good grammar is always important. As you will see in the chapters ahead, the scoring guidelines clearly state that poorly written essays (i.e., those with serious grammatical errors) will not receive an upper-level score.

In what order should I answer the essay questions?

Some students feel most comfortable working in the order that the questions are given. Others prefer to scan all three and begin with the one they feel most confident about. Still others know that a particular question (often one requiring poetry analysis) is the most difficult for them. They therefore answer that one last—or first. You will not be penalized for the order in which you present your essays.

How long should my essays be?

Answer each question completely and with specific references to the text for each point you make. If your handwriting is of average size, try for at least a page and a half. Essays shorter than that usually lack substance, even if they are accurate or well written. Remember, the College Board saw merit in the prompt, so your essay should show that you do as well.

How important is it to outline my essays?

Very important.

Plan, plan, plan, and plan some more. In the chapters ahead, you will learn specific strategies for planning your answers and balancing your time. If you have approximately 40 minutes in which to answer a given question, you should allot a few minutes for reading the prompt and 5 to 10 minutes for planning your answer.

Should I title my essays?

No. Titles can often be distracting, and will gain no credit.

Must my essay be five paragraphs?

The five-paragraph essay is an acceptable format for expository writing; however, an essay written in cookie-cutter fashion will probably receive only a medium score. As you develop confidence and practice the necessary skills, both your thinking and writing will reflect your growth. You will find yourself writing four- and seven-paragraph essays. You will be rewarded for breaking the mold. Creativity and originality are always to your advantage—as long as you stay focused on the topic and answer the question.

One thing is certain: Your essay should have more than one or two paragraphs, because they serve to organize ideas for the reader. They help you guide the reader's thinking.

How do I pace myself?

Wear a watch. The proctor will not inform you of the passage of time.

What is a rubric?

A rubric is a scoring guideline that helps the AP readers score your essays. It is a set of criteria that specifies what qualities should and should not be present in essays. It dictates elements of correct answers that are rewardable and establishes a norm by which all essays are measured.

The question leader presents a rubric indicating the characteristics of each possible score for an essay. The table leaders meet a day before the reading (session during which essays are scored), look at student essays, and fine-tune the rubric based on the way that year's group of students responded to the questions.

Here is a sample AP scoring rubric:

RUBRIC (Generic)

Score	Explanation
9–8	Writers of these eloquent essays clearly understand the text. These essays accurately analyze the text and the methods by which the author achieves his/her purpose. Examples include: tone, structure, point of view, or contrast. Writers of these essays demonstrate a sophisticated mastery of sentence structure, word choice, and organization. While the writing need not be flawless, it must reveal the writer's ability to address the prompt with flair and efficiency.
7–6	These essays also accurately discuss the text, but they do so with less insight than do the essays in the 9–8 range. They may misinterpret one part of the text. Their discussion of the *how* (the techniques employed) will be less well developed. While these essays are well written with a strong sense of audience, they are less sophisticated than the top-range essays. Lucid and insightful, these essays fulfill the task.
5	These essays are adequately written, yet superficial. They do not demonstrate stylistic maturity or confident control over the elements of composition. These essays discuss the text vaguely or inadequately analyze the author's techniques. They may cite stylistic techniques without sufficiently supporting how they work in developing the author's purpose.
4–3	Essays in this range are adequately written, but either summarize or misinterpret the work. Even a well-written plot summary will receive no higher than a 4. These essays may simply list stylistic techniques, providing no discussion, evidence, or support. The writing also may be significantly flawed with syntactical errors and a lack of organization. Note: Essays that refer to the movie version of the work will automatically score a 3 or lower.

2–1	These essays are poorly written and show consistent errors in diction, spelling, or syntax. They may use the passage merely as a springboard for an essay on a general topic. There is serious misinterpretation of the text. They are often too short and replete with errors, or simply illegible.
0	An essay with a score of zero is nothing more than a restatement of the prompt.
–	This symbol is reserved for the response that has nothing to do with the question. Should you decide to write about the sex life of a tsetse fly or your personal problems, your score will be a dash.

Notice that nowhere does the rubric specify a number of paragraphs, or the necessity of an introduction or conclusion. Readers are cautioned to read to the end, and to read quickly and holistically. Therefore, the essay must be focused, should have several paragraphs to indicate several points, and should get to those points quickly, succinctly, and clearly.

Can I write a good essay on a topic other than the prompt?

No. There are no choices on the essay questions. A brilliant essay on another topic will receive no credit.

Is this a difficult exam?

Yes, the examination is designed to be challenging. If this were not so, it would not be a fair test of your skills. Because you will be receiving college credit, you are expected to demonstrate college-level proficiency in all aspects of the test.

What will the essay questions ask for?

The essay questions will probably ask you how the authors use specific literary techniques to develop meaning. More importantly, this section of the exam assesses your ability to analyze a text and express your analyses in writing.

Where can I find out more about the exam?

You can visit the College Board website at **www.collegeboard.org** to download sample exam questions and a course outline and read specific scoring guidelines for previous essay questions. You will also find two practice tests at the end of this book.

On the next page is a suggested timetable for you to do your reviewing and studying for the test. Put in time and effort, and you *will* see results!

5-Week Cram Table

Week	Day	Activity	Time
1	1 & 2	Organize all English work into categories such as: vocabulary/rhetorical terms, books, poems, essays. Have a number of prompts for prose and poetry.	15–30 minutes
	3 & 4	Pick a book from the beginning of the year. Gather all notes from class lectures, or your own questions and comments from the book. Make an outline of the book, spending little time on the plot and a lot of time on theme, tone, key characters, etc.	60–90 minutes
	5	Pick a poem you have not worked on in class. Cluster/web/outline and write the first paragraph of an essay about it.	15–30 minutes
	6 & 7	GO TO THE BEACH.	all day
2	1 & 2	Go over your cluster/web/outline and try to pick out any other main points or ideas in the poem. Write at least five multiple-choice questions on the poem, using the ones in this book as a guide.	20–30 minutes
	3 & 4	Write an essay out of the cluster/web/outline you made for the poem. Try to keep within the suggested time limit that will be required on the test.	30–45 minutes
	5 & 6	Pick another book from your class. Make an outline of the book, spending little time on the plot and a lot of time on the theme, tone, key characters, etc.	60–90 minutes
	7	CHOCOLATE BREAK	the whole day
3	1 & 2	Pick a prose passage that you have not worked on in class. Cluster/web/outline the passage and write the first paragraph of an essay.	15–30 minutes
	3 & 4	Go over the cluster/web/outline you did of an essay and try to pick out any other main points or ideas from the passage.	10–20 minutes
	5	Write an essay out of the cluster/web/outline you made for the passage. Remember to watch your time.	30–45 minutes
	6	This is a good time to take a practice AP test. Allot yourself 3 hours and try one of the tests at the end of this book. Grade yourself. Then you'll know your strengths and weaknesses. Personalize this guide accordingly.	3 hours

	7	SLEEP	your choice
4	1 & 2	Pick another poem from your class. Make an outline of the poem, spending little time on the plot, and a lot of time on the theme, tone, key characters, etc.	60–90 minutes
	3 & 4	Go over the cluster/web/outline you did and try to pick out any other main points or ideas from the poem. Write some multiple-choice questions on the poem using the ones in this book as models.	30–40 minutes
	5 & 6	Write an essay based on the cluster/web/outline you made for the poem. Remember to watch your time.	30–45 minutes
	7	GO SHOPPING.	until the bank drops
5	1 & 2	Pick another book from your class. Make an outline of the book, spending little time on the plot and a lot of time on the theme, tone, key characters, etc.	60–90 minutes
	3 & 4	Write what you think could be a possible AP open question. Choose a book that you have outlined over the last couple of weeks. Cluster/web/outline and write an essay answering the prompt. **DO NOT USE YOUR NOTES! AND STAY WITHIN THE TIME LIMIT!**	no more than 45 minutes
	5	Do a complete practice AP test—use one from the back of this book. Find a quiet place with good lighting and time yourself. Do all the multiple-choice questions in 1 hour, take a five-minute break, and then do three essays: poem, prose, and open question in 2 hours.	3 hours
	6	Review the practice test you took yesterday. Make sure you understand what you did well—and what you need to work on.	as long as necessary
	7	IT'S OVER.	forever

PART 2
Literary Elements

1

Essential Literary Elements

You are taking a test that assesses your understanding of literature and ability to read and analyze critically. What does that really mean? Is it enough to have read volumes and volumes and to have memorized scores of dates, names, and plots? Can you breeze through the AP on your intelligence and determination alone?

As you can probably guess, we believe the answer to be a resounding *no*. After all, an AP score of 4 or 5 can help you bypass freshman English in many of the country's top colleges and universities. Therefore, to obtain a 4 or 5, you will be expected to demonstrate a college-level understanding of literature—and that requires much more than intelligence and determination alone: It requires critical insight. While this might seem an overwhelming task at first, it is something that can be achieved through hard work, a voracious appetite for reading, and your teacher's guidance.

As with any other endeavor, the first step toward success on the AP Literature and Composition Examination entails knowing what is expected of you. By understanding the exact requirements of your task, you will best be able to formulate a focused plan for succeeding.

Essentially, your task will be fourfold. You will be required to closely read poetry and prose, analyze the material you have read, answer multiple-choice questions, and write essays in response to specific prompts. This process is illustrated in the box below.

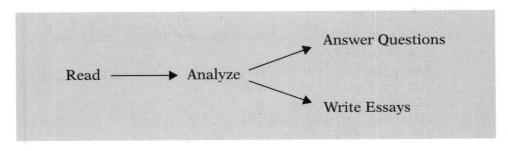

Analysis

The word *analysis* was first used by the Greek philosopher Aristotle and means "to break into pieces or parts." Analysis enables you to examine the many parts that make up a whole. In literature, these "parts" can include everything from the author's use of diction (choice of words) to syntax (the arrangement of the words on the page), to use of rhetorical devices (e.g., figurative language, symbolism, tone, and irony). A solid understanding of these literary elements will enable you to achieve a deeper level of understanding when you read—and, ultimately, a higher AP score.

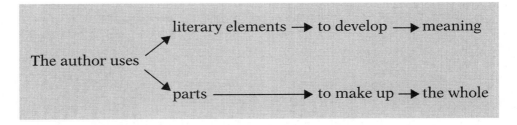

In other words, to truly gain insight into a work of literature, it is not enough merely to understand *what* that piece means; you must also understand *how* the author uses the tools at his or her disposal (the literary elements) to achieve this meaning. For example, you should be able to identify the way in which Edgar Allan Poe uses elements such as tone and diction to create a sense of morbid terror in "The Raven," or the role that irony plays in Jonathan Swift's "A Modest Proposal."

☛ *AP Tip*

When analyzing a literary piece, ask yourself the following questions:

WHAT is the meaning of the text?

HOW does the author achieve the goal?

Of course, no single AP question (multiple-choice or essay question) will ask you to identify all of the elements in one fell swoop. Rather, you will be required to answer questions that have a narrow focus. Here are examples of the types of questions to expect:

Multiple Choice:

1. In stanza two, which of the following literary devices are most in evidence?
   (A) hyperbole and allusion
   (B) analogy and alliteration
   (C) satire and irony
   (D) chiasmus and hyperbole
   (E) personification and synecdoche

Essay:
All cultures have rituals which reflect their values. From the list below, choose a novel or play containing a scene in which an important ritual takes place. In a focused essay, discuss how the scene contributes to the novel, play, or poem as a whole.

You may choose a work of similar quality that is not listed.
(A list of about 30 novels and plays typically follows the prompt.)

Being able to recognize literary elements will assure you 5 to 10 points on the multiple-choice section of the exam. Being able to identify them and intelligently discuss how they help to develop an author's thesis, focus, purpose, and meaning will give you an upper-half score in the essay portion of the exam.

In the next section of this lesson, you will have the opportunity to review those literary elements with which you are already familiar and gain a working knowledge of the ones with which you are not. Armed with this vocabulary, you will then be prepared to move on to Lessons 2 and 3 for a more in-depth exploration of such literary elements as symbolism, irony, and tone.

Although you might at first be intimidated by the lengthy list of terms that starts on page 19, don't worry. You are probably already familiar with many more of the terms than you think. Do you know the ones in the box below? See if you can match these elements to the quotes that utilize them in the activity below.

A Few Common Literary Elements

rhetorical question	apostrophe	allusion
onomatopoeia	personification	simile
iambic pentameter	metaphor	synecdoche
paradox	hyperbole	alliteration

Literary Elements: Activity 1

1. "To the tintinnabulation that so musically wells
    From the bells, bells, bells, bells,
       Bells, bells, bells—
    From the jingling and the tinkling of the bells."

2. "It was the summer of 1963. Was emancipation a fact? Was freedom a force?"

   _____

3. "The governor of Buenos Aires took everything, but left me your heart. Come; your presence will either return me to life or cause me to die of joy."

   _____

4. "In his blue gardens, men and girls came and went *like moths*. . . . Fresh faces drifted here and there *like rose petals* blown by the sad horns around the floor."

   _____

5. "I was seized with a great sense of insecurity and loneliness. I was yet liable to be taken back, and subjected to all the tortures of slavery. . . . There I was *in the midst of thousands and yet a perfect stranger.*"

   _____

6. "There shall your master have a thousand loves,
   A mother and a mistress and a friend . . ."

   _____

7. "The angels, not *half* so *happy* in *heaven*
   Went envying *her* and me."

   _____

8. "O death, where is thy sting?"

   _____

9. "The pearl *beckoned* to him; it *winked.*"

   _____

10. Lear: "Art not ashamed to look upon this *beard?*"

    _____

11. "An aged man is but a paltry thing,
    A tattered coat upon a stick, unless . . ."

    _____

12. "In Spenser, Shakespeare, Milton, Keats, we can follow the tradition of the liquid diction, the fluid movement, of Chaucer."

    _____

Turn to page 38 to see how you did.

1. Edgar Allan Poe, "The Bells" 2. Martin Luther King, Jr., "Why We Can't Wait" 3. Voltaire, *Candide* 4. F. Scott Fitzgerald, *The Great Gatsby* 5. Frederick Douglass, *Narrative of the Life of Frederick Douglass, An American Slave* 6. William Shakespeare, *All's Well That Ends Well* 7. Edgar Allen Poe, "Annabel Lee" 8. Corinthians I 9. John Steinbeck, *The Pearl* 10. William Shakespeare, *King Lear* 11. William Butler Yeats, "Sailing to Byzantium" 12. Matthew Arnold, "The Study of Poetry"

Literary Terms: A Quick Review

For each term, read the definition and the example provided. Then on a separate piece of paper practice writing your own examples.

Sample:

ad misericordiam: An appeal to the audience's sympathy; an attempt to persuade another, using a hard-luck story rather than logic or reason. For example, if you slapped your little sister and then told your parents you did it because you're under a lot of stress at school, that would be pleading *ad misericordiam*.

Example:

"Oh, Mom, everyone in my class is going to the party. Do you want me to be left out?"

alliteration: The repetition of accented consonant sounds at the beginning of words that are close to each other, usually to create an effect, rhythm, or emphasis.

> Big, bad, barking dog. The noisy gnat knit nine sweaters. (Note in the latter example that the *n* sound is the same, although the spelling is not.)

allusion: A reference in literature or in art to previous literature, history, mythology, pop culture/current events, or the Bible.

> "It may be we shall touch the Happy Isles
> And see the great Achilles, whom we knew."
>   (Tennyson, "Ulysses")

Here Tennyson alludes to the Happy Isles, or Elysium, where warriors, according to Greek mythology, spent the afterlife. He also makes an allusion to Achilles, a heroic leader in the Trojan War. Note that the title of the poem, "Ulysses," is an allusion in itself, this time to the hero of the *Odyssey*, Odysseus—aka Ulysses.

ambiguity: Quality of being intentionally unclear. Events or situations that are ambiguous can be interpreted in more than one way. This device is especially beneficial in poetry, as it tends to grace the work with the richness and depth of multiple meanings.

> "Thou still unravished bride of quietness."
>   (Keats, "Ode on a Grecian Urn")

Does "still" mean that she is dead, that she never was alive, that the vase still exists, or that she is still virginal?

anachronism: An element in a story that is out of its time frame; sometimes used to create a humorous or jarring effect. Beware: This can also occur because of careless or poor research on the author's part.

> In *Julius Caesar*, Shakespeare mentions caps, which the Romans did not wear. Or, imagine Shakespeare's Romeo (from *Romeo and Juliet*, which is set in the 16th century) riding to Mantua in a Porsche.

analogy: An analogy clarifies or explains an unfamiliar concept or object, or one that cannot be put into words, by comparing it with one which is familiar. By explaining the abstract in terms of the concrete, an analogy may force the reader to think more critically about a concept. Analogies tend to appear more often in prose than in poetry. They enliven writing by making it more interesting, entertaining, and understandable. Similes and metaphors are two specific types of analogies.

> "Knowledge always desires increase: it is like fire, which must first be kindled by some external agent, but which will afterwards propagate itself."—Samuel Johnson

> The island in *Lord of the Flies* before the boys arrived is analogous to the Garden of Eden.

analysis: The process of examining the components of a literary work.

> An analysis of Charlotte Brontë's *Jane Eyre* might make reference to the novel's Gothic setting, elements of suspense, the author's style, romantic and feminist themes, the use of symbolism and figurative language, and the novel's religious aspects.

anapest: The poetic foot (measure) that follows the pattern unaccented, unaccented, accented. The poet is usually trying to convey a rollicking, moving rhythm with this pattern.

> "I am **mon**arch of **all** I sur**vey**."
> (William Cowper, "The Solitude of Alexander Selkirk")

anecdote: A short and often personal story used to emphasize a point, to develop a character or a theme, or to inject humor.

> In F. Scott Fitzgerald's *The Great Gatsby* there is the anecdote about Tom Buchanan's liaison with the chambermaid during his honeymoon that speaks volumes about his character.

antagonist: A character who functions as a resisting force to the goals of the protagonist. The antagonist is often a villain, but in a case where the protagonist is evil (for example, in *Macbeth*), the antagonist may be virtuous (i.e., Macduff).

> Iago from *Othello* and Tybalt from *Romeo and Juliet* are antagonists.

antecedent: The word or phrase to which a pronoun refers. It often precedes a pronoun in prose (but not necessarily in poetry).

> "O that this too, too solid flesh would melt,
> Thaw and resolve itself into a dew."
>   (Shakespeare, *Hamlet*)

Flesh is the antecedent; *itself* is the pronoun that refers to it.

anticlimax: An often disappointing, sudden end to an intense situation.

> Many critics consider Jim's capture and rescue in *The Adventures of Huckleberry Finn* an example of an anticlimax.

antihero: A protagonist who carries the action of the literary piece but does not embody the classic characteristics of courage, strength, and nobility.

> Holden Caulfield in *The Catcher in the Rye*, Yossarian in *Catch-22*, and Meursault in *The Stranger* are considered to be antiheroes.

antithesis: A concept that is directly opposed to a previously presented idea.

> In the popular *Star Wars* movie trilogy, Darth Vader, of the dark side of the Force, represents ideas that are diametrically opposed (that is, antithetical) to those of the Jedi Knights.

aphorism: A terse statement that expresses a general truth or moral principle; sometimes considered a folk proverb.

> Ralph Waldo Emerson's "A foolish consistency is the hobgoblin of little minds" or Benjamin Franklin's "Early to bed, early to rise, makes a man healthy, wealthy, and wise."

apostrophe: A rhetorical (not expecting an answer) figure of direct address to a person, object, or abstract entity.

> John Donne's sonnet, "Death, Be Not Proud," or Antony's address to the dead Caesar in *Julius Caesar*.

apotheosis: Elevating someone to the level of a god.

> Many people revere Martin Luther King. Helen of Troy is considered the apotheosis of beauty.

archetype: A character, situation, or symbol that is familiar to people from all cultures because it occurs frequently in literature, myth, religion, or folklore.

> *Character:*
> The archetypal gunslinger, having been forced to kill once more, rides off into the sunset, leaving behind a town full of amazed and awestruck citizens.

Situation:
Just when it looks like the battle will be won by the enemy,
reinforcements arrive.

Symbol:
the dove of peace

aside: A short speech or remark made by an actor to the audience
rather than to the other characters, who do not hear him or her. Shakespeare's characters often share their thoughts with us in this way.

In a room full of people, Macbeth uses an aside to tell the audience his
plans: "To the castle of Macduff I will surprise . . ."

 assonance: The repeated use of a vowel sound.

How now brown cow. Twice five miles in a mazy motion.

attitude: The author's feelings toward the topic he or she is writing
about. Attitude, often used interchangeably with "tone," is usually revealed through word choice.

In her novel, *To Kill a Mockingbird,* Harper Lee uses an innocent and
unjaded child narrator to express her own attitude toward prejudice. In
Liam O'Flaherty's *The Sniper*, the narrator's objectivity and ambiguity in
referring to the men as "brothers" underscore the author's attitude
toward the horror of civil war.

aubade: A poem or song about lovers who must leave one another in
the early hours of the morning.

"Hark, hark, the lark at heaven's gate sings,
And Phoebus 'gins arise,
His steeds to water at those springs
On chaliced flowers that lies;
And winking Mary-buds begin
To ope their golden eyes;
With every thing that pretty is,
My lady sweet, arise:
Arise, arise!"
 (Shakespeare, *Cymbeline*)

ballad: A folk song or poem passed down orally that tells a story which
may be derived from an actual incident or from legend or folklore. Usually composed in four-line stanzas (quatrains) with the rhyme scheme
abcb. Ballads often contain a refrain.

Barbara Allen (anonymous)

blank verse: Unrhymed poetry of iambic pentameter (five feet
of two syllables each—unstressed and stressed); favored technique of
Shakespeare.

"When honour's at the stake. How stand I then,
That have a father kill'd, a mother stain'd . . ."
    (Shakespeare, *Hamlet)*

cacophony: Harsh, discordant sounds, unpleasant to the ear; the sound of nails scratching a blackboard is cacophonous. Cacophony is used by poets for effect.

"And squared and stuck there squares of soft white chalk,
And with a fish-tooth, scratched a moon on each,"
    (Browning, "Caliban Upon Setebos")

Notice all the *cacophonous* sounds in these two lines: *sq, st, ck, ft, t, k, sc, ch.*

carpe diem: Latin for "seize the day"; frequent in 16th- and 17th-century court poetry. Expresses the idea that you only go around once; refers to the modern saying that "life is not a dress rehearsal."

Gather ye rosebuds while ye may,
    Old time is still a-flying;
And this same flower that smiles today,
    Tomorrow will be dying.
    (Robert Herrick, "To the Virgins, to Make Much of Time")

catharsis: In his *Poetics,* Aristotle wrote that a tragedy should "arouse pity and fear in such a way as to accomplish a catharsis of such emotions in the audience." The term refers to an emotional cleansing or feeling of relief.

Many cry at the end of *Gone With the Wind,* empathizing with Scarlett O'Hara and her losses. They are experiencing catharsis.

chiasmus: The opposite of parallel construction; inverting the second of two phrases that would otherwise be in parallel form.

parallel construction: "I like the idea; I don't like its execution."
chiasmus: "I like the idea; its execution, I don't."

colloquial: Of or relating to slang or regional dialect, used in familiar everyday conversation. In writing, an informal style that reflects the way people spoke in a distinct time and/or place.

Pap's speech in Mark Twain's *The Adventures of Huckleberry Finn* is rife with colloquialisms:

"Well, I'll learn her how to meddle. And looky here—you drop that school, you hear? I'll learn people to bring up a boy to put on airs over his own father and let on to be better'n what HE is."

"'Here's what the law does: The law takes a man worth six thousand dollars and up'ards, and jams him into an old trap of a cabin like this, and lets him go round in clothes that ain't fitten for a hog. They call that govment!'"

comic relief: Humor that provides a release of tension and breaks up a more serious episode.

> Some of the nurse's speeches in *Romeo and Juliet* and the grave-digging scene in *Hamlet* provide perfectly timed comic relief.

conceit: A far-fetched comparison between two seemingly unlike things; an extended metaphor that gains appeal from its unusual or extraordinary comparison.

> "Oh stay! three lives in one flea spare
> Where we almost, yea more than married are.
> This flea is you and I, and this
> Our marriage-bed and marriage-temple is."
>   (John Donne, "The Flea")

Donne begs his beloved not to kill the flea that has bitten both of them because their blood is mingled in the flea, representing three lives (theirs and the flea's). The conceit is that he compares the flea to a marriage-bed and a temple.

connotation: Associations a word calls to mind. *House* and *home* have the same denotation, or dictionary meaning—a place to live. But *home* connotes warmth and security; *house* does not. The more connotative a piece is, the less objective its interpretation becomes. Careful, close reading often reveals the writer's intent.

> Some very connotative words are *light, fire, mother, father, rose, water, home.*

consonance: Same consonant sound in words with different vowel sounds.

> The following word groups reflect consonance: *work, stack, ark, belong, among.*

conventional character: A character with traits that are expected or traditional. Heroes are expected to be strong, adventurous, and unafraid. Conventional female characters often yearn for a husband, or once married, stay at home and care for their children; conventional men are adventurers. If married, they tend to "wear the pants in the family."

> Mrs. Bennet in Jane Austen's *Pride and Prejudice* is a conventional wife and mother who wants to see her daughters married.

couplet: Two successive rhyming lines of the same number of syllables, with matching cadence.

"Hope springs eternal in the human breast: / Man never is, but always to be blest." (Alexander Pope, *An Essay on Man*)

dactyl: Foot of poetry with three syllables, one stressed and two short or unstressed. Think of the waltz rhythm.

"Just for a handful of silver he left us."
  (Robert Browning, "The Lost Leader")

"This is the forest primeval. / The murmuring pines and the hemlocks."
  (Henry Wadsworth Longfellow, *Evangeline*)

denotation: The dictionary or literal meaning of a word or phrase. Compare to connotation.

Thin's denotation is "not fat." *Skinny* and *scrawny* also refer to someone or something that is not fat, but they imply or connote "underfed" or "unattractively thin."

dénouement: The outcome or clarification at the end of a story or play; the winding down from climax to ending.

In Nathaniel Hawthorne's *The Scarlet Letter*, the dénouement occurs after Dimmesdale's death.

deus ex machina: Literally, when the gods intervene at a story's end to resolve a seemingly impossible conflict. Refers to an unlikely or improbable coincidence; a cop-out ending.

In Greek mythology, Medea murders her children and is whisked away by a chariot of the gods. In "Sleeping Beauty," the handsome prince kisses the beautiful princess and she awakes from her seemingly eternal slumber.

diction: The deliberate choice of a style of language for a desired effect or tone. Words chosen to achieve a particular effect that is formal, informal, or colloquial.

The diction of Hawthorne in *The Scarlet Letter* is formal, whereas Mark Twain's diction is often highly informal.

Hawthorne: "The founders of a new colony, whatever Utopia of human virtue and happiness they might originally project, have invariably recognised it among their earliest practical necessities to allot a portion of the virgin soil as a cemetery, and another portion as the site of a prison."

Twain: "While Tom was eating his supper, and stealing sugar as opportunity offered, Aunt Polly asked him questions that were full of guile, and very deep—for she wanted to trap him into damaging revealments."

didactic: A didactic story, speech, essay or play is one in which the author's primary purpose is to instruct, teach or moralize.

Many of Aesop's fables fall into this category, ending with moral lessons. For example, "Gratitude and grief go not together" is the moral at the end of "The Wolf and the Crane."

distortion: An exaggeration or stretching of the truth to achieve a desired effect.

Gregor Samsa waking up as a large insect in Kafka's *The Metamorphosis* is a distortion of reality.

enjambment: In poetry, the running over of a sentence from one verse or stanza into the next without stopping at the end of the first.

I like to see it lap the Miles
And lick the Valleys up—
And stop to feed itself at Tanks—
And then, prodigious, step

Around a Pile of Mountains
    (Emily Dickinson, "I like to see it lap the Miles")

epigram: A short, clever poem with a witty turn of thought.

Oh, life is a glorious cycle of song,
A medley of extemporanea;
And love is a thing that can never go wrong;
And I am Marie of Roumania.
    (Dorothy Parker, "Comment")

epigraph: A brief quotation found at the beginning of a literary work, reflective of theme.

Toni Morrison's *Beloved* opens with the epigraph "Sixty Million and more," which says volumes about slavery. In Chinua Achebe's *Things Fall Apart,* the following lines from William Butler Yeats's poem "The Second Coming" appear at the beginning of the book, foretelling the story's theme:

"Turning and turning in the widening gyre
The falcon cannot hear the falconer;
Things fall apart; the centre cannot hold;
Mere anarchy is loosed upon the world."

epiphany: Eureka! A sudden flash of insight. A startling discovery and/or appearance; a dramatic realization.

Jocasta's sudden realization that her husband is her son is an epiphanous moment in Sophocles' *Oedipus Rex.*

epistolary novel: A novel in letter form written by one or more of the characters. The novelist can use this technique to present varying first-person points of view and does not need a narrator.

> C. S. Lewis' *The Screwtape Letters* and Alice Walker's *The Color Purple* are epistolary works.

essay: A short composition on a single topic expressing the view or interpretation of the writer on that topic. The word comes from the French *essayer* ("to attempt," "to try"). It is one of the oldest prose forms.

> Jonathan Swift's "A Modest Proposal" is one of the most famous essays ever written.

euphemism: Substitution of an inoffensive word or phrase for another that would be harsh, offensive, or embarrassing. A euphemism makes something sound better than it is but is usually more wordy than the original.

> "He passed on" rather than "he died." A dishwasher calling herself a "utensil maintenance technician."

euphony: The quality of a pleasant or harmonious sound of a word or group of words as an intended effect. Often achieved through long vowels and some consonants, such as "sh."

> "The gray sea and the long black land;
> And the yellow half-moon large and low"
>   (Robert Browning, "Meeting at Night")

farce: A kind of comedy that depends on exaggerated or improbable situations, physical disasters, and sexual innuendo to amuse the audience. Many situation comedies on television today might be called farces.

> Shakespeare's *The Taming of the Shrew*, Brandon Thomas' *Charley's Aunt*, Woody Allen's *Bullets Over Broadway*

figurative language: Unlike literal expression, figurative language uses *figures of speech* such as metaphor, simile, metonymy, personification, and hyperbole. Figurative language appeals to one's senses. Most poetry contains figurative language.

> Sweet daughter of a rough and stormy sire,
> Hoar Winter's blooming child; delightful Spring!
> Whose unshorn locks with leaves
> And swelling buds are crowned . . .
>   (Anna Laetitia Barbauld, "Ode to Spring")

first person: A character in the story tells the story, using the pronoun *I*. This is a limited point of view since the narrator can relate only events that he or she sees or is told about.

Fitzgerald's *The Great Gatsby* is written in first person. The narrator is Nick Carraway:

> "Yet high over the city our line of yellow windows must have contributed their share of human secrecy to the casual watcher in the darkening streets. . . . I saw him too, looking up and wondering. I was within and without."

flashback: Interruption of a narrative by the introduction of an earlier event or by an image of a past experience.

> Tim O'Brien's *In the Lake of the Woods* uses this technique at crucial points to help the reader better understand John Wade and what happened in the past to make him the way he is now.

flat character: A simple, one-dimensional character who remains the same, and about whom little or nothing is revealed throughout the course of the work. Flat characters may serve as symbols of types of people, similar to stereotypical characters.

> Mrs. Micawber, in Dickens' *David Copperfield*, is the ever-loyal wife who repeatedly says "I never will desert Mr. Micawber." Mme. Ratignolle is portrayed as a Mother Earth figure throughout Kate Chopin's *The Awakening*. Another example is the morally reprehensible Tom Buchanan in *The Great Gatsby*.

foil: A character whose contrasting personal characteristics draw attention to, enhance, or contrast with those of the main character. A character who, by displaying opposite traits, emphasizes certain aspects of another character.

> Fortinbras is Hamlet's foil; Tybalt serves as Romeo's.

foreshadowing: Foreshadowing hints at what is to come. It is sometimes noticeable only in hindsight, but usually it is obvious enough to set the reader wondering.

> The rosebush at the beginning of *The Scarlet Letter* foreshadows some of the tale; so does the picture of David and Bathsheba in Dimmesdale's bedroom.

free verse: Poetry that does not have regular rhythm or rhyme.

> On a flat road runs the well-train'd runner,
> He is lean and sinewy with muscular legs,
> He is thinly clothed, he leans forward as he runs,
> With lightly closed fists and arms partially rais'd.
> (Walt Whitman, *Leaves of Grass*)

genre: The category into which a piece of writing can be classified—poetry, prose, drama. Each genre has its own conventions and standards.

Robert Frost's "Stopping by Woods on a Snowy Evening" is a poem; Ernest Hemingway's *The Sun Also Rises* is prose; Arthur Miller's *The Crucible* is a drama.

heroic couplet: In poetry, a rhymed couplet written in iambic pentameter (five feet, each with one unstressed syllable followed by a stressed syllable).

> Alexander Pope used this form almost exclusively in his poetry:
> "The bookful blockhead, ignorantly read,
> With loads of learned lumber in his head."
> *(An Essay on Criticism)*

hubris: Insolence, arrogance, or pride. In Greek tragedy, the protagonist's hubris is usually the tragic flaw that leads to his or her downfall.

> The swaggering protagonist of *Oedipus Rex* is ultimately made to suffer because of his hubris. He defies moral laws by unwittingly killing his father and marrying his mother, and then bragging about how his father's murderer will be punished.

hyperbole: An extreme exaggeration for literary effect that is not meant to be interpreted literally.

> "A greenhouse arrived from Gatsby's."
> (F. Scott Fitzgerald, *The Great Gatsby*)

By using this hyperbolic term to describe the abundance of flowers sent to Nick's, where Gatsby would soon meet Daisy, Fitzgerald conveys the extent of Gatsby's anxiety about seeing Daisy and his wish for everything to be perfect.

iambic pentameter: A five-foot line made up of an unaccented followed by an accented syllable. It is the most common metric foot in English-language poetry.

> "When I have fears that I may cease to be
> Before my pen has gleaned my teeming brain."
> (John Keats, "When I Have Fears")

imagery: Anything that affects or appeals to the reader's senses: sight, sound, touch, taste, or smell.

> Wait for a while, then slip downstairs
> And bring us up some chilled white wine,
> And some blue cheese, and crackers, and some fine
> Ruddy-skinned pears.
> (Richard Wilbur, "A Late Aubade")

in medias res: In literature, a work that begins in the middle of the story.

> The *Odyssey, Medea,* and *Oedipus Rex* all begin *in medias res*.

interior monologue: A literary technique used in poetry and prose that reveals a character's unspoken thoughts and feelings. An interior monologue may be presented directly by the character, or through a narrator. (See also *stream of consciousness*.)

> That's my last Duchess painted on the wall,
> Looking as if she were alive. I call
> That piece a wonder, now: Frà Pandolf's hands
> Worked busily a day, and there she stands.
>> (Robert Browning, "My Last Duchess")

internal rhyme: A rhyme that is within the line, rather than at the end. The rhyming may also be within two lines, but again, each rhyming word will be within its line, rather than at the beginning or end.

> *Within the line:*
> A **narrow fellow** in the grass
> Occasionally rides;
>> (Emily Dickinson, "A Narrow Fellow in the Grass")

> *Within two lines:*
> We had gone back and forth all **night** on the ferry.
> It was bare and **bright** and smelled like a stable—
>> (Edna St. Vincent Millay, *Recuerdo*)

inversion: A switch in the normal word order, often used for emphasis or for rhyme scheme.

> Strong he was.

Italian (Petrarchan) sonnet: Fourteen-line poem divided into two parts: the first is eight lines (*abbaabba*) and the second is six (*cdcdcd* or *cdecde*).

From *Sonnets from the Portuguese* by Elizabeth Barrett Browning

	Rhyme Scheme
The first time that the sun rose on thine oath	a
To love me, I looked forward to the moon	b
To slacken all those bonds which seemed too soon	b
And quickly tied to make a lasting troth.	a
Quick-loving hearts, I thought, may quickly loathe;	a
And, looking on myself, I seemed not one	b
For such man's love!—more like an out-of-tune	b
Worn viol, a good singer would be wroth	a
To spoil his song with, and which, snatched in haste,	c
Is laid down at the first ill-sounding note.	d
I did not wrong myself so, but I placed	c
A wrong on *thee*. For perfect strains may float	d
'Neath master-hands, from instruments defaced—	c
And great souls, at one stroke, may do and dote.	d

litotes: Affirmation of an idea by using a negative understatement. The opposite of hyperbole.

> He was not averse to taking a drink.
> She is no saint.

lyric poem: A fairly short, emotionally expressive poem that expresses the feelings and observations of a single speaker.

> He clasps the crag with crookèd hands;
> Close to the sun in lonely lands,
> Ring'd with the azure world, he stands.
> The wrinkled sea beneath him crawls;
> He watches from his mountain walls,
> And like a thunderbolt he falls.
> (Tennyson, "The Eagle")

metamorphosis: A radical change in a character, either physical or emotional.

> In Kafka's aptly titled *The Metamorphosis*, a man is transformed overnight into a large bug. In Stevenson's *The Strange Case of Dr. Jekyll and Mr. Hyde*, a gentle doctor experiences repeated violent shifts in personality after imbibing a potent solution.

metaphor: A figure of speech which compares two dissimilar things, asserting that one thing *is* another thing, not just that one is *like* another. Compare with analogy and simile.

> "Life's but a walking shadow"
> (Shakespeare, *Macbeth*)

meter: The rhythmical pattern of a poem. Just as all words are pronounced with accented (or stressed) syllables and unaccented (or unstressed) syllables, lines of poetry are assigned similar rhythms. English poetry uses five basic metric feet.

> iamb—unstressed, stressed: *before*
> trochee—stressed, unstressed: *weather*
> anapest—unstressed, unstressed, stressed: *contradict*
> dactyl—stressed, unstressed, unstressed: *satisfy*
> spondee—equally stressed: One-word spondees are very rare in the English language; a spondaic foot is almost always two words, for example, "*Woe, woe* for England . . ."

metonymy: A figure of speech that replaces the name of something with a word or phrase closely associated with it. Similar to synecdoche (many authors do not distinguish between the two).

> "the White House" instead of "the president" or "the presidency"; "brass" to mean "military officers"; "suits" instead of "supervisors"

myth: A story, usually with supernatural significance, that explains the origins of gods, heroes, or natural phenomena. Although myths are fictional stories, they contain deeper truths, particularly about the nature of humankind.

The Greek myth of Demeter and Persephone explains the seasons.

narrative poem: A poem that tells a story.

Noyes's *The Highwayman*; Longfellow's *Paul Revere's Ride*

near, off, or slant rhyme: A rhyme based on an imperfect or incomplete correspondence of end syllable sounds.

Common in the work of Emily Dickinson, for instance:
It was not death, for I stood up,
And all the dead lie down.
It was not night, for all the bells
Put out their tongues for noon.
("It Was Not Death")

onomatopoeia: Words that imitate sounds.

meow, clip-clop, whirr, clang, pop, bang

oxymoron: A figure of speech that combines two contradictory words, placed side by side: *bitter sweet, wise fool, living death.*

Feather of lead, bright smoke, cold fire, sick health,
Still-waking sleep, that is not what it is!
(Shakespeare, *Romeo and Juliet*)

parable: A short story illustrating a moral or religious lesson.

The story of the Good Samaritan and the tale of the Prodigal Son are both parables.

paradox: A statement or situation that at first seems impossible or oxymoronic, but which solves itself and reveals meaning.

"Fair is foul and foul is fair"
(Shakespeare, *Macbeth*)

"The Child is father of the Man."
(Wordsworth, "My Heart Leaps Up When I Behold")

"My only love sprung from my only hate!"
(Shakespeare, *Romeo and Juliet*)

parallelism: The repeated use of the same grammatical structure in a sentence or a series of sentences. This device tends to emphasize what is said and thus underscores the meaning. Can also refer to two or more stories within a literary work that are told simultaneously and that re-inforce one another.

In a sentence: "I came, I saw, I conquered."(Plutarch)
We went to school, to the mall, and then to a movie.

In a literary work: Presented alternately within *King Lear* are the stories of both King Lear and his daughters, and Gloucester and his sons.

parody: A comical imitation of a serious piece with the intent of ridi-culing the author or his work.

Fielding's *Shamela* is, in large part, a parody of Richardson's overly sentimental *Pamela*. Alexander Pope's *The Rape of the Lock* parodies the epic poem. Epic poetry, especially the work of John Milton, which focused mainly on Christian parables, was particularly popular at the time Pope wrote this piece. *The Rape of the Lock* is about the foibles of 18th-century high society—hardly traditional "epic" material!

pastoral: A poem, play, or story that celebrates and idealizes the simple life of shepherds and shepherdesses. This highly conventional form was popular until the late 18th century. The term has also come to refer to an artistic work that portrays rural life in an idyllic or idealistic way.

Marlowe's "The Passionate Shepherd to His Love" and Milton's *Lycidas*

pathos: The quality of a literary work or passage which appeals to the reader's or viewer's emotions—especially pity, compassion, and sympathy. Pathos is different from the pity one feels for a tragic hero in that the pathetic figure seems to suffer through no fault of his or her own.

King Lear is a tragic figure, but Cordelia's situation represents pathos. Hamlet is tragic, Ophelia pathetic. The deaths of Romeo and Juliet and Desdemona represent pathos.

periodic sentence: A sentence that delivers its point at the end; usu-ally constructed as a subordinate clause followed by a main clause.

At the piano she practiced scales.

personification: The attribution of human characteristics to an ani-mal or to an inanimate object.

Wordsworth's daffodils "tossing their heads in a sprightly dance" in "I Wandered Lonely as a Cloud"

point of view: Perspective of the speaker or narrator in a literary work.

> First person: Charlotte Brontë's *Jane Eyre:*
> "Raw and chill was the winter morning: my teeth chattered as I hastened down the drive."
> (The story is told by Jane herself.)

> Third person limited: Bret Harte's "The Outcasts of Poker Flat":
> "Mr. Oakhurst seldom troubled himself with sentiment, still less with propriety; but he had a vague idea that the situation was not fortunate."
> (The story is told from Mr. Oakhurst's point of view, but through a narrator.)

> Third person omniscient: Jane Austen's *Pride and Prejudice:*
> "Elizabeth related to Jane the next day what had passed between Mr. Wickham and herself."
> (The story is told by an all-seeing narrator.)

protagonist: The main or principal character in a work; often considered the hero or heroine.

> Hamlet, Macbeth, Oedipus, Anna Karenina, and Tom Sawyer are the protagonists of the eponymous works in which they appear.

pun: Humorous play on words that have several meanings or words that sound the same but have different meanings.

> In *Romeo and Juliet*, Mercutio's "You will find me a grave man" refers both to the seriousness of his words and the fact that he is dying.

quatrain: Four-line stanza.

> Spirit, that made those heroes dare
>   To die, and leave their children free,
> Bid Time and Nature gently spare
>   The shaft we raise to them and thee.
>   (Ralph Waldo Emerson, "Concord Hymn")

refrain: Repetition of a line, stanza, or phrase.

> In Poe's "The Raven," the following phrase appears as a refrain: "Quoth the Raven, 'Nevermore.'"

repetition: A word or phrase used more than once to emphasize an idea.

> Coleridge's "Water, water everywhere" in *Rime of the Ancient Mariner* serves to emphasize the sense of frustration that the poet seeks to convey in describing a situation where a man is dying of thirst while surrounded by water.

rhetorical question: A question with an obvious answer, so no response is expected; used for emphasis or to make a point.

> "Were it not madness to deny
> To live because we're sure to die?"
>   (Etherege, "To a Lady Asking Him How Long He Would Love Her")

satire: The use of humor to ridicule and expose the shortcomings and failings of society, individuals, and institutions, often in the hope that change and reform are possible.

> Swift's suggestion in "A Modest Proposal" that Irish babies be butchered and sold as food to wealthy English landlords in order to alleviate poverty in Ireland is a classic example of satire because Swift was really savagely attacking the English for exploiting the Irish. Oscar Wilde's *The Importance of Being Earnest* satirizes Victorian social hypocrisy. If you've ever watched "Saturday Night Live," you've enjoyed satire.

sestet: A six-line stanza of poetry; also, the last six lines of a sonnet.

> "But thy eternal summer shall not fade,
> Nor lose possession of that fair thou ow'st,
> Nor shall Death brag thou wander'st in his shade,
> When in eternal lines to time thou grow'st;
>   So long as men can breathe, or eyes can see,
>   So long lives this, and this gives life to thee."
> (Shakespeare, Sonnet XVIII)

shift: In writing, a movement from one thought or idea to another; a change.

> Tennyson's poem *Ulysses* begins with Ulysses speaking of—and to—himself, then shifts to lines about his son (which are directed toward an unspecified audience), and finally ends with Ulysses addressing his aged mariners, urging them to continue their adventures.

simile: A comparison of unlike things using the word *like*, *as*, or *so*.

> "O, my Love is like a red, red rose."
>   (Robert Burns, "A Red, Red Rose")

soliloquy: A character's speech to the audience, in which emotions and ideas are revealed. A monologue is a soliloquy only if the character is alone on the stage.

> Macbeth's famous "Is this a dagger I see before me?" speech, Act II, scene i

sonnet, English or Shakespearean: Traditionally, a fourteen-line love poem in iambic pentameter, but in contemporary poetry, themes and form vary. A conventional Shakespearean sonnet's prescribed rhyme scheme is *abab, cdcd, efef, gg.* The final couplet *(gg)* sums up or resolves the situation described in the previous lines. Milton, Donne, Sidney, Rossetti, and the Brownings also wrote sonnets, but not necessarily in Shakespearean form. (Also see *Italian [Petrarchan] sonnet*.)

EXAMPLE: (Boldfaced syllables are accented, showing five feet per line.)

Sonnet XCI	Rhyme Scheme
Some **glory in** their **birth**, some **in** their **skill**,	a
Some **in** their **wealth**, some **in** their **body's force**;	b
Some **in** their **garments**, **though** new-**fan**gled **ill**;	a
Some **in** their **hawks** and **hounds**, some **in** their **horse**;	b
And **every hum**our **hath** his **ad**junct **pleas**ure,	c
Where**in** it **finds** a **joy** a**bove** the **rest**;	d
But **these** particulars are **not** my **measure**,	c
All **these** I **bet**ter **in** one **gen**eral **best**.	d
Thy **love** is **bet**ter **than** high **birth** to **me**,	e
Ri**cher** than **wealth**, prou**der** than **garments'** **cost**,	f
Of **more** de**light** than **hawks** and **hors**es **be**;	e
And, **having thee**, of **all** men's **pride** I **boast**.	f
Wret**ched** in **this** alone, that **thou** mayst **take**	g
All **this** away and **me** most **wretch**ed **make**.	g

stanza: A grouping of poetic lines; a deliberate arrangement of lines of poetry.

"Hope" is the thing with feathers
That perches in the soul,
And sings the tune without the words,
and never stops—at all.
   (Dickinson, " 'Hope' is the thing with feathers")

stock character: A stereotypical character; a type. The audience expects the character to have certain characteristics. Similar to conventional character and flat character.

The wicked stepmother, the dizzy blonde, and the absent-minded professor are all stock characters.

stream of consciousness: A form of writing which replicates the way the human mind works. Ideas are presented in random order; thoughts are often unfinished. (Also see *interior monologue*.)

Morrison's *Beloved*; Joyce's *Ulysses*; Faulkner's *The Sound and the Fury*

structure: The particular way in which parts of a written work are combined.

The structure of a sonnet is 14 lines. The structure of a drama is a certain number of acts and scenes. Plot structures a novel, and poems are organized by stanzas. Other structural techniques include chronological, nonlinear, stream of consciousness, and flashback.

style: The way a writer uses language. Takes into account word choice, diction, figures of speech, and so on. The writer's "voice."

> Hemingway's style is simple and straightforward. Fitzgerald's style is poetic and full of imagery. Virginia Woolf's style varies, but she is often abstract.

symbol: A concrete object, scene, or action which has deeper significance because it is associated with something else, often an important idea or theme in the work.

> Many critics feel that Melville's white whale in *Moby-Dick* symbolizes good, while Ahab the whale hunter embodies evil.

synecdoche: A figure of speech where one part represents the entire object, or vice versa.

> All *hands* on deck; lend me your *ears*.

 syntax: The way in which words, phrases, and sentences are ordered and connected.

> Many of Mark Twain's characters speak in dialect, so their syntax is ungrammatical.

> "'Jim, this is nice,' I says. 'I wouldn't want to be nowhere else but here. Pass me along another hunk of fish and some hot cornbread.'" (Twain, *The Adventures of Huckleberry Finn*)

theme: The central idea of a literary work.

> The theme of George Eliot's *Silas Marner* is that love can soften even the hardest hearts. *Candide*'s themes include Voltaire's humorous indictment of human gullibility, greed, and optimism. In Arthur Miller's *Death of a Salesman*, one of the themes is the emptiness of the American dream.

tone: Refers to the author's attitude toward the subject, and often sets the mood of the piece.

> In Chinua Achebe's *Things Fall Apart*, the depiction of the District Commissioner and other British government officials shows the author's disdain for the colonial power's rule.

tongue in cheek: Expressing a thought in a way that appears to be sincere, but is actually joking.

> "How do you like this neon cowgirl outfit? I think I'll wear it to my job interview tomorrow."

tragic flaw: Traditionally, a defect in a hero or heroine that leads to his or her downfall.

Oedipus' pride; Othello's jealousy; Hamlet's indecisiveness

transition/segue: The means to get from one portion of a poem or story to another; for instance, to another setting, to another character's viewpoint, to a later or earlier time period. It is a way of smoothly connecting different parts of a work. Authors often use transitional sentences or phrases to achieve this.

Transition phrases include "the next day," "thereafter," and other phrases that mark the passage of time. Section breaks also help segue the reader to a different place or time in the work.

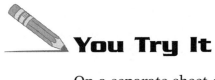

You Try It

On a separate sheet of paper, write your own examples for the literary terms you've just reviewed. The first one is done for you.

ad misericordium

My little brother was sick last night and I had to take him to the hospital. Then my dog had to go to the vet. By this time it was midnight. I typed my paper and then my printer broke down and the disk is stuck in the computer. Please give me extra time to finish my paper.

Lesson 1: Answers

Literary Elements: Activity 1

1. onomatopoeia
2. rhetorical question
3. hyperbole
4. simile
5. paradox
6. iambic pentameter
7. alliteration
8. apostrophe
9. personification
10. synecdoche
11. metaphor
12. allusion

L E S S O N

Symbolism and Allusion

> In Shakespeare's *Romeo and Juliet,* which of the following does Juliet wish for when she says, "Gallop apace, you fiery-footed steeds, / Towards Phoebus' lodging"?
>
> **(A)** Her lover's arrival
>
> **(B)** The darkness of night
>
> **(C)** The light of day
>
> **(D)** A swift journey to Romeo
>
> **(E)** Nurse's return with Romeo's message

To correctly answer this question, you must not only have a thorough understanding of the play *Romeo and Juliet,* but you must also know that Phoebus Apollo was the Greek god of the sun. According to Greek mythology, each day his "steeds" pulled his chariot across the sky; when he returned to his lodging at the end of the day, night would fall. So the correct answer is B.

You may ask why it is necessary to have knowledge of classical Greek mythology, which predates Shakespeare's work by over two thousand years, in order to fully understand *Romeo and Juliet*. Shouldn't a close reading of the play suffice? In truth, authors employ many different literary devices to give their text complex layers of meaning. In the last chapter, you reviewed a number of these. While some (e.g., alliteration, synecdoche, and assonance) develop meaning through the manipulation of textual elements, others go farther and harness the power of art, religious belief, and mythology. An author's influences are based largely on cultural traditions: The work of Shakespeare, an English playwright, is informed by the Bible and Greek mythology; a modern Chinese playwright is very likely to be influenced by Confucian or Buddhist ideas.

39

Modern American literature draws upon an increasingly rich, diverse range of cultural traditions, but the Bible and classical Greek literature and mythology are most prevalent in the literature you will encounter on the AP exam. Knowing these elements will enhance your ability to critically analyze what you read. Two important devices—symbolism and allusion—draw heavily on history, art, literature, religion, mythology, and nature. For instance, the quote above contains an allusion to Phoebus Apollo. Some allusions are so familiar to us that they have become symbolic of certain traits or events. Yet while these two devices are intertwined, there are some distinct differences.

Symbolism

In its most basic sense, a symbol is a thing that represents, or stands for, something else. The "something else" is usually abstract and intangible, such as an idea, a feeling, or a theme. Symbols enable authors to convey these intangibles concretely. This is usually quite powerful and effective. For example, consider this poem by the 18th-century poet William Blake.

The Sick Rose

O Rose, thou art sick!
    The invisible worm,
That flies in the night,
    In the howling storm,

Has found out thy bed
    Of crimson joy,
And his dark secret love
    Does thy life destroy.

On the surface, this poem appears to be about a flower that is at risk of being destroyed by some sort of worm. The poet laments the destruction of something so joyful by something so dark. The average reader might walk away with little more than an appreciation of Blake's use of language. But is that all there is? Is it possible that there is more at work here? After all, there seem to be some unanswered questions: Why is the worm *invisible*? What is the dark secret love? Let's look at some of the words. Can you separate them into categories?

Light	Dark
rose	invisible worm
bed of crimson joy	night
	howling storm
	dark secret love

A rose is a flower, but it can also be a person's name. Flowers grow in flowerbeds, but people sleep in beds, as well. A worm is similar in form to a serpent. And *a* serpent is reminiscent of *the* serpent in the Garden of Eden. Traditionally, the serpent symbolizes sin and specifically the temptation that led to the knowledge of good and evil.

Now read the poem again. Is it possible that the rose symbolizes innocence? Chastity? Could the invisible worm be a symbol of desire, tempting the innocent girl as the serpent tempted Eve? Could it signal the loss of childhood, the loss of innocence, and the emergence of sexuality?

One final note: Knowing a particular author's style and body of work is helpful when analyzing a piece with which you are unfamiliar. Christianity was the centerpiece of Blake's poetical landscape. But his views differed radically from those of most of his contemporaries. For Blake, it was not so much the existence of desire that was destructive, but the *denial* of it. In "The Sick Rose," it is not the love per se that destroys the rose, but rather the nature of that love—dark and secret, delivered through something invisible on a stormy night.

The Universal Nature of Symbolism

All cultures throughout history have created myths, folktales, and other stories to express their views about the world. Although the particulars of these tales differ from culture to culture, and from century to century, certain patterns—threads—can nevertheless be traced. Certain themes seem to recur. These timeless and universal symbols are called archetypes.

For example, the well-known tale of Cinderella has reared its head elsewhere. Whether we call the heroine Cinderella (France), Aschenputtel (Germany), or Cordelia (in *King Lear*), she is the sweet and virtuous daughter (or stepdaughter) who is tortured and betrayed by her evil sisters/stepsisters.

In most versions, virtue and sweetness are triumphant; the evil sisters are defeated. In the hands of a tragedian, the heroine may die, but she is still viewed as spiritually triumphant, and good vanquishes evil—even in the tragedy.

The story "Snow White and the Seven Dwarfs" provides a good example of the symbolism that exists in most of these tales. The heroine's name tells us of her character, purity, and innocence. The huntsman who spares her life is a man in tune with nature and life (comparable to the herdsman who spares the life of Oedipus). There are seven dwarfs—not six or eight. Seven is a mystical number, found to be significant in mythology, religion (seven deadly sins, seven sacraments), and cosmology (there were supposed to be seven concentric spheres around the Earth in the early medieval philosophical view of the universe); even in gambling, seven is considered a lucky number.

The wicked queen/witch/stepmother looks into her magic looking glass and asks, "Mirror, mirror on the wall, who is the fairest of them all?" Unfailingly, the mirror answers truthfully because, symbolically, the mirror represents truth, clarity, and self-knowledge, as well as vanity. Of course, breaking the mirror promises seven years of bad luck to the careless party (if, indeed, the careless party believes in such things).

The mirror has no choice but to "reflect" the truth, leading the queen to seek Snow White and try to poison her. With what? An apple.

The apple is a potent symbol. The juicy red apple represents love and fertility. It has also represented temptation (even though it was Milton who first called the serpent's tempting fruit an apple, it has stuck for centuries). Fortunately for Snow White, the apple symbolically leads to redemption, even though the story gives the credit to Prince Charming. This story, like most others of its genre, is filled with secondary meanings such as these. Most of the time we understand the "hidden" meaning without quite realizing it; sometimes it just lodges in the subconscious. But make no mistake: The symbols are making an impression on us at one level or another.

Allusion

Imagine that you are at a party with your friends on a Friday night. You have been having such a great time that your midnight curfew is the farthest thing from your mind. Glancing at your watch, you realize in horror that it's already 11:45! Mumbling about your need to get home by midnight, you dash for the door. Your friend calls after you, "What's wrong? Is your carriage going to turn into a pumpkin?"

Your friend is obviously making a sarcastic reference to the story of Cinderella. And since your knowledge of fairy tales is excellent, you know exactly what she means. But what if you didn't? Her words would be confusing, to say the least.

Such a reference is called an *allusion*. Authors pepper their poetry and prose with allusions because these references add depth and complexity to their work. But if you are unfamiliar with the events and works to which they allude, you will miss out on this depth and complexity.

Most of the Western literature of the past 600 years (the source of most AP literature) is characterized by the use of allusions to mythology, classical literature, history, and the Bible. Why is this? As you know, authors write with their audiences firmly in mind. After all, complex layers of meaning are wasted if they fall on deaf ears. Most published Western writers of the past 600 years wrote for an audience that—like the authors themselves—had been steeped in those traditions.

However, such allusions are not relegated solely to works of the past. For example, did you know that Luke Skywalker is a modern incarnation of the Greek god Phoebus Apollo? Luke (from the Latin word for "light") is the "skywalker," striding with his light across the expanse of the Empire. Many of the allusions that enrich classic literature continue to appear in the popular music, film, and literature of today.

Allusion: Seeing It in Action

Now read the following excerpts from the poem *L'Allegro* by John Milton. For 370 years, scholars have praised this poem, trying to understand its complex meanings. *L'Allegro*, which means "the cheerful man," contains

152 lines describing how the cheerful man spends his happy days in the sunny countryside and his cheery nights at the parties and theater performances in the lively city. For the record, everything in this poem is in marked contrast to its companion piece, *Il Penseroso*, which is about the meditative man who spends his days browsing among his beloved books and his nights in meditative walking through the woods. The following are the first 40 and the last nine lines of the poem.

L'Allegro

by John Milton

Hence, loathed Melancholy,
Of <u>Cerberus</u> and blackest Midnight born
In <u>Stygian</u> cave forlorn
'Mongst horrid shapes, and shrieks, and sights unholy!
5   Find out some <u>uncouth</u> cell,
Where brooding Darkness spreads his jealous wings,
And the night raven sings;
There, under <u>ebon</u> shades and low-browed rocks,
As ragged as thy locks,
10   In dark <u>Cimmerian</u> desert ever dwell.
But come, thou Goddess fair and free,
In heaven <u>yclept</u> <u>Euphrosyne</u>,
And by men heart-easing Mirth;
Whom lovely <u>Venus</u> at a birth,
15   With two sister Graces more,
To ivy-crownèd <u>Bacchus</u> bore:
Or whether (as some sager sing)
The frolic wind that breathes the spring,
<u>Zephyr</u>, with <u>Aurora</u> playing,
20   As he met her once a-Maying,
There, on beds of violets blue,
And fresh-blown roses washed in dew,
Filled her with thee, a daughter fair,
So <u>buxom</u>, blithe, and debonair.
25   Haste thee, Nymph, and bring with thee
Jest, and youthful Jollity,
And <u>Quips and Cranks</u> and Wanton Wiles,
Nods and Becks and wreathed Smiles,
Such as hang on <u>Hebe</u>'s cheek,
30   And love to live in dimple sleek;
Sport that wrinkled Care derides,
And Laughter holding both his sides.
Come, and trip it, as you go,
On the light fantastic toe;
35   And in thy right hand lead with thee,
The mountain-nymph, sweet Liberty;
And, if I give thee honour due,
Mirth, admit me of thy crew,
To live with her, and live with thee,
40   In unreproved pleasures free . . .

. . . The hidden soul of harmony;
That Orpheus' self may heave his head
From golden slumber on a bed
Of heaped Elysian flowers, and hear
45   Such strains as would have won the ear
Of Pluto to have quite set free
His half-regained Eurydice.
These delights if thou canst give,
Mirth, with thee I mean to live.

Analysis: *L'Allegro*

Can you summarize Milton's poem? Don't worry if you can't. It is filled with complex language and imagery. When confronted with difficult pieces such as this, it is often hard to know where to start. The task can seem overwhelming.

As discussed on page 16, to analyze means to break into parts. You can begin an analysis by first isolating specific literary devices and then examining how they are used to contribute to the poem's meaning. A reader familiar with classical allusions would be able to glean quite a bit of information from Milton's choice of words. That reader might quickly generate the following list.

Cerberus: the three-headed dog/monster who guards the gate of Hades

Stygian cave: The Styx is one of the five major rivers in classical hell.

uncouth: strange, dreadful

ebon: black, dark (like ebony)

Cimmerian: Morpheus, the god of sleep, was supposed to have a cave in this proverbially dark land of Cimmeria.

yclept: archaic way of saying "named"

Euphrosyne: goddess of mirth (joy)

Venus: the goddess of love, supposedly the mother of Euphrosyne

Bacchus: god of revelry, the father of Euphrosyne, at least in one myth

Zephyr (the warm nurturing wind) and **Aurora** (the goddess of dawn) are Mirth's parents in another myth. In any case, Mirth is the offspring of happy, positive parents.

buxom: jolly; lively; here, means "full of gaiety"

Quips and Cranks: smart jests and clever witticisms

Hebe: goddess of youth who pours nectar into Jove's (Jupiter's) cup

Using the explanations in the list above, see if you can paraphrase each line of the poem. The first one is done for you.

1. "Hence, loathed Melancholy, / Of Cerebus and blackest Midnight born" *(lines 1–2)*

   First, the cheerful man tells Melancholy to go away. This poor, sad creature was born of Cerberus and darkest midnight.

2. "In Stygian cave forlorn / 'Mongst horrid shapes, and shrieks, and sights unholy!" *(lines 3–4)*

_____

_____

3. "Find out some uncouth cell, / Where brooding Darkness spreads his jealous wings," *(lines 5–6)*

_____

_____

4. "And the night raven sings; / There, under ebon shades and low-browed rocks," *(lines 7–8)*

_____

_____

5. "As ragged as thy locks, / In dark Cimmerian desert ever dwell."*(lines 9–10)*

_____

_____

6. "But come, thou Goddess fair and free, / In heaven yclept Euphrosyne," *(lines 11–12)*

_____

_____

7. "And by men heart-easing Mirth; / Whom lovely Venus, at a birth," *(lines 13–14)*

_____

_____

8. "With two sister Graces more, / To ivy-crownèd Bacchus bore:" *(lines 15–16)*

_____

_____

9. "Or whether (as some sager sing) / The frolic wind that breathes the spring, / Zephyr, with Aurora playing, / As he met her once a-Maying," *(lines 17–20)*

_____

_____

10. "There, on beds of violets blue, / And fresh-blown roses washed in dew, / Filled her with thee, a daughter fair, / So buxom, blithe, and debonair." *(lines 21–24)*

_____

_____

11. "Haste thee, Nymph, and bring with thee / Jest, and youthful Jollity, / And Quips and Cranks and Wanton Wiles / Nods and Becks and wreathed Smiles," *(lines 25–28)*

_____

_____

12. "Such as hang on Hebe's cheek, / And love to live in dimple sleek;" *(lines 29–30)*

_____

_____

Now can you tell what this complex poem is saying? Basically, Milton has taken all these lines to say: "Go away Melancholy and all the dark and sad things that accompany you, and welcome Mirth (joy or jollity), daughter of parents who bring happiness."

Symbolism and Allusion: Activity 1

Usually reserved for gravestones, an epitaph sums up a person's life or achievements in a few well-chosen lines. It can also help you test your knowledge of many of the mythological, classical, literary, and biblical characters with whom you must be familiar.

Write epitaphs for the characters below. The first few, written by other AP students, are done for you.

1. Achilles

    a. Fighting and killing have been my whole life,
       But why did I fight this war over another's wife?

    b. With all the ingenuity in the Greek army's fleet
       You'd think they'd invent armor for the feet.

    c. Never trust a woman.

2. Clytemnestra

    My husband was away for years numbering ten,
    But when he came home, I shouldn't have done him in.

3. Iphigenia

    My father sent for me saying he had given me away,
    So in my homeland I no longer wanted to stay.
    But when I went to him what a terrible deed he performed—
    He sacrificed me so there would be no more storm.

4. Brutus

    _____

    _____

    _____

5. Hester Prynne

_____

_____

_____

6. Pip

_____

_____

_____

7. Ophelia

_____

_____

_____

8. Tom Sawyer

_____

_____

_____

9. Herod

_____

_____

_____

10. Zeus

_____

_____

_____

Symbolism and Allusion: Activity 2

The analogies below are based on mythological, literary, and biblical characters. For each one, choose the answer that best completes the relationship. (Answers are on page 63.)

1. Solomon : wisdom :: Hermes :
  (A) honesty
  (B) humor
  (C) malevolence
  (D) swiftness

2. Whitney : cotton gin :: Daedalus :
  (A) conundrum
  (B) Icarus

(C) labyrinth
(D) minotaur

3. Hercules : weakness :: Penelope :
   (A) infidelity
   (B) infirmity
   (C) marriage
   (D) strength

4. Damocles : sword :: Sisyphus :
   (A) fire
   (B) pendulum
   (C) stone
   (D) hill

5. Electra : Oedipus :: David :
   (A) Absalom
   (B) Bathsheba
   (C) Saul
   (D) Goliath

6. Job : faith :: Cain :
   (A) flock
   (B) greed
   (C) envy
   (D) pride

7. Newcastle : coals :: swine :
   (A) bacon
   (B) pearls
   (C) purse
   (D) stitches

A Profusion of Allusions

The following characters and events are common allusions in poetry and prose. Knowing them well will help you raise your AP score.

Abraham and Isaac: In Genesis, Abraham was asked by God to sacrifice his beloved son, Isaac. Abraham made ready to obey. At the last moment, his hand was stayed by an angel of the Lord. Isaac was spared and Abraham received the Lord's blessing. This story is symbolic of man's willingness to make the ultimate sacrifice to demonstrate his faith and trust in God. It is also symbolic of the idea that faith shall be rewarded.

Absalom: In Samuel II, Absalom was David's favorite son who was killed in battle while attempting to usurp his father's throne. David grieved: "O my son Absalom, my son, my son Absalom!" The word alludes to paternal grief, and to a lost and faithless son. William Faulkner used *Absalom! Absalom!* as the title of a novel.

Achilles: In Greek legend, Achilles was the hero of Homer's *Iliad* who was the model of valor and beauty. He slew the Trojan hero Hector but was himself invulnerable to wounds because his mother Thetis had held him by the heel and dipped him in the river Styx. Later he was slain by Paris who shot an arrow into his heel, which had not gotten wet. Today the term "Achilles' heel" refers to the vulnerable part of a person's character.

Agamemnon: In Greek mythology, he was the king who sacrificed his daughter Iphigenia to win the gods' favor for his war against Troy. Also father of Orestes and Electra and unfaithful husband of Clytemnestra.

Antigone: Daughter of Oedipus who performed funeral rites over her brother Polynices in defiance of Creon's order. Her story can be seen as symbolic of the choice between the gods' authority and civil authority, or the choice between justice and law.

Armageddon: In Revelation, which predicts apocalypse, Armageddon is the location of the final cosmic battle between the forces of good and evil. The term is often used in literature to refer to an apocalyptic climax, or to a time of judgment.

Atalanta: In Greek mythology, she was a huntress who promised to marry any man who could outrun her in a footrace. She was defeated by Hippomenes, who threw three golden apples to distract her as she ran. She is the archetype of speed, strength, and daring foiled by a trick of the intellect.

Atlas: In Greek mythology, Atlas was one of the Titans who rebelled against Zeus. As punishment for his actions, he was condemned to forever hold up the heavens on his shoulder (literally: "has the weight of the world on his shoulders").

blind leading the blind: "And if the blind lead the blind, both shall fall into the ditch." In the Bible, blindness frequently represents a lack of spiritual enlightenment. This particular reference from Matthew implies that wisdom cannot be attained through the teachings of the unenlightened.

burning bush: In Exodus, God used this device to catch Moses' attention when he wished to assign him the task of bringing the Israelites out of Egypt. Because the bush burns but is not consumed, this tale is symbolic of initial reluctance, followed by proof of authoritative truth. The burning bush also represents physical proof of divinity.

by bread alone: In Matthew, Christ said "Man shall not live by bread alone, but by every word . . . of God." In other words, not all human needs are met by food; human kindness is important too. (An example is Lear's "O! Reason not the need" speech.) Also refers to the idea that faith can provide spiritual sustenance.

Cain and Abel: In Genesis, Cain murdered his brother Abel out of jealousy. This became a theological reference to innocent blood, and the archetypal brother-versus-brother conflict.

camel through a needle's eye: Jesus criticized the Pharisees for striving to strain out a gnat, yet being willing to swallow a camel. In Matthew and Luke, he stated that it would be easier for a camel to pass through the eye of a needle than for a rich man to get into heaven.

Cassandra: In Greek mythology, Cassandra was a daughter of Priam, king of Troy, who possessed the gift of prophecy but was fated by Apollo never to be believed. As an allusion, she represents an accurate but unheeded prophet of doom.

cast the first stone: In John, a woman caught in adultery was to be publicly stoned. But Jesus said, "He that is without sin among you, let him first cast a stone at her. . . ." This is a warning against hypocrisy.

cast thy bread upon the waters: From Ecclesiastes, this injunction advises us to share our wealth with those who need it and says that it shall be returned to us.

conversion of Saul: In Acts, Saul, a Roman citizen, actively persecuted the new Christian believers. While on the road to Damascus, Saul was blinded by a "light from heaven" and heard the words of God. Three days later, he accepted baptism and "the scales" fell from his eyes. Saul is known as St. Paul, one of the major figures in the early Christian church.

Crucifixion: The death of Christ on the cross, believed by Christians to be the sacrifice that redeemed fallen humankind.

Daedalus and Icarus: In Greek mythology, Daedalus, the great architect, designed the labyrinth that held captive the Minotaur of Crete. Imprisoned along with his son Icarus, he designed wings of wax and feathers that would allow them to escape. Despite warnings not to fly too high, Icarus soared too close to the sun god Apollo. The wax on his wings melted, and he plunged to his death. It is symbolic of the danger involved in daring to enter "the realm of the gods." James Joyce's protagonist Stephen Dedalus, in *A Portrait of the Artist as a Young Man*, dared to question the strict teachings of his Cathloic upbringing.

Damocles, sword of: A symbol of impending peril in Greek mythology. Damocles was seated at a sumptuous banquet only to look up to see a sword suspended by a thread over his head. This spoiled his pleasure. In modern literary usage, the term indicates impending disaster.

Damon and Pythias: In Greek mythology, these were two inseparable friends who would lay down their lives for one another. They symbolize lasting friendship.

Daniel: This biblical hero was cast into the lions' den to punish him for his fidelity to his Christian God; he was divinely delivered. The tale of Daniel in the lions' den is representative of extreme bravery and unwavering faith in the face of adversity. Daniel also interpreted Nebuchadnezzar's dream; thus an allusion to Daniel in literature may also be interpreted as referring to an uncanny ability to "read the handwriting on the wall."

David and Bathsheba: In Samuel, David had an adulterous relationship with Bathsheba. When she became pregnant, David sent her husband, Uriah, into battle, where he was killed. David and Bathsheba married. The child conceived during their affair died, but Bathsheba later gave birth to Solomon.

David and Goliath: As a young man, David slew the "giant" (6 feet 9 inches!) Philistine champion, Goliath. The battle and victory become symbolic of the just defeating the unjust, despite the latter's superior strength. Modern example: "Jack and the Beanstalk."

Dionysus or Bacchus: Greek and Roman name, respectively, of the god of wine, revelry, the power of nature, fertility, and emotional ecstasy. He is usually thought of in terms of overuse or excess. Ancient drama festivals were dedicated to him. Today he is representative of the Nietzschean philosophy, the creative-intuitive principle. Modern example: the movie *Animal House.*

divide the sheep from the goats: This phrase refers to the biblical parable explaining the time of judgment, when the faithful (good and saved) would be separated from the unfaithful (condemned). It alludes to the division of the true from the false, the worthy from the unworthy.

eye for an eye: In Leviticus, the passage "Breach for breach, eye for eye, tooth for tooth" recommends the practice of exacting specific and equal punishment for a transgression or injury; for example, killing a murderer for his crime of killing another. (This was later revised in Matthew: ". . . whoever shall smite thee on thy right cheek, turn to him the other also.")

four horsemen of the apocalypse: In Revelation, John prophesies the end of the world, the final struggle between good and evil. He uses the metaphor of four enormously powerful horsemen as the ultimate destructive forces of divine retribution: war, death, plague, and famine. In literature, the four horsemen remain symbolic of powerful destructive forces.

garden of Gethsemane: This is the garden outside Jerusalem where the agony and betrayal of Jesus took place. Symbolically, a place of great physical or psychological suffering.

good Samaritan: In spite of a long-standing mutual hatred between Jews and Samaritans, a good Samaritan stopped to help a Jew who had been waylaid by thieves, thereby becoming the prototype of a good neighbor. The term has come to mean anyone who stops to help a stranger in need.

Grail or Holy Grail: Subject of multiple legends, most prominently as the chalice or cup that caught the blood from Christ's side and which he had used at the Last Supper; probably of even more ancient origin as a fertility symbol. In Arthurian legend, it is the object of a quest on the parts of the Knights of the Round Table. The Holy Grail brings health and sustenance to those who hold it and may be found only by the pure of heart. Modern examples: *Indiana Jones*, *Monty Python*.

heap coals of fire: In Proverbs, it is said that if you treat your enemy with kindness, it will sting him as though you had "heap[ed] coals of fire" upon him. Teaches a lesson in mercy and cautions "be kind to your enemy."

Herod: King of the Jews who ruled Judaea at the time of Jesus' birth. In order to assure his reign, he is reputed to have ordered the massacre of Bethlehem's male children born within a year of Christ's birth. ("To author Herod" is to surpass the evil of the worst tyrant.)

house has many mansions: In John, Christ assured Peter that his father's house (i.e., heaven) has many mansions. In other words, there is room in heaven for all who believe.

Iphigenia: In Greek mythology she was the eldest child of Agamemnon and Clytemnestra. She was sacrificed by her father in exchange for a guarantee of fair winds for the Greek fleet on its way to Troy. (Compare to Abraham and Isaac.)

Isaac: In Genesis, Isaac's son Jacob was a recipient of the promise or covenant with God.

Jacob: The biblical patriarch whose twelve sons were the founders of the twelve tribes of Israel; his name was later changed to Israel.

Jacob and Esau: In Genesis, Jacob and Esau were the twin sons of Isaac and Rebekah. Esau, who was born first, was stronger than his brother, but Jacob was the more clever of the two. Esau sold Jacob his birthright in a moment of weakness; later, through artful manipulation, Jacob received his father's blessing, originally meant for Esau. A literary reference to the pair may allude to discord between siblings, to the politics of the birthright, or to the idea of the fortunate or favored son.

Jacob's ladder: In Genesis, Jacob dreamed of a ladder from Earth to heaven and heard the voice of God promise land and favor to his descendants. He awoke to place the stone on which he had been sleeping as the first stone of a future temple of God. The ladder is symbolic of the path to God and to heaven. The dream also contains references to the Promised Land and to the covenant with the "chosen people."

Jephthah's daughter: In Judges, this is the story of another father's sacrifice of a daughter to keep a vow. Jephthah vowed to sacrifice whatever living creature emerged first from his house in return for victory over the Ammonites. His daughter, who was the first to leave the house, would not let him break his vow but asked for two months' respite to walk the mountains and mourn her virginity—which she retained. She is the model for later Christian saints who died to protect their virginity. Modern example: Keats' "The Eve of St. Agnes."

Jezebel: In Kings, she was a Phoenician princess who married King Ahab and urged him to sin; she became a formidable enemy of the prophet Elijah. In Revelation, Jezebel is the name given to a false prophet. In literature the term usually refers to a seductive woman who leads the hero astray. Modern example: Margaret Atwood's *The Handmaid's Tale.*

John the Baptist: The prophet who prepared the way for his cousin Jesus as Messiah; the forerunner of Christ's ministry. He was beheaded by Herod at the request of Salome.

Joseph and his brothers: In Genesis, Joseph was the eleventh of Jacob's sons. His brothers became jealous of him and sold him into slavery. He accurately interpreted the pharaoh's dream of seven lean cattle swallowing up seven fat cattle to mean that famine would follow years of plenty. The pharaoh heeded his warning, grain was stored, and Egypt was saved. Joseph ultimately forgave his brothers and shared grain with their tribes.

Joseph and Potiphar's wife: In Genesis, Potiphar's wife tried to seduce Joseph. When he refused, she accused him of attempted rape, and he was imprisoned. He was released by the pharaoh in order to interpret his dream.

Joseph in Egypt: Joseph was made governor of all the lands of Egypt, shared grain with his brothers' tribes, and brought about the migration of Jacob and all his family to Egypt.

Jonah: Old Testament prophet commanded by God to warn Nineveh of its sinful condition. Instead, he took his ship in the opposite direction. God struck the ship with a terrible storm, and the crew threw Jonah overboard. God caused Jonah to be swallowed by a huge whale. Jonah prayed and repented, and after three days the whale deposited Jonah safely onto dry land. This event is thought to prefigure Christ's death, three days in the tomb, and resurrection. Modern example: *Pinocchio.*

Judas Iscariot: One of the original twelve Apostles, he betrayed Jesus by selling him out for thirty pieces of silver and identifying him with a kiss. Later he committed suicide. Regarded as the prototype of the ultimate betrayer.

judgment of Paris: In Greek mythology, a beauty contest was held to determine the fairest of the goddesses. Paris, the handsomest man in the world, was the judge; the contestants were Hera, Athena, and Aphrodite (representative of greatness, prowess in battle, and love, respectively). Angered at not being invited to Thetis' wedding, Eris, the goddess of discord, threw an apple marked "To the Fairest" into the gathering, provoking the goddesses to fight over it. Paris ultimately chose Aphrodite and was promised the love of Helen in return. This sparked the events that led to the Trojan War. Consider similar elements in "Snow White" ("Mirror, mirror, who is the fairest?"); the apple as fruit of discord; the disastrous choice of love and beauty over less ephemeral attributes. Consider also the following similarities between Paris and Oedipus: both were exposed on a hillside as infants to protect their fathers; both were rescued by shepherds; and both were cursed by fate.

know them by their fruits: In Matthew, Christ warns against wolves in sheep's clothing. He instructs his followers to know them by their fruits: "A good tree cannot bring forth evil fruit, neither can a corrupt tree bring forth good fruit." This injunction entreats us to judge others by their actions, rather than by appearances.

labors of Hercules: In Greek mythology, Hercules had to perform 12 fabulous tasks of enormous difficulty before becoming immortal: killing the Nemean lion; killing the Hydra; capturing the hind of Artemis; killing the man-eating Stymphalian birds; capturing the oxen of Geryon; cleaning the Augean stables; capturing the Cretan bull; capturing the horses of Diomedes; capturing the girdle of Hippolyta (queen of the Amazons); killing the monster Gorgon; capturing Cerberus; and taking the golden apples of Hesperides.

Laius: In Greek mythology, Laius was the father of Oedipus and the original husband of Jocasta. Killed by Oedipus in fulfillment of the oracle, Laius is a major figure in the Laius-Jocasta-Oedipus myth in which the son kills his father and takes his place as both king and husband. The tale is symbolic of the inevitable usurpation of father by son, a familiar theme in folklore.

lamb to the slaughter: Originally, in Isaiah's prophecy, this was the servant of the Lord who took the sins of his people on himself and sacrificed himself for their expiation, much as actual goats or lambs were sacrificed. In the New Testament, Christ is frequently referred to as the sacrificial lamb. The Christian belief is that he atoned for the sins of all men by taking them upon himself and sacrificing his life in fulfillment of Isaiah's very specific prophecy.

Last Supper: The Last Supper was Jesus' last meal with his disciples before his crucifixion. Virtually every aspect of the story has both literal and symbolic associations. During this dinner, Christ instituted a number of sacraments, especially Communion, in which bread and wine after transubstantiation become the "body and blood" of Christ. In consuming the bread and wine, followers of Christ accept him as their savior.

Lazarus: In the New Testament, he is the brother of Martha and Mary of Bethany, whom Jesus raised from the dead after four days, prefiguring the resurrection. Lazarus is symbolic of one who lives after a declared death. (Compare to Sisyphus.)

Leda: In Greek mythology, Zeus is said to have come to Leda in the shape of a swan to father four legendary children: Castor, Clytemnestra, Pollux, and Helen. The story of Leda and the swan is a favorite theme of artists from Michelangelo to Dali.

lilies of the field: In Matthew, this is used as an example of the way God cares for the faithful. If he "dresses" the lilies so beautifully, surely he will provide raiment for his children.

lion lies down with the lamb: In Isaiah, this is the classic image of the idyllic harmony and universal peace of the earthly paradise that will come into being when the Messiah arrives.

loaves and fishes: In Matthew, Christ multiplied five loaves of bread and two fishes into a sufficient amount to feed a crowd of 5,000 (not counting women and children). When all had eaten their fill, there were still 12 baskets of scraps left over.

Lot/Lot's wife: In Genesis, Lot was a moral inhabitant of the sinful city of Sodom. A nephew of Abraham, Lot escaped the destruction of the city by the angels of the Lord. Abraham had argued with the Lord over his intended destruction of the innocent along with the guilty. Lot and his family were warned of their impending doom, but his sons-in-law "thought he were joking." Lot took his wife and daughters and fled. God warned them not to look back, but Lot's wife could not resist, and was turned into a pillar of salt. The tale of Lot's wife is illustrative of the idea that God punishes those who are disobedient.

magi: Latin plural of *magus*, "wise man." Traditionally, they have the names Melchior, Gaspar, and Balthazar. The gifts the magi brought to the Christ child were gold (symbolic of royalty); frankincense (the emblem of divinity); and myrrh (the symbol of death). The Christmas story of the three wise men visiting the manger represents the "showing forth" of the newborn Christ child to the Gentiles (non-Jews). This moment of awareness is known liturgically as "the Epiphany," the term James Joyce used for his and his characters' moments of enlightenment. Modern example: O. Henry's short story "The Gift of the Magi."

mammon: From the Aramaic word for *wealth*, as used in the Bible. Mammon became the evil personification of riches and worldliness, and the god of avarice. Modern examples: In Spenser's *The Faerie Queen* and Milton's *Paradise Lost*, Mammon personifies the evils of greed and wealth.

Mary (the Virgin): In the gospels of Matthew, Mark, Luke, and John, Mary is the mother of Jesus and wife of Joseph. Symbolic of purity, virginity, and maternal love, she is the object of special devotion in the Roman Catholic church and the major subject, along with her son, of thousands of works of art, especially the art of the Renaissance. (Compare to the Greek/Roman goddess Artemis/Diana, known variously as goddess of the hunt, virginity, and motherhood.)

Mary Magdalene: She is the reformed prostitute who may have been the woman saved from the mob in the "let him cast the first stone" story. She washed Jesus' feet with her tears and dried them with her hair. She was present at the Crucifixion and is said to have been one of the first to see the tomb open three days later (Easter Sunday). She represents the meaning of true contrition and the power of forgiveness.

massacre of the innocents: At the time of the birth of Jesus, Herod, the king of Judaea, hoping to squelch any possible threat to his throne, ordered the death of all male babies born in Bethlehem during a two-year period determined by the appearance of an extraordinary "star in the East." Joseph, warned in a dream, took Mary and Jesus and fled to Egypt, thus escaping the massacre. (See *Herod*.)

Medusa: In Greek mythology, Medusa was the chief of the three Gorgons—monsters who had snakes for hair, and faces so horrifying that just the sight of them turned men to stone. She was killed by Perseus, who took her head with a sword given to him by Hermes. Pegasus, the winged horse, sprang from her blood.

Minotaur: In Greek mythology, this was a monster with a bull's head and a man's body. Poseidon sent a bull from the sea as a signal of favor to Minos. As a result, Minos was crowned king of Crete, but he neglected to sacrifice the bull to Poseidon. Angered, Poseidon caused Minos' wife Pasiphaë to become enamored of the bull. The offspring of their union was the Minotaur, which was imprisoned by Minos in the labyrinth designed by Daedalus. Modern examples: Mary Renault's novels *Bull From the Sea* and *The King Must Die*.

Moses: He received the Ten Commandments from Jehovah on Mt. Sinai. Following the pattern of the archetypal hero's life, Moses was a foundling child rescued by Pharaoh's daughter and raised to be a prince of Egypt. As an adult, he led his own people, the children of Israel, out of bondage in Egypt, through the Red Sea on dry land, and on a 40-year journey searching for the Promised Land. Because he committed one arrogant sin—striking a rock to bring forth needed water—he himself was not permitted to enter the Promised Land. (Compare to all cautionary tales from mythology that warned heroes not to fly too high, or to assume godlike powers. Like Moses, Icarus, Prometheus, and Bellerophon also suffered for their arrogance.)

Myrmidons: In Greek mythology, these were people from Thessaly who accompanied Achilles at the siege of Troy. They were known for their brutality and savagery. According to legend, they were originally ants who were turned into human beings to populate one of the Greek islands.

Nebuchadnezzar's dream: Nebuchadnezzar was the most powerful and longest-reigning king of Mesopotamia. He brought Babylon to the heights of its power during the sixth century B.C. and is credited with creating the fabled Hanging Gardens of Babylon. He conquered Jerusalem, burned the Temple of Solomon, and exiled the Israelites to Babylon. During his reign, he had a series of prophetic dreams or visions, which he was unable to interpret. He questioned all the wise men of his kingdom and condemned them to death because they could not interpret his dreams. Then Daniel came forward and explained that the dream of a statue with a head of gold, chest and arms of silver, belly and thighs of bronze, legs of iron, and feet of iron and clay foretold the succession of kingdoms that would follow Nebuchadnezzar's— each less glorious than the last. Daniel also foretold the emergence of an indestructible kingdom of God. Daniel was rewarded with a high position.

Nemesis: In Greek mythology, she was the personification of righteous anger. Nemesis punished those who transgressed upon the natural order of things, either through hubris or through excessive love of material goods. Currently, the word usually refers to an unbeatable enemy.

nirvana: This Sanskrit word means "going out," like a light. Buddhists believe that in this doctrine of release, a state of perfect bliss is attained in life through the negation of all desires and the extinction of the self. Nirvana is union with the Buddha, an ideal condition of harmony.

Noah and the flood: In Genesis, when God decided to punish the wicked of the world with a terrific flood, he chose Noah, a good man, to build an ark. Noah, his family, and pairs of the animals of the world lived on the ark during the 40 days and 40 nights of the deluge, while everyone and everything else perished. After the ark came to rest on the top of Mt. Ararat, Noah, his wife, his sons and their wives, and the animals emerged to repopulate Earth. The rainbow that appeared represents God's promise that never again would he destroy Earth by flood. Flood themes appear frequently in mythology. Examples: the epic of Gilgamesh in Sumerian legend; Vishnu in Hindu mythology, Deucalion in Greek mythology.

***Odyssey*:** Ninth-century B.C. epic poem, attributed to Homer, which recounts the story of the ten-year-long homeward journey of Odysseus and his men after the Trojan War. The *Odyssey* is a source of our knowledge of many of the major Greek myths and legends, as well as the basis for many modern works. The most outstanding of these is James Joyce's *Ulysses*. More recently, the movie *O Brother, Where Art Thou?* was based loosely on the *Odyssey*.

Oedipus: In Greek mythology, Oedipus was the son of Laius and Jocasta. In response to an oracle, Oedipus was abandoned at birth and raised as the son of Polybus and Merope, king and queen of Corinth. When grown, Oedipus learned of the prophecy that foretold that he would kill his father and marry his mother—two of the worst taboos in human civilization. In an attempt to avoid fulfilling the prophecy, he left his adopted land, Corinth, and fled to Thebes, his actual birthplace. En route, he encountered—and in his pride and ignorance slew—Laius, the king of Thebes. He also answered the riddle of the sphinx, saving Thebes from paying the annual tribute of its best youth to the monster. As a reward, he was made king of Thebes and he married Jocasta, the queen and his mother, thus fulfilling the prophecy and continuing the curse of the House of Atreus. Freud based his well-known theory of the "Oedipus complex" on this myth.

Pandora: In Greek mythology, she was the first woman, comparable to Eve in biblical allusion. Like Eve, Pandora, whose name means "all gifts," was given the power to bring about the ruin of mankind. Zeus gave her a closed box filled with all the evils of the world and warned her not to open it. Her curiosity got the better of her, and when she opened the box, all the evils flew out, and they have continued to harm human beings ever since. Today, Pandora's box refers to a gift that turns out to be a curse. It also refers to the unanticipated consequences of one's actions, as in "opening a can of worms."

Persephone: (Roman name: Proserpine) In Greek and Roman mythology she was the goddess of fertility and queen of the underworld. The daughter of Zeus and Demeter (Ceres), she was kidnapped by Pluto (Hades). Her mother grieved so deeply that all earthly crops died and perpetual winter threatened. A bargain was struck: Persephone would spend half the year with Hades—hence autumn and winter—and return to her mother for half the year, allowing the revival of the crops during spring and summer. The myth of Persephone is the classical explanation for the seasons.

Pharisees: In Matthew, these were members of an ancient Jewish sect that emphasized strict observance of the Law. Self-righteous and separatist, they refused contact with any not of their kind. Consequently, the term *Pharisees* developed a negative connotation, and is usually interpreted to mean *hypocrites*.

Philistines: These traditional enemies of the Israelites fought against Samson, David, and other major Jewish heroes. In contemporary usage the term connotes an ignorant, crude, and rude person lacking in culture and artistic appreciation and characterized by materialistic values.

phoenix: This mythical bird lived for 500 years, burned to death, and then rose from its own ashes to begin life anew. For this reason, the phoenix frequently symbolizes death and resurrection, or eternal life.

Pontius Pilate: The Roman governor before whom Jesus was tried. When he could not convince the mobs to release Jesus, he washed his hands, symbolically cleansing himself of what was to follow, and turned Jesus over for crucifixion. In contemporary usage, a Pontius Pilate is one who betrays his own moral convictions and submits to the pressure of others, "washing his hands of the matter."

Procrustes: In Greek mythology, Procrustes was a thief of Attica who placed anyone he captured on an iron bed. If the person was too tall, he cut off whatever hung over; if too short, he stretched the person until he fit. The term "Procrustean bed" connotes a rigid standard to which exact conformity is enforced.

Prodigal Son: In one of Jesus' parables, this is the younger son who wastes his "portion," or his inheritance. His father forgives him and celebrates his homecoming over his older brothers' protests. Modern examples: Prince Hal in Shakespeare's *Henry IV, Part II*; the children's tale "Peter Cottontail."

Prometheus: (Greek for "forethought") A Titan and the champion of men against the gods, Prometheus stole fire from Mount Olympus and gave the precious gift to humans. As punishment for his transgression, Zeus had him chained (or nailed) to a mountain where an eagle tore out his entrails each day. The organs regenerated overnight. He was eventually freed by either Hercules or Zeus (accounts differ). He is the hero of Aeschylus' *Prometheus Bound* and Shelley's poem "Prometheus Unbound." He is also the subject of the golden statue above the skating rink at Rockefeller Center in New York City.

Proteus: In Greek mythology, Proteus was Poseidon's herdsman and a prophet. He was a sea god who could assume any form or shape he wished. In current usage, *protean* means *versatile*.

Pygmalion: In Greek mythology, Pygmalion was a sculptor and king of Cyprus who created a statue of Aphrodite. He fell in love with his own creation, and Aphrodite herself answered his prayer: The statue came to life, and he married her. The statue is named Galatea in other versions of the story. George Bernard Shaw's play *Pygmalion* and the musical *My Fair Lady*—the story of Professor Higgins and his "creation," Eliza Doolittle—are based on this myth.

Pyrrhus: King of Epirus in ancient Greece. For 25 years he waged a series of wars. He often won, but lost too many soldiers in the process.

At the time of his death, he had succeeded only in bringing Epirus to ruin. A pyrrhic victory is one that was won at much too high a price.

Rachel and Leah: In Genesis, these are the two wives of Jacob. Jacob had been promised Rachel in marriage if he worked seven years for her father. He was tricked into marrying Leah, Rachel's older sister. After promising to work another seven years for Laban, the girls' father, he also married Rachel. Rachel and Leah are referred to together as the matriarchs of Israel.

Romulus and Remus: In Roman mythology, these are legendary twins, sons of Mars and a vestal virgin who was put to death at their birth. The boys were thrown into the Tiber but were washed ashore (compare to Moses) and suckled by a she-wolf. They were found by a herdsman and his wife, who brought them up as their own. As adults, Romulus and Remus decided to found a city (Rome) on the spot where they had been rescued from the Tiber. When an omen declared Romulus to be the true founder of the city, the brothers fought, and Romulus killed Remus. Note the similarities between this story and that of Cain and Abel (the demigod status of the founding father) and Oedipus (the coincidental raising by a herdsman). Virgil's great Roman epic poem, the *Aeneid,* was so titled because the twins were said to be descendants of Aeneas.

Ruth: Ruth was a Moabite widow who refused to abandon her mother-in-law, Naomi. Her lovingly loyal behavior became the model for good women to follow. Eventually, she married Boaz and became the great-grandmother of David. Her intertribal marriage to Boaz also represents openness to the world.

Sabine women, rape of: In Roman legend, Romulus "solved" the problem of finding wives for the men in his new settlement by stealing and raping the virgins of the Sabines after luring the men away to a celebration. After a subsequent war, the tribes intermarried by accord, and the settlement flourished.

Salome: In Matthew, because Salome so pleased Herod, the governor of Judaea, by dancing at his birthday feast (legend has it that it was the "Dance of the Seven Veils"), Herod promised her anything she asked for. Salome's mother had divorced her husband and married Herod. John the Baptist had denounced the marriage and was imprisoned for doing so. Salome asked for John the Baptist's head, and she was given it on a platter.

satyrs: In Greek mythology, a race of goat-men, sometimes considered woodland demigods, with the tail and ears of a horse and the legs and horns of a goat. They were followers of Dionysus and were best known for chasing wood nymphs. Satyrs were a major feature of the satyr play, which traditionally followed a tragic trilogy. The satyr play treated serious matters in a grotesquely comic way. Shakespeare used vestiges of the form in plays such as A *Midsummer Night's Dream.*

Salman Rushdie alludes to the satyr figure in *Satanic Verses*. Also, e. e. cummings' "goat-footed balloon-man."

Scylla and Charybdis: In Greek mythology, a jealous Circe turned the nymph Scylla into a sea monster with twelve feet, six heads on long necks, and menacing rows of teeth with which she devoured sailors. The terrible Charybdis, hurled into the sea by Zeus, hid under rocks and created a whirlpool. Together they were a formidable danger to ships passing through the Straits of Messina. They came to be understood as metaphors for the dangerous rocks on one side of the passage and a devastating whirlpool on the other. The popular phrase related to the pair is "between a rock and a hard place."

Sermon on the Mount: This is the sermon given by Jesus (as recorded by Matthew) in which he expresses the essence of his teachings. The sermon begins with the beatitudes: "Blessed are the poor," the meek, the sorrowful, etc. The beatitudes (the word means "happiness") promise religious happiness for those who lack material goods and are in need of the spiritual blessings of God. The sermon as a whole outlines rules for behavior according to God's law. The speech is usually interpreted as the fulfillment of the law of the Old Testament.

Sisyphus: In Greek mythology, Sisyphus cheated death by telling his wife to forgo the usual burial rites when he died, thus giving him permission to return from the underworld to punish her. This angered Zeus, and when Sisyphus died a second time, many years later, he was condemned to eternally roll a huge rock up a hill, only to have it roll back down as he was about to reach the top. Albert Camus used Sisyphus as the metaphor for modern man's situation in *The Myth of Sisyphus*. He serves as a constant metaphor for the never-ending struggle to complete one's task, only to be thwarted by still more hurdles.

Sodom and Gomorrah: The two major cities, according to Genesis, which were destroyed by heaven with fire and brimstone (traditional elements of hell) because of their wickedness. They stand as symbols of debauchery.

Solomon: Traditionally the wisest and grandest of the kings of Israel, Solomon was the son of David and Bathsheba. When asked by Jehovah what gift he most wanted, he responded "an understanding heart," and ever after he was renowned for his wisdom. The story of the two women who both claimed to be the mother of the same baby remains as the model of the "Solomon-like" decision. Solomon decreed the baby be cut in half to give each woman her "just" due. The false mother agreed, but the true mother was willing to give up her claim so the baby would live. Solomon returned the baby to the true mother, of course. He also directed the construction of the great temple that bore his name.

sphinx: In Greek mythology, the sphinx was a monster with the face of a woman, the body of a lion, and the wings of a bird. She posed a riddle to the citizens of Thebes and devoured the young men who could not answer it. When Oedipus, en route to Thebes, correctly answered the riddle, the sphinx killed herself in chagrin. The riddle is usually given as, "What walks on four legs in the morning, on two at midday, and on three in the evening?" (Answer: Man, who crawls on all fours as a baby, walks upright as an adult, and uses a cane in old age.) In Egypt the sphinx was usually seen as a huge statue with the body of a lion and the head of a man, representing the sun god Ra. The largest remaining sphinx is two-thirds the length of a football field. The sphinx also represents monumental silence in literary references.

stealing the apples of the Hesperides: In Greek mythology, the Hesperides were the daughters of Hesperus whose golden apples were guarded by a dragon. One of Hercules' labors was to slay the dragon and steal the apples. (Compare to the serpent and the tree in the Garden of Eden.)

Styx: In Greek mythology, the Styx was one of the five rivers of hell (the others are Acheron, Cocytus, Phlegethon, and Lethe). Charon ferried the dead across the river Styx to the underworld. The Styx figures heavily in Dante's *Inferno*. Lethe turns up frequently in literature as an allusion to forgetfulness.

swords into ploughshares: Although the sword appears as a weapon of war or a symbol of wrath more than 400 times in the Bible, this use in Isaiah refers to the hope that a peaceful age will eventually eliminate the needs for weapons of war. Beating swords into farm implements is comparable to the practice of converting munitions factories into home appliance factories after times of war in the twentieth century. The phrase is often used by speakers advocating peace.

Tantalus: In Greek mythology, Tantalus was a progenitor of the House of Atreus (source of many of the extended Greek tragedies from Agamemnon to Orestes) who is best known for his punishment in Hades. He suffers eternal hunger and thirst while standing in the middle of a body of clear, cold water that dries up as he reaches for it. The fruit of a heavily laden bough hangs above his head, but remains just out of reach. His name gives us the word *tantalize*.

thirty pieces of silver: This is the amount paid to Judas Iscariot for betraying Jesus by identifying him with a kiss, leading to Jesus' arrest and Crucifixion. Legend has it that he threw it back at the Jewish priests just before he hanged himself. The phrases "thirty pieces of silver" and "Judas' kiss" refer to betrayal and treachery.

through a glass darkly: Writing to the Corinthians on the gift of Christ's perfect love, Paul prophesied a time of perfect love and clarity of knowledge of God, in contrast to the time when people saw God indistinctly or "through a glass darkly." This passage is used frequently in wedding ceremonies and, conversely, by writers who wish to convey the opposite of perfect love and clear knowledge through irony.

Tower of Babel: In Genesis, after the flood, the descendants of Noah built a tower that was meant to reach to heaven. But Jehovah, unhappy with their arrogance and hubris, "confounded" their speech so they could not understand one another, and then he scattered them over the Earth. This is the biblical explanation for the diversity of languages in the world. The Tower of Babel has come to represent a madly visionary scheme, and the word *babel* now means a senseless uproar in which nothing can be understood. It is also related to the word *babble*. Once again, this is a cautionary tale warning that humankind should not aspire to the heights of the gods.

Trojan horse: A large wooden horse designed and built by the Greeks, supposedly as a gift to Athena. Because the Greeks had been unable to take the walled city of Troy during their ten-year siege, they instead tried deception. Placing a troop of soldiers inside the hollow wooden horse, the Greeks pretended that they were sailing homeward. The unsuspecting Trojans brought the horse inside the walls. Late that night, the Greeks crept out of the horse and opened the gates of the city, letting in their comrades, and they took Troy at last. The phrase "beware of Greeks bearing gifts" has its origins in this tale.

Utopia: In literature, the title of the 1516 book by Sir Thomas More, who gave the name, meaning *nowhere* in Greek, to his imaginary island. More describes the ideal society according to the ideals of the English humanists, who dreamt of a land where ignorance, crime, poverty, and injustice did not exist. Since then the name has been applied to all attempts to describe or establish a society in which these ideals would prevail. Interestingly, many twentieth-century writers have focused on the anti-utopian, or dystopian, world. Examples of this kind of work include Aldous Huxley's *Brave New World*, George Orwell's *1984*, and Ray Bradbury's *Fahrenheit 451*.

Waterloo: The town in Belgium where Napoleon was resoundingly defeated in 1815. In current usage, the term refers to a crushing and final defeat.

Lesson 2: Answers

Symbolism and Allusion: Activity 2

1. swiftness (d)
2. labyrinth (c)
3. infidelity (a)
4. stone (c)
5. Saul (c)
6. envy (c)
7. bacon (a)

3 LESSON

Irony and Tone

In this chapter you will learn about two important literary elements: irony and tone. You are no doubt familiar with both of these terms. In fact, you probably use them all the time. How many times have you heard someone say, "Don't use that tone with me!" or "That sure is ironic"? Yet this familiarity can be dangerous. These terms—especially irony—have very specific meaning when used in a literary context.

Irony

Irony always implies some sort of discrepancy or incongruity. Something is ironic when reality is in sharp contrast to appearance. Irony spices up your life, makes you laugh at yourself at even the most unexpected moments, and promotes a sardonic appreciation of this intriguing journey called life.

For example, the high school football captain plays a fierce season and escapes unscathed, then breaks his arm on the curb outside the movie theater. Or perhaps your school officials seem more interested in what kids wear than in their intellectual progress. These are examples of ironic situations.

Aristotle defined irony as a "dissembling toward the inner core of truth." According to Cicero, "Irony is the saying of one thing and meaning another." In literature, irony lends complexity to character, to plot, and to conclusions.

O. Henry's famous story "The Gift of the Magi" is an excellent example of irony. It tells the heart-rending story of a poor young married couple who are celebrating their first Christmas together. The wife sells her hair (her most precious possession) to buy her husband a watch chain, or fob, for his most prized possession—his watch. Of course, as you've guessed, he's already sold his watch to buy combs for her glorious hair. This tale reflects irony at its best!

In poetry, also, irony can provide surprise, insight, and closure. Take, for example, the poem "To an Athlete Dying Young" by A. E. Housman, in which the speaker praises the smart boy who slips away instead of becoming one of many "lads that wore their honors out." The speaker implies that it's better to die in glory at age 22 than to live long enough to see that glory usurped by others.

Irony: Activity 1

Read this short poem. What do you think is ironic about it? Write your answer on the lines that follow.

Lines for a Christmas Card

May all my enemies go to hell,
Noel, Noel, Noel, Noel.

—Hilaire Belloc

_____

_____

_____

_____

Now try another.

Earth

"A planet doesn't explode of itself," said dryly
The Martian astronomer, gazing off into the air.
"That they were able to do it is proof that highly
Intelligent beings must have been living there."

—John Hall Wheelock

What do you make of this poem? Where is its central irony?

_____

_____

_____

_____

To see sample student responses to these questions, turn to page 79.

Irony and the AP Exam

In your preparation for the AP English literature and composition exam, you should explore the concept of irony thoroughly. Doing so will enhance your ability to look deeper, to make connections, and to show the literary significance of the connections you make.

The exam will most likely focus on three specific types of irony: *dramatic, verbal,* and *situational.*

Dramatic Irony

In dramatic irony, the discrepancy is between what the *speaker says* and what the *audience knows to be true.*

Example:

Oedipus exhausts every avenue to find his father's murderer, only to discover that he *himself* is the murderer. Oedipus, that unwilling pawn of fate, tells Creon:

> "Whoever killed King Laius might—who knows?—
> Lay violent hands even on me and soon.
> I act for the murdered king in my own interest."
> (Sophocles, *Oedipus Rex*)

We, the audience, are drawn into the incredible vulnerability of Oedipus, for we have already guessed the truth: Oedipus is the killer of Laius. And he will indeed lay his own violent hands upon himself.

Thus, another function of dramatic irony is to provide much of the intrigue in a story or play because the reader or audience enjoys being in on the secret; in other words, dramatic irony is a form of *suspense.*

Example:

When the villain Iago is referred to as "honest Iago" in Shakespeare's *Othello,* we are part of the intrigue, the mounting morass that will envelop the too-trusting Othello. From his first appearance, when Iago utters racial and personal slurs about his general (and yet compliments his superior officer when speaking to him), we realize Iago is evil and deceitful, and decidedly not honest. The sobriquet "honest" becomes an ironic refrain, underscoring one of the play's major themes—that things are not necessarily as they appear.

Irony: Activity 2

On the lines below, list three books, stories, or movies that provide examples of dramatic irony. Explain why they are ironic.

Work #1 _____

_____

_____

_____

Work #2 _____

_____

_____

_____

Work #3 _____

_____

_____

_____

Verbal Irony

In verbal irony, the intended meaning of a work or statement is often the opposite of what the work or statement literally "says." Verbal irony carries with it the implication of a meaning opposite to a direct statement.

Perhaps the classic example of verbal irony can be found in Jonathan Swift's "A Modest Proposal," in which he suggests that the babies of the poor be butchered and sold for food to the English landlords in order to alleviate the problems of a starving Ireland. The careful reader understands that Swift's outrageous proposal is not meant to be taken literally. Swift directs his anger at those who have exploited the Irish, hoping that this will lead to reform.

Irony: Activity 3

List three books, stories, or movies that contain verbal irony. Explain the irony.

Work #1 _____

_____

_____

_____

Work #2 _____

_____

_____

_____

Work #3 _____

_____

_____

_____

☞ *AP Tip*

Sarcasm is similar to verbal irony, but it is not the same. Generally, a statement is considered to be sarcastic only if the person to whom it is directed *knows* that it is meant that way. If he or she takes the statement at face value, then it becomes ironic.

Some of the devices through which verbal irony is achieved include:

- understatement
- exaggeration
- satire

Situational Irony

In situational irony, there is an occurrence that is contrary to what is intended or expected, a reversal of events. As mentioned earlier, "The Gift of the Magi" is a perfect example of situational irony. Still another example is Guy de Maupassant's "The Necklace." In this story, Madame Loisel loses her beauty, her youth, and her position in society because she loses a diamond necklace she borrowed from a friend and works for the rest of her life to pay for it—only to discover that it was, in fact, a fake. And in O. Henry's "The Ransom of Red Chief," it is indeed ironic that the bumbling kidnappers of the incorrigible brat Red Chief end up paying his parents to take him back, instead of collecting the ransom themselves.

☞ *AP Tip*

While it is important to recognize irony, it is more important to perfect your ability to show its **significance to the meaning** of a literary work.

Still another example of situational irony is seen in Shakespeare's famous soliloquy from *Henry IV, Part II*. The king laments his inability to sleep while his poorer subjects rest easily despite their harsh physical conditions. It is ironic that the king, with all the comforts his position can provide, cannot enjoy sleep, the most basic of human functions. This instance serves to reveal the king as a human being with depth, needs, and frailties and thus makes his character more appealing and more universal.

Irony: Activity 4

List three books, stories, or movies that contain situational irony. Explain your choices.

Work #1 _____

_____

_____

_____

Work #2 _____

_____

_____

_____

Work #3 _____

_____

_____

_____

Irony is common in poetry, drama, prose, and all other forms of written expression. Whole genres, such as Greek tragedy, incorporate irony as a fundamental technique. Shakespeare's works abound with irony. One example, found in *Romeo and Juliet*, is the timing of the death scene. Another is King Lear's disowning the daughter who loves him the most. In one of the most famous ironic speeches ever written, Marc Antony addresses the Roman mob with the stated purpose of saying farewell to Caesar, who has just been assassinated by Senate members led by his trusted friend, Brutus.

Irony: Activity 5

Which of the following indicate irony? Why or why not?

1. We've been planning this picnic for months! Why did it have to rain today?

_____

_____

_____

2. Mom: "I love your navel ring. Will you buy me one?"

   _____

   _____

   _____

3. Student: "But I don't understand! What does it mean?"
   Teacher: "It's a bit difficult to understand a book you haven't read, isn't it?"

   _____

   _____

   _____

4. Write three essays this weekend? Sure! There's nothing I'd rather do.

   _____

   _____

   _____

5. An Olympic hurdle jumper trips on her doorstep and breaks her leg.

   _____

   _____

   _____

To see answers to these questions, turn to page 80.

Irony and the AP Prompt

A typical AP question might look like this:

> **Prompt**
>
> Read the following passage from Shakespeare's *Julius Caesar* carefully. Then, in a well-written essay, discuss how Marc Antony's goals are achieved in the speech. Consider such literary techniques as irony, synecdoche, imagery, syntax, diction, and tone.

As you can see, this prompt requires you to show how various literary techniques—including irony—contribute to the speech's meaning. In Part 4, you will be given a step-by-step explanation of how to analyze and respond to a prompt such as this. For the moment, however, focus only on the use of irony in the speech.

Try It Out

Read the speech and answer the questions that follow.

from Julius Caesar

Marc Antony: Friends, Romans, countrymen, lend me your ears;
         I come to bury Caesar, not to praise him.
         The evil that men do lives after them,
         The good is oft interred with their bones;
5   So let it be with Caesar. The noble Brutus
         Hath told you Caesar was ambitious.
         If it were so, it was a grievous fault,
         And grievously hath Caesar answer'd it.
         Here, under leave of Brutus and the rest,
10   (For Brutus is an honourable man
         So are they all, all honourable men)
         Come I to speak in Caesar's funeral.
         He was my friend, faithful and just to me:
         But Brutus says he was ambitious
15   And Brutus is an honourable man.
         He hath brought many captives home to Rome
         Whose ransoms did the general coffers fill:
         Did this in Caesar seem ambitious?
         When that the poor have cried, Caesar hath wept;
20   Ambition should be made of sterner stuff:
         But Brutus says he was ambitious,
         And Brutus is an honourable man.
         You all did see that on the Lupercal
         I thrice presented him a kingly crown,
25   Which he did thrice refuse. Was this ambition?
         Yet Brutus says he was ambitious,
         And sure he is an honourable man.
         I speak not to disprove what Brutus spoke,
         But here I am to speak what I do know.
30   You all did love him once, not without cause;
         What cause withholds you then to mourn for him?
         O judgment! thou art fled to brutish beasts,
         And men have lost their reason. Bear with me,
         My heart is in the coffin there with Caesar,
35   And I must pause till it come back to me.

Analysis, Activity 1: Marc Antony's speech from *Julius Caesar*

Answer the questions below. If necessary, refer to the speech or prompt.

1. Summarize the speech.

_____

_____

_____

_____

_____

2. List the lines or phrases that contain irony.

_____

_____

_____

_____

_____

3. Identify any literary devices or techniques that help the author convey irony.

_____

_____

_____

To see sample student responses to these questions, turn to page 80.

Try It Out

Now read "aesop revised by archy" by the poet Don Marquis. As you can see, this piece is harder to read because there is no punctuation or capitalization. (That is because archy is a cockroach, and he can't reach all the keys on the typewriter.)

aesop revised by archy

a wolf met a spring
lamb drinking
at a stream

and said to her
you are the lamb
that muddied this stream
all last year
so that I could not get
a clean fresh drink
i am resolved that
this outrage
shall not be enacted again
this season
i am going to kill you
just a moment
said the lamb
i was not born last
year so it could not
have been i
the wolf then pulled
a number of other
arguments as to why the lamb
should die
but in each case the lamb
pretty innocent that she was
easily proved
herself guiltless
well well said the wolf
enough of argument
you are right and i am wrong
but i am going to eat
you anyhow
because i am hungry
stop exclamation point
cried a human voice
and a man came over
the slope of the ravine
vile lupine marauder
you shall not kill that
beautiful and innocent
lamb for i shall save her
exit the wolf
left upper entrance
snarling
poor little lamb
continued our human hero
sweet tender little thing
it is well that i appeared
just when i did
it makes my blood boil
to think of the fright
to which you have been

subjected in another
moment i would have been
too late come home with me
and the lamb frolicked
about her new found friend
gamboling as to the sound
of a wordsworthian tabor
and leaping for joy
as if propelled by a stanza
from william blake
these vile and bloody wolves
went on our hero
in honest indignation
they must be cleared out
of the country
the meads must be made safe
for sheepocracy
and so jollying her along
with the usual human hokum
he led her to his home
and the son of a gun
did not even blush when
they passed the mint bed
gently he cut her throat
all the while inveighing
against the inhuman wolf
and tenderly he cooked her
and lovingly he sauced her
and meltingly he ate her
and piously he said a grace
thanking his gods
for their bountiful gifts to him
and after dinner
he sat with his pipe
before the fire meditating
on the brutality of wolves
and the injustice of
the universe
which allows them to harry
poor innocent lambs
and wondering if he
had not better
write to the papers
for as he said
for god s sake can t
something be done about it

                   archy

Analysis, Activity 2: "aesop revised by archy"

Now answer the questions below. If necessary, refer to the poem.

1. Summarize the poem.

_____

_____

_____

_____

2. List the lines or phrases that contain irony.

_____

_____

_____

_____

_____

_____

_____

3. Identify any literary devices or techniques that help the author convey irony.

_____

_____

_____

_____

4. What do you think the author is saying about self-knowledge, self-deception, hypocrisy, good and evil, and the vulnerability of the weak, the less fortunate, and the innocent of the world?

_____

_____

_____

_____

_____

To see sample student responses to these questions, turn to page 81.

> ☞ *AP Tip*
>
> Don't worry if you don't know the meanings of all the words in a selection. No one is expected to know everything. You must do the best you can with what you know in the time allotted. Outside of the testing situation, however, you should do your best to look up the definitions of unfamiliar words. Some of the unusual words you might need to look up in "aesop revised by archy" are:
>
> | | |
> |---|---|
> | gamboling | hokum |
> | lupine | meads |
> | piously | tabor |
> | grace | inveighing |
> | marauder | mint bed |
> | ravine | Wordsworthian |

Tone

Although we normally think of tone as something we *hear*, as in a tone of voice, it also plays a crucial role on the printed page. Just as the tone of a person's voice clues us in as to the speaker's intended meaning, literary tone reveals meaning on the printed page. This is especially important in poetry, since the poet must compensate for the inability to convey inflection through other devices.

In literature, tone refers to the writer's *attitude* toward the subject. Often, it sets the mood of the poem or prose piece. For example, many of Poe's short stories have a foreboding, mysterious tone. Many of Mark Twain's stories have a humorous tone. For some authors, tone is an integral part of their style. Hemingway tends to be noncommittal and objective, while Gabriel García Márquez is mystical and cryptic.

In other cases, authors adjust their tone to convey meaning in a particular piece. For example, in Dickens' *A Christmas Carol*, consider the tone when the ghost of Christmas Future comes to visit and contrast that with the celebratory tone of Scrooge in the book's final chapter.

tone ⟶ author's attitude

When you take the AP, you may be asked to show how an author's choice of tone helps him or her convey the meaning of a poem or prose passage. Or you may be asked to identify devices or techniques that the author utilizes to achieve a specific tone. These can include everything from word choice to figurative language.

A typical AP tone question might take the following form:

1. The overall tone of this passage can be described as
   - **(A)** insolent and flippant
   - **(B)** didactic and moralistic
   - **(C)** snooty and condescending
   - **(D)** biting and sarcastic
   - **(E)** cynical but hopeful

Tone: Shades of Meaning

To appreciate the power of tone, think of how it can affect a simple two-letter word: *no* (defiantly); *no* (hesitantly); *no* (fearfully); *no* (in horror); *no* (teasingly); *no* (doubtfully); *no* (triumphantly).

For authors, conveying a specific tone is often difficult because they must give the reader the clues necessary for "hearing" the tone through the words on the page. The reader's task is to detect those clues and thus understand the "tone of voice" the author intended. If you miss the tone, you miss the meaning.

Tone, Activity 1

The words in the table below are commonly used to describe tone and have been used in past AP exam questions. The exercise that follows will familiarize you with these important tools.

Place the word *I'm* before the first word: *I'm* admiring. Say it aloud. What tone or lilt comes into your voice when you admire something? How about your body language? Your facial expression? Now complete the sentence. Imagine a situation when you are admiring something—a Mustang, a football pass, the hottest video star's moves. Try this with some of the other words listed below: I'm agitated . . . I'm angry . . . Sometimes the sound of the word helps you get the tone. *Benevolent* is pleasant-sounding, euphonious; *contemptuous* is harsh-sounding.

admiring	colloquial	diffident
agitated	compassionate	disdainful
angry	complimentary	disgusted
annoyed	concerned	dramatic
apathetic	condescending	ecstatic
apologetic	confident	effusive
apprehensive	consoling	elegiac
authoritative	contemptuous	facetious
bantering	contentious	factual
benevolent	contradictory	fanciful
biting	cynical	flippant
bitter	dejected	haughty
brash	desperate	hopeful
candid	detached	humble
cheery	determined	impartial
clinical	didactic	incisive

indignant	moralistic	scornful
inflammatory	mournful	sentimental
informative	neutral	snooty
inquisitive	nostalgic	solemn
insipid	objective	somber
insolent	passive	soothing
instructive	patronizing	sympathetic
ironic	pedantic	taunting
irreverent	persuasive	threatening
learned	petty	turgid
lighthearted	pretentious	urbane
lugubrious	respectful	urgent
manipulative	restrained	vibrant
melancholic	romantic	whimsical
miserable	sarcastic	wistful
mock-heroic	sardonic	worshipful
mock-serious	satiric	
mocking	scholarly	

Tone, Activity 2

Now read the following fable by James Thurber.

The Courtship of Arthur and Al

Once upon a time there was a young beaver named Al and an older beaver named Arthur. They were both in love with a pretty little female. She looked with disfavor upon the young beaver's suit because he was a harum-scarum and a ne'er-do-well. He had never done a single gnaw of work in his life, for he preferred to eat and sleep and to swim lazily in the streams and to play Now-I'll-Chase-You with the girls. The older beaver had never done anything but work from the time he got his first teeth. He had never played anything with anybody.

When the young beaver asked the female to marry him, she said she wouldn't think of it unless he amounted to something. She reminded him that Arthur had built thirty-two dams and was working on three others, whereas he, Al, had never even made a bread board or a pin tray in his life. Al was very sorry, but he said he would never go to work just because a woman wanted him to. Thereupon she offered to be a sister to him, but he pointed out that he already had seventeen sisters. So he went back to eating and sleeping and swimming in the streams and playing Spider-in-the Parlor with the girls. The female married Arthur one day at the lunch hour (he could never get away from work for more than one hour at a time). They had seven children and Arthur worked so hard supporting them he wore his teeth down to the gum line. His health broke in two before long and he died without ever having had a vacation in his life. The young beaver continued to eat and sleep and swim in the streams and play Unbutton-Your-Shoe with the girls. He never Got Anywhere, but he had a long life and a Wonderful Time.

Moral: It is better to have loafed and lost than never to have loafed at all.

Analysis: "The Courtship of Arthur and Al"
Answer the questions below. If necessary, refer to the selection.

1. Summarize the tale.

_____

_____

_____

2. List the words or lines that influence tone.

_____

_____

_____

_____

_____

3. Identify any literary devices or techniques that help the author convey tone.

_____

_____

_____

To see student responses to these questions, turn to page 82.

Lesson 3: Answers

Irony, Activity 1

Sample Student Responses

"Lines for a Christmas Card"

the irony of using the day on which most of the Western world celebrates the concept of peace to curse your enemies

"Earth"

Highly intelligent beings would not destroy themselves.

Irony, Activity 5

Sample Student Responses

1. This indicates irony. It's ironic that no matter how much planning you do, you can't plan the weather.
2. This indicates irony. Most moms would be horrified that their daughter got a navel ring, but this mom wants one too.
3. This doesn't indicate irony. The teacher is being sarcastic.
4. This doesn't indicate irony. The student is being sarcastic.
5. This indicates irony. The hurdle jumper can jump high hurdles, but can't get past her own little doorstep without breaking her leg.

Analysis, Activity 1: Marc Antony's speech from *Julius Caesar*

Sample Student Responses

1. Although charged not to speak in a manner that would detract from Caesar's killers, Marc Antony manages not only to speak of the good done by Caesar but also takes away from the honor of the assassins. In his speech, he refutes Brutus' accusation that Caesar was ambitious. To achieve this, Antony reminds the crowd that Caesar had been offered the crown three times, but had refused it each time. Antony also reminds them of how much they had loved Caesar, how much Caesar had loved them.

2. In the course of the speech, Antony repeats the phrase, "Brutus is an honourable man," each time condemning him even more effectively. By the fourth repetition, we know that Brutus is anything but honorable.

   Shakespeare develops irony by having Antony declare that his purpose is not to honor the dead, and then goes on and praises Caesar. He uses Brutus' own words to praise Caesar and condemn Brutus. He says, "I speak not to disprove what Brutus spoke, / But here I am to speak what I do know." Antony leaves no doubt of his true feelings for Brutus and the other conspirators.

3. "Honourable man" repeated four times. The repetition of the phrase builds to a searing condemnation of Brutus as dishonorable. Calling a murderer honorable is in itself ironic.

   metonymy/synecdoche/form of direct address: "Friends, Romans, countrymen, lend me your ears." A stark call to attention sets the tone for the speech. Also appeals to Romans' patriotism.

   chiasmus: "I come to bury Caesar, not to praise him." This assures the assassins that he'll abide by their agreement, yet he clues his listeners in to his actual intent.

   rhetorical questions: "Did this in Caesar seem ambitious?" "Was this ambition?" "What cause withholds you then to mourn for him?" Provoke the audience to respond to these questions. Sets up, by implication, the idea that it was the assassins, not Caesar, who suffered from ambition. Ironic contrast of ambitious and honorable throughout the speech should be noted.

Analysis, Activity 2: "aesop revised by archy"

Sample Student Responses

1. A lamb and a wolf meet by a stream. Angrily, the wolf accuses the lamb of dirtying the water, thus justifying his killing of the lamb. Further arguments ensue, and although the lamb is innocent, the wolf, true to his nature, declares that he will eat the lamb anyway because "i am hungry." A man rescues the lamb, criticizing the wolf's intended actions. The man takes the lamb home, kills it, cooks it, and eats it. After his meal, he continues to rail against the "brutality of wolves and the injustice of the universe."

2.
words	how they work (effect they have)
muddied	it is incongruous with the image of a lamb, especially a spring lamb
I am resolved	the wolf sounds like a lawyer
outrage	inappropriate for a wolf to describe natural behavior this way
am going to kill you	moves from formal declaration that sounds like a legal brief to a matter-of-fact announcement of intended lambicide
just a moment	understatement: the lamb responds not in terror but politely
vile lupine marauder	incongruous language for a hunter
you shall not kill	sounds like hero chasing villain away
exit the wolf	moves from woodland scene to stage directions

3. allusion: Wordsworth and Blake celebrated nature in their poetry yet the wolf is part of the natural world and is only acting instinctively, while the human's behavior should be "above" that of the wolf.

   stock characters: All three characters are stock characters in one sense, but not in the way they talk, which is where the irony comes in.

   paradox: The man refers to the wolf as vile, bloody, and inhuman but he is the one who cuts the lamb's throat and eats it. He even piously says grace. He never sees his own hypocrisy.

4. The author seems to be saying that people deceive themselves to get what they want. They are blind to everything that would make them uncomfortable or think badly of themselves. The weak and the innocent will always be victims of the strong and powerful.

Tone, Activity 2: "The Courtship of Arthur and Al"

Sample Student Responses

1. Al was a young beaver who never did any work and just liked to play and chase the girls. Arthur was an older beaver who did nothing but work. They were both in love with a female beaver, but she would have nothing to do with a lazy beaver like Al, so she married Arthur. Arthur worked himself literally to death, and Al, who continued to enjoy himself, lived a long time.

2. "harum-scarum," "never done a single gnaw of work," "never done anything but work from the time he got his first teeth," "had never even made a bread board or a pin tray," "already had seventeen sisters," "wore his teeth down to the gum line"

3. The tone of this piece is mock-serious. The author uses situational irony. The hard-working beaver never had any fun and died young, while the good-for-nothing beaver lived a long and happy life. The author uses tongue-in-cheek humor throughout the piece. The moral is a pun on the line, "It is better to have loved and lost than never to have loved at all."

PART 3
AP Multiple Choice

Scoring Big on the AP Multiple-Choice Section

In Section One of the AP examination, you will read five or six literary passages and answer multiple-choice questions about each. These passages will consist of both poetry and prose, and will be representative of the type of literature that freshmen read in college. This section accounts for 45% of your total grade and takes approximately one hour.

AP Test Breakdown

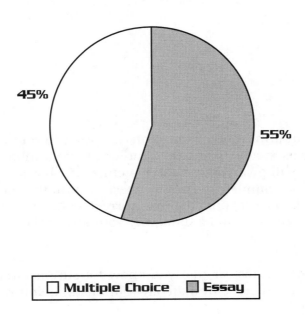

45%

55%

☐ **Multiple Choice** ▨ **Essay**

The primary purpose of Section One is to assess your ability to understand the meaning of a given passage and to identify the literary elements that the author uses to express this meaning. To prepare for this, you should have a solid understanding of the literary elements reviewed in Part 2 (pages 13–82), as well as a familiarity with the types of multiple-choice questions that will be asked.

Multiple-Choice Items: A Question of Structure

The way that multiple-choice questions are worded on the AP test can give you clues as to how to answer. Studying the question types and examples below will give you a clearer picture of what to expect on the exam. When you complete the practice test items at the end of the book, don't just check to see if your answer is correct. Instead, study each question and make sure you understand *why* your answer is right or wrong.

"I, II, III"

First of all, find an answer that you know for sure is either correct or incorrect. Then you can eliminate any options that contradict this.

Example:

1. In line 149, "speck" refers to which of the following?
   I.   a water sprite (line 155)
   II. the specter bark (line 202)
   III. naked hulk (line 195)
   (A) I only
   (B) II only
   (C) I and III only
   (D) II and III only
   (E) I, II, and III

"According to the Speaker"

Read the lines before and after the line in question, and then read all of the answer choices before deciding on one. Look only for what the speaker means at this particular point, not necessarily for the overall message of the piece. This deals with what the speaker is doing, saying, or implying. These questions are usually specific to the passage and depend on the subject material. Be careful not to assume the literal meaning, but check the answers in the context of the piece.

Example:

1. According to the speaker, Appomattox was actually a victory
for
   (A) New England idealism
   (B) the Rosicrucians
   (C) the proletariat
   (D) the plutocracy
   (E) "a forlorn intelligentsia"

"Allusion"

This asks what an allusion is referring to, or how it aids the idea/meaning of the piece. This is the perfect question to skip if you don't recognize the allusion, and a perfect example of why recognizing allusions is beneficial (see Part 2). If time remaining is very slim, this type of question can usually be answered without a great understanding of the passage if you are familiar with the allusion.

Example:

1. In the line, "That's Ophelia, that Cordelia," Yeats is referring to
   (A) the protagonists of *Othello* and *The Crucible*
   (B) tragic female figures in *Hamlet* and *King Lear*
   (C) wives of Odysseus and Agamemnon
   (D) Lear's daughters
   (E) tragic female figures in *Macbeth* and *King Lear*

"Context"

This type of question asks you to identify the meaning of a word used in the context of a passage. Remember that many words have several meanings, and that there are subtle shades of meaning as well. You must make sure the definition you choose matches the way the author intended the word to be interpreted in the specific piece. Try replacing the word in the passage with the possible definitions given. Choose the one that does not change the meaning of the sentence.

Example:

1. What does the word *chagrin* mean as used in the context of
the story?
   (A) optimism
   (B) foreboding
   (C) cheerfulness
   (D) embarrassment
   (E) pessimism

"Dominant Device"

Some questions will ask for the "dominant device" or technique of an excerpt. In addition, some will ask what effect this device produces. In such questions, there are usually a few options you can eliminate. Once this is done, eliminate answers demonstrating correct technique, but incorrect effect.

Example:

1. The dominant device used by the author is
   (A) comparison and contrast
   (B) appeal to emotion
   (C) extended analogy
   (D) hyperbole
   (E) interior monologue

"Effect"

This question asks you to understand the technique of lines in a question and also to choose why they are used (what effect they have on the passage). This is a good type to skip if time is running out. Be sure to get the lines in context, because this is the only way to understand the effect in addition to the meaning of the lines. The purpose of a sentence or line is usually to introduce an idea, set the tone, solidify something that was said before it, or serve as a thesis.

Example:

1. The speaker includes descriptions of Barton Williams primarily to provide all of the following except
   (A) an example of the type of man Shirley is expected to marry
   (B) a parallel with Bethune Street
   (C) a symbol of the boring future to which Shirley sees herself doomed
   (D) a contrast to the dreamy but exciting Arthur
   (E) an interlude of comic relief

"Excerpted Words"

Read and reread the entire sentence in which the word is found, as well as a few lines before and after the excerpted words. If you are still unable to ascertain the meaning, identify the device, etc., reread the entire paragraph or stanza. Eliminate the obviously incorrect answers and work with what's left.

Example:

1. In line 11, "convolutions" refers to
   (A) convictions
   (B) coils
   (C) irregular folds
   (D) intricate passages
   (E) agitations

"Infer/Suggest"

Some questions will ask you to construe the meaning of an excerpt based on the context and connotations of the piece. Avoid taking a literal view of the question: Look for deeper meaning. At the same time, do not be afraid to choose an obvious answer if you think it is the correct one.

Example:

1. It can be inferred that the speaker
   (A) teaches biology
   (B) is a native Californian
   (C) sees parallels between humans and animals
   (D) does not enjoy camping alone
   (E) is allergic to cats

"Literary Devices"

Find clear examples of the devices that you are looking for, if possible. Try to eliminate the ones that you know are not used within the piece. Good knowledge of the literary vocabulary is particularly helpful in ruling out distracters and incorrect answers.

Example:

1. In lines 46–48, the speaker employs which of the following literary devices?
   (A) euphemism
   (B) allusion
   (C) metaphor
   (D) chiasmus
   (E) paradox

"Modifying"

Pay attention to the line numbers. Go to the beginning of the sentence in question and imagine someone saying it aloud. Read slowly and comprehend what the speaker is saying. If you can follow what the imaginary speaker is saying to you, you should be able to find what the clause or word is modifying.

Example:

1. In line 8, "avalanching" modifies
   (A) horses (line 8)
   (B) night (line 4)
   (C) flare (line 9)
   (D) darkness (line 8)
   (E) quake (line 9)

"Not/Except"

This type of question appears in many forms, but the most basic is "all of the following EXCEPT." These questions can be time-consuming, because you must examine all the answers in order to determine which one is correct. Always read all of the answers before making your selection. Cross off the true answers rather than the false ones.

Example:

1. According to the speaker, the American male is seeking a wife who fits all of the following descriptions EXCEPT:
   (A) an educated woman
   (B) a woman who "does something"
   (C) a woman who agrees that marriage is a matter of give and take
   (D) a woman who cries at sad movies
   (E) a woman who nurtures him

"Passage as a Whole"

This type of question always refers to an idea that is present throughout the work. Look back at the parts in the poem or passage that most obviously support the clue, and then eliminate the answer choices that have no relation at all. Take into account everything in the passage. If an answer choice fits for only one part of the piece, it's not right. Choices that contain exact words from the piece are usually not right. The most abstract answer is also usually incorrect.

Example:

1. The passage as a whole is best described as
   (A) a dramatic monologue
   (B) an objective commentary
   (C) an extended metaphor
   (D) a villanelle
   (E) an allegorical fable

"Pronoun/Antecedent"

This type of question asks which antecedent (noun) the pronoun is referring to. It is usually not the most obvious one nor the one closest to the pronoun. This can be a time-consuming question, and it should be avoided if little time is left. One technique is to replace the word with the antecedent you think is the correct answer and reread it to make sure it makes sense in context.

Example:

1. In line 47, the antecedent for the pronoun "they" is
   (A) officials at the bus station
   (B) black passengers on the bus
   (C) children waiting for the bus
   (D) white passengers on the bus
   (E) bus drivers

"Quotes"

This type of question asks you to choose a quote from the passage that either best expresses a specific idea, or best supports another quote. Reread and make sure you understand the parts immediately before, after, and including the quote. Usually the correct answer is not the one closest to the idea within the passage. A full understanding of the passage is required to relate the choices with the section in question.

Example:

1. With which of the following quotes does the speaker illustrate what he means by "Youth is impulsive"?
   (A) "It matters little where we pass the remnant of our days. They will not be many."
   (B) "Revenge by young men is considered gain, even at the cost of their own lives."
   (C) "His brave warriors will be to us a bristling wall of strength."
   (D) "To us the ashes of our ancestors are sacred and their resting place is hallowed ground."
   (E) "Even the little children who lived here and rejoiced here for a brief season will love these somber solitudes and at eventide they greet shadowy returning spirits."

"Rhetorical Function"

This type of question asks you to explain the purpose of a sentence, group of sentences, whole paragraph, or line or stanza of poetry in relation to the rest of the piece. Ask yourself what the selected part of the passage or poem does. For example, it may draw a comparison, state the thesis of the piece, or give an example.

Example:

1. Which of the following best describes the rhetorical function of the sentence beginning "You must go at your life with a broadax . . ."?
   (A) It restates the thesis of the passage.
   (B) It provides an example of the speaker's innocence.
   (C) It provides support for the thesis.
   (D) It draws an analogy between a writer's life and a moth's life.
   (E) It gives factual information.

"Structure"

This type of question asks you to identify the structure of a poem. Scan the poem to determine meter and rhyme scheme, if any, and then look for the answer. Remember that in many poems, especially longer ones, the structure may not be consistent.

Example:

1. The structure of this poem is
   (A) four-line stanzas of iambic pentameter rhymed *abab*
   (B) a pantoum
   (C) a classic Petrarchan sonnet
   (D) four-line stanzas of iambic pentameter rhymed *abab* alternating with a refrain of two lines of iambic hexameter
   (E) blank verse

"Style"

When answering questions about a writer's style, be sure that both of the descriptors fit. In fact, for any question that combines two answers in one, check both carefully to be sure they both apply. In the following example, you can eliminate answer C because the two words are antonyms, so both cannot be correct.

Example:

1. The style of the passage as a whole is most accurately characterized as
   (A) disjointed and abstract
   (B) formal and complex
   (C) unemotional and effusive
   (D) pedantic and didactic
   (E) rambling and descriptive

"Tone"

This asks you to identify the tone of the passage (or a selection from the passage). (Read Lesson 3 carefully to increase your understanding of this concept.) If the answer choices involve pairs of words, like those in the example below, you should be able to eliminate some choices because one of the words in the combination does not apply. Make sure you know whether the question is asking for the author's tone or the speaker's tone. They may not be the same.

Example:

1. The overall tone of the passage is
   (A) accusatory and pessimistic
   (B) humorous and ironic
   (C) insightful and penetrating
   (D) mournful and nostalgic
   (E) whimsical and charming

5

Analyzing Poetry for the Multiple-Choice Section

This lesson will focus on strategies for responding to AP multiple-choice questions about poetry. Questions relating to poetry make up approximately 40% of the AP English test, broken down as follows:

Section One (Multiple Choice)	Section Two (Essay Portion)
At least two poems	At least one poem

Many people find poetry harder to read than prose because of its heavy use of figurative language, symbolism, and allusion. Because a poem says so much in so few words, it is a challenging means of communication.

In addition, poems often contain multiple levels of meaning. The danger in such cases is that a superficial reading often leads in turn to a superficial understanding of the poem's meaning. This can prove disastrous if the reader is taking a test, such as the AP exam. Close reading, and rereading, is the key to successfully analyzing a piece of poetry.

Upon close inspection, even the simplest nursery rhyme can hint at deeper levels of meaning.

JACK AND JILL

Jack and Jill went up the hill,
To fetch a pail of water,
Jack fell down and broke his crown,
And Jill came tumbling after.

"Jack and Jill": Interpreting Meaning

You have probably read this poem many times before. But have you ever thought about what it means? On the surface, it seems very simple: A boy and a girl climb a hill to fill a bucket with water. Unfortunately, the boy falls, hitting his head, and the girl tumbles after him. Upon a closer reading, however, the poem may suggest a deeper meaning. Consider these possibilities:

Interpretation #1:
Man is destined to struggle forever, only to meet with disaster.

Interpretation #2:
The poem gives us another version of Adam and Eve's expulsion from the Garden of Eden.

Now that we've introduced the *what* of "Jack and Jill," we can go further with the idea, and think about how different schools of interpretation might look at the poem.

"Jack and Jill": The feminist perspective
Why is Jill always following Jack? Why is his name first? Why was she so distraught over his fall that she fell after him? Should she have played Florence Nightingale and cared for him? Who was carrying the pail?

"Jack and Jill": The religious perspective
Were Jack and Jill being punished for a transgression? Was the punishment commensurate with the sin? Are they representative of Adam and Eve? Does the water signify a baptism? Were they redeemed after their fall?

"Jack and Jill": The sociological perspective
Was this an argument for child labor laws? Are they representative of the poor, underprivileged working class? Or does the hill represent their attempt to rise above their class in society? Is the crown a railing against the monarchy?

"Jack and Jill": Recognizing Literary Devices

☞ AP Tip: Techniques for Interpreting a Poem

To interpret a poem, you should first examine it to see what literary devices the poet uses. This means checking for:

structure	allusion	apostrophe	conceit
alliteration	analogy	euphony	cacophony
assonance	consonance	imagery	internal rhyme
symbolism	onomatopoeia	metaphor	simile

Taking It Apart: "Jack and Jill"

While being able to identify different literary techniques is certainly necessary in order to analyze poetry, you must be able to show how these devices contribute to meaning. For example, look at the use of alliteration in the names themselves: *Jack* and *Jill*.

Do you see any connection between this repeated beginning sound and the poem's meaning? _____

_____

Is assonance used in this poem? _____

No doubt you've already chosen *Jill* and *hill*, *down* and *crown*. Do these sounds emphasize meaning? If so, how? _____

_____

_____

_____

Remember, for this lesson you are developing your expertise in taking the poetry multiple-choice portion of the test, but in order to do that, you must first reinforce your ability to analyze poetry.

Multiple Choice: "Jack and Jill"

Try answering these sample questions about "Jack and Jill":

1. What is the tone of the poem?
    (A) optimistic
    (B) foreboding
    (C) cheerful
    (D) mournful
    (E) pessimistic

2. Who is the speaker?
    (A) Mother Goose
    (B) a second-grade teacher
    (C) a concerned parent
    (D) an AP teacher
    (E) a six-year-old

3. The hill symbolizes
    (A) insurmountable obstacles
    (B) sexual fulfillment
    (C) social climbing

(D) Golgotha
(E) surmountable obstacles

You can probably see that, depending on your interpretation of the poem, your answers could be any or all of these!

Literary Origins: "Jack and Jill"

Interestingly, *People* magazine reported a supposedly true story of the derivation of "Jack and Jill." According to folklore, a young man named Jack did die of a "broken crown" or cracked skull in Kilmersdon, England, sometime in the 1400s. His sweetheart, Jill, died grief-stricken after giving birth to their son.

Not every poem is open to interpretation; some have a very specific meaning. In such cases, it may be necessary to have a greater understanding of the historical, personal, or social context in which the poem was written. Another familiar nursery rhyme illustrates this quite clearly:

Ring Around the Rosy

Ring around the rosy
A pocket full of posies
Ashes! Ashes! We all fall down.

Happy children have sung this nursery rhyme for centuries. However, its roots lie in a dark period of human history. During the Middle Ages, one of the primary symptoms of the bubonic plague—the Black Death—was a red ring on the skin, called a *rosy*. Posies—common flowers—were thought to ward off the deadly disease. When plague victims died, their bodies were burned in the hope that the plague germs would burn with them. Of course "falling down" refers to the fate of those infected with bubonic plague—death.

Finally, not every poem you will ever read will have a hidden meaning. Some will be truly simplistic, others purely experiential. For example, read the following poem from Shakespeare's play *Love's Labour's Lost*.

Winter

When icicles hang by the wall,
    And Dick the shepherd blows his nail,
And Tom bears logs into the hall,
    And milk comes frozen home in pail,
When blood is nipped, and ways be foul,
Then nightly sings the staring owl,
    Tu-whit;

Tu-who, a merry note,
While greasy Joan doth keel the pot.

When all aloud the wind doth blow,
    And coughing drowns the parson's saw,
And birds sit brooding in the snow,
    And Marian's nose looks red and raw,
When roasted crabs hiss in the bowl,
Then nightly sings the staring owl,
    Tu-whit;
Tu-who, a merry note,
While greasy Joan doth keel the pot.

This poem beautifully describes a winter's day in Renaissance England. You feel cold just reading it, but it does not hint at a deeper meaning.

Review

Although you reviewed general literary terms in Lesson 1, you should familiarize yourself with those that are specific to poetry. These are listed below.

Poetry Terminology

alliteration	elegy	near (or slant)
allusions	epigram	rhyme
ambiguity	euphony	occasion
analogy	figurative language	octave
anapest	form	onomatopoeia
antecedent	free verse	organization
apostrophe	heroic couplet	oxymoron
assonance	hexameter	paradox
attitude	hyperbole	pastoral
aubade	iamb	pentameter
ballad	imagery	personification
blank verse	interior monologue	quatrain
cacophony	internal rhyme	refrain
carpe diem	inversion	repetition
central purpose	irony	rhetorical questions
(meaning)	Italian	rhythm
conceit	(Petrarchan)	sarcasm
connotation	sonnet	satire
consonance	litotes	sestet
couplet	(understatement)	shift
dactyl	lyric poetry	simile
denotation	metaphor	soliloquy
diction	meter	sonnet
didactic	metonymy	speaker
effect	narrative poetry	stanza

structure	terza rima	trimeter
stylistic devices	tetrameter	trochee
symbols	theme	understatement
synecdoche	title	villanelle
syntax	tone	

Part I: The "What"

Now it is time to try your hand at analyzing some poetry. Quickly scan "Rites of Passage" by Sharon Olds. This will give you a sense of the poem's meaning. Then slowly and carefully do a close reading. Pay special attention to *what* the author says, as it will help you to determine *what* she means! As you read, underline, circle, or otherwise mark the poem to identify significant words, phrases, and literary elements.

Rites of Passage

As the guests arrive at my son's party
They gather in the living room—
short men, men in first grade
with smooth jaws and chins.
5   Hands in pockets, they stand around
jostling, jockeying for place, small fights
breaking out and calming. One says to another
How old are you? Six. I'm seven. So?
They eye each other, seeing themselves
10   tiny in the other's pupils. They clear their
throats a lot, a room of small bankers,
they fold their arms and frown. *I could beat you*
up, a seven says to a six,
the dark cake, round and heavy as a
15   turret, behind them on the table. My son,
freckles like specks of nutmeg on his cheeks,
chest narrow as the balsa keel of a
model boat, long hands
cool and thin as the day they guided him
20   out of me, speaks up as a host
for the sake of the group.
We could easily kill a two-year-old,
he says in his clear voice. The other
men agree, they clear their throats
25   like Generals, they relax and get down to
playing war, celebrating my son's life.

You have just begun the most important process you can use in analyzing poetry: a careful, close reading. Poetry is never meant to be read only once. We read poetry that moves us again and again. A great poem unfolds like a lovely rosebud, revealing more of itself on each reading. It will show its color and shape, and delight our senses anew each time we read it.

However, for the AP test, you will not have the luxury of as many readings as possible. Instead, you are limited to approximately ten minutes per poem or passage for the multiple-choice section, so you will need to train yourself to scan the poem quickly first to get the gist of it. Then you must give it that careful and close reading we discussed earlier. Always feel free to mark the passage with your ideas as you read—this can help save time later.

To assist you in becoming as adept as possible at understanding and analyzing poetry and thus able to respond accurately to multiple-choice questions about it, we are now going to do what we would do in the classroom. We will break the poem down into lines and groups of lines to determine *what* the poet is saying. After that is accomplished, we will examine *how* she says it. During the exam, you should answer these questions as you read the piece.

Analysis: "Rites of Passage"

1. Paraphrase the poem by putting as much of it as you can in your own words.

   _____

   _____

   _____

2. Make a determination of the poet and poem's purpose. What is it? Use the space below to write a one-sentence interpretation of the poem's reason for being.

   _____

   _____

   _____

3. Now read the first four lines again:

   As the guests arrive at my son's party
   They gather in the living room—
   short men, men in first grade
   with smooth jaws and chins.

   Who is the speaker?

   _____

4. Read lines 12 to 15:

   . . . I could beat you
   up, a seven says to a six,
   the dark cake, round and heavy as a
   turret, behind them on the table. . . .

   What simile does the poet use to emphasize the belligerent motif?

   _____

5. Now read lines 15 to 21.

> . . . My son,
> freckles like specks of nutmeg on his cheeks,
> chest narrow as the balsa keel of a
> model boat, long hands
> cool and thin as the day they guided him
> out of me, speaks up as a host
> for the sake of the group.

What images does the speaker use to emphasize the youth and fragility of her son?

_____

6. Despite these characteristics, what role does he assume?

_____

7. Lines 22 and 23 serve as the poem's climax:

> *We could easily kill a two-year-old*,
> he says in his clear voice.

Why are these lines startling in the context of the poem?

_____

_____

8. What is ironic about the last four lines?

_____

_____

9. This is an appropriate time to revisit the title. Think about the connotations of the words *rites* and *passage*. What other "rites of passage" do you know of?

_____

_____

_____

10. Why is this an apt title?

_____

_____

_____

11. What do you think the poet is saying about human behavior (i.e., the poem's theme) even as it is exhibited in small children?

_____

_____

Part II: The "How"

It is time to attack the other aspect of analysis: the *how*. What techniques does the poet employ to achieve her purpose? This is the time to recall as much as you can of that long list of words on pages 97–98. Focus your responses on the devices the author uses. What imagery reinforces the depiction of little boys playing grown-up men? Remember, imagery appeals to all the senses. To assist you in determining the extent to which this device is used, look at the descriptions of the boys, their posture, their speech, the tone of voice implied by their speech, the cake, the nutmeg freckles.

Now that you have established a strong basis for an understanding of the poem "Rites of Passage" and the techniques the poet Sharon Olds uses, it's time for you to take a multiple-choice test on the poem. The following multiple-choice strategies will prove useful. Peruse them carefully, and then take the test.

☞ *AP Tip: Multiple Choice*

Here is a helpful five-step strategy for answering multiple-choice AP exam questions.

1. Read the poem quickly to get the gist of it.

2. Pass over what you do not fully understand, since time is of the essence. You may find that you pick up clues from subsequent questions. This will lead you to a greater understanding of the poem. You may find that you will wish to change one or two previous answers. Do so only if you are *sure* that your first response was incorrect.

3. Read the questions. Write directly on the test, crossing out those responses that are obviously incorrect. The process of elimination is valuable in narrowing your field while answering multiple-choice questions. In order to do this quickly, eliminate a response if any portion of it seems wrong. In the AP test, as in the SAT, you are not penalized for leaving a question blank. However, if you can eliminate at least one of the choices, you should attempt to guess the answer. Statistically, if you get one question right, you make up for four incorrect choices. The penalty for an incorrect response is 1/4 point off your score.

4. Concentrate on correctly answering 40 to 45 questions out of a possible 55 or so, rather than on answering all of the questions.

5. When you go back to answer a particular question, make sure that you go back and read from the beginning of the sentence, not the beginning of the last line.

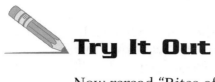

Try It Out

Now reread "Rites of Passage" and answer the questions that follow.

Multiple Choice: "Rites of Passage"

1. The central purpose of the poem is to show that
   - **(A)** parents don't truly know their children
   - **(B)** children are not innocent to begin with
   - **(C)** we need to know ourselves in order to understand ourselves
   - **(D)** the behavior of children often mirrors that of adults
   - **(E)** we are savage at heart

2. Calling the guests "short men" and "Generals . . . playing war" serves to do which of the following?
   - **(A)** It foreshadows the boys' future.
   - **(B)** It intensifies the tragedy of innocence being lost at such a young age.
   - **(C)** It emphasizes that both children and adults desire dominance.
   - **(D)** It points out that short men are prone to be belligerent.
   - **(E)** It shows that little boys like to play soldiers at war.

3. What is the speaker's tone?
   - **(A)** regretful sorrow
   - **(B)** observant chagrin
   - **(C)** puzzled anxiety
   - **(D)** ironic lightheartedness
   - **(E)** caustic sarcasm

4. The phrase, *"We could easily kill a two-year-old,"* emphasizes
   - **(A)** social unity through superiority over a common foe
   - **(B)** the tendency to strive for power and dominance even at such an early age
   - **(C)** the maturity of the young guests
   - **(D)** that children are naturally destructive
   - **(E)** the unexpressed horror of the mother upon hearing the statement

5. Why does the speaker choose a birthday party as a setting for the poem?
   - **(A)** to emphasize the innocence of childhood
   - **(B)** to add ironic contrast
   - **(C)** to lighten the horror
   - **(D)** to juxtapose life with death
   - **(E)** to highlight a rite of passage

6. Which of the following best describes the effect produced by the phrase, "they relax and get down to playing war, celebrating my son's life"?
   (A) It illustrates the calm nature of the mother.
   (B) It illustrates the imagination of the children.
   (C) It illustrates the consciousness of the children.
   (D) It illustrates the irony of playing war to celebrate life.
   (E) It illustrates the mother's concern.

7. Which best describes the children's behavior between lines 6 and 13?
   (A) acculturated hostility
   (B) ridiculing threats
   (C) insecure belligerence
   (D) pompous loathing
   (E) pedantic ambivalence

8. The image of "Generals" suggests all of the following EXCEPT
   (A) decisiveness
   (B) power
   (C) preparedness
   (D) anger
   (E) leadership

9. By comparing the boys first to bankers and then to generals, the speaker
   (A) increases their loss of innocence
   (B) heightens their capability for increasing evil
   (C) portrays them as little boys playing at being adults
   (D) is injecting levity into the occasion
   (E) is projecting her son's future

10. The speaker of the passage is
    (A) an insightful but biased narrator
    (B) a disillusioned parent
    (C) a perceptive and concerned mother
    (D) a nonjudgmental commentator
    (E) a loving mother

11. Which statement best defines the mother's attitude toward her son?
    (A) "Narrow as the balsa keel of a model boat" *(lines 17–18)* shows that she still finds innocence within her son's image.
    (B) "Dark cake, round and heavy as a turret" *(lines 14–15)* is ominous: she expects turbulence between her son and his guests.
    (C) *"We could easily kill a two-year-old" (line 22)* expresses her realization that he is entirely unknown to her at the moment.
    (D) "Long hands cool and thin" *(lines 18–19)* implies that she is concerned about his frailty.
    (E) "In his clear voice" *(line 23)* reveals his mother's sense of pride; he is clearly the leader of the group.

Lesson 5: Answers

Analysis: "Rites of Passage"

Sample Student Responses

1. Children come to a birthday party and are feeling rather uncomfortable at first. Then the challenges and fights begin. They even talk about beating up two-year-olds because they know they could kill a toddler. The boys then begin to relax and play "war" or boyish games while the mother watches the stages of her boy's life.

2. Human nature is instinctively violent, regardless of age. Children learn from observation. Man, no matter how young or apparently civilized, is, at his core, primal. Men are always children; children are always men. All men are created with an innate desire for violence which reveals itself during rites of passage.

3. the mother

4. She compares the cake to a gun turret.

5. The speaker emphasizes her son's fragility by comparing his freckles to specks of nutmeg, a spice, and his narrow chest to balsa wood, which is a very light and flimsy wood.

6. a commander's role, one of a leader with whom they all agree

7. These lines are startling because the children are six or seven years old. They should be thinking about building forts and sailing boats, not killing babies when they are still babies themselves.

8. They are playing war, pretending to kill, yet they are celebrating life through a birthday party. They "relax" by "playing war," but war is not relaxing. They are called men, yet they are children.

9. bar and bat mitzvah, confirmation, quinceana, and walkabout

10. Being a kid and playing these types of games is a rite of passage, a part of a normal childhood since we are living in a violent world.

11. Boys and men see everything in terms of fighting, war, and power. They think of it as a game.

Multiple Choice: "Rites of Passage"

Answers

1. *D* The metaphors used by the poet—jockeying, weaponry, adult postures—reinforce their mimicking of adult behavior. Both *A* and *C* are generalizations that are not relevant to the central purpose. Answers *B* and *E* touch on what may be universal truths, but neither reflects the central purpose of this poem.

2. *B* It demonstrates that although very young, they have already observed enough violence to bring it into their play experience.

3. *B* Use the process of elimination for this one. The mother is watching the children and relating the scene she has observed with obvious distress; thus, "observant chagrin" is the best answer. Choice *A*, "regretful sorrow," is not correct since she does not express regret (remember, if one part of the answer is wrong, you should eliminate it). Choice *C*, "puzzled anxiety," is not correct, for the mother sees clearly what is occurring. As for *D*, "ironic lightheartedness," although irony exists, there is no lightheartedness here. Even though some of the images in another context might strike the reader as humorous, in this context, they inspire horror instead. Choice *E*, "caustic sarcasm," is obviously wrong.

4. *A* Mirroring adults and recognizing that nothing unites faster than a common enemy, whether real or imagined, strengthens the social unit and raises the group's self-esteem. Choice *B* is distracting because it seems like a very possible answer, but it is not the best choice. Answer *C* is obviously wrong, while *D* and *E* are not relevant in context.

5. *B* This is correct because of the ironic contrast of the presumably benign occasion, the young child's birthday party, and the potential for violent behavior observed by the mother. Answers *A* and *D* are obviously wrong. Choice *C* is incorrect because it does not lighten the horror. Choice *E* is the distracter. While a birthday is indeed a rite of passage, it is nowhere nearly as profound a rite of passage as the one which the children undergo in this poem.

6. *D* Playing at war is a markedly ironic way to celebrate life. Choice *A* is incorrect, since this phrase says nothing about the mother's nature. Choice *B* is incorrect, as the children could play far more imaginative games, while *C* and *E* are obviously wrong.

7. *A* The lines that begin with "jostling, jockeying . . ." and end with ". . . seven says to a six" (lines 6–13) clearly point to "acculturated hostility" as the correct answer. Acculturation is the process by which the culture of a particular society is instilled in a human being from infancy onward. Answers *B*, *C*, and *E* can be eliminated, since there is no evidence of ridicule, insecurity, pomposity or pedantic ambivalence (it might be a good idea to look these words up, as the multiple-choice test is very much a measure of the breadth of your vocabulary).

8. *D* The generals were not angry at all. It is important to note the word EXCEPT, which always makes a question challenging.

9. *C* This is the correct answer, because generals and bankers are adult roles. Choice *B* is incorrect, since neither being a

banker nor being a general implies inherent evil. Choice *D* is wrong, since levity implies humor and this is not funny, while *E* is obviously wrong.

10. *C* The mother is perceptive and concerned. Her perceptions are obvious; her concern is implied. Choice *A*, "an insightful but biased narrator," is not the best answer. Although insightful, she does not appear to be biased. Choice *B*, "a disillusioned parent," is incorrect. Although she may be unhappy with the situation, she is not expressing disillusionment or disenchantment. Choice *D* can be eliminated since the poem implies her dismay, which is judgmental. And we can also eliminate *E*. She probably is a loving mother, but this is not the best answer.

11. *A* Throughout the poem there is an obvious contrast between the children's ages and their actions, but they are still children. They remain relatively innocent.

Analyzing Prose for the Multiple-Choice Section

Much of the advice given on the poetry multiple choice applies to the prose multiple choice as well. Since you've been speaking prose all your life, it may seem the easier of the two sections. Once again, having a solid understanding of vocabulary, allusion, and other linguistic techniques will enable you to unlock meaning.

Try It Out

In 1981, the AP exam included a prose piece written by George Bernard Shaw. Below is the passage and some multiple-choice questions based on it. On the actual test, you will probably want to allow yourself about 15 minutes for this exercise (since there are usually four passages and 52–55 questions). Since this is practice, try not to take more than a half hour.

Cognitive research has shown that we remember and understand better when we can connect new knowledge to information and ideas we already have. This exercise is a good example. If you already know that Shaw is remembered for his wit, you will be expecting irony and subtle humor when you read this piece.

Untitled

At the passage "earth to earth, ashes to ashes, dust to dust" there was a little alteration of the words to suit the process. A door opened in the wall: and the violet coffin mysteriously passed out through it and vanished as it closed. People think that door is the door of the furnace: but it isn't. I went behind the scenes at the end of the service and saw the real thing. People are afraid to see it; but it is wonderful. I found there the violet coffin opposite another door, a real unmistakable furnace door this time: when it lifted there was a plain little chamber of cement and fire-brick. No heat, no noise. No roaring draught. No flame. No fuel. It looked cool, clean, sunny. You would have walked in or put your hand in without misgiving. Then the violet coffin moved again and went in, feet first. And behold! The feet burst miraculously into streaming ribbons of garnet coloured lovely flame, smokeless and eager, like pentecostal tongues, and as the whole coffin passed in, it sprang into flame all over; and my mother became that beautiful fire. . . . The door fell; well, they said that if we wanted to see it all through to the end, we should come back in an hour and a half. I remembered the wasted little figure with the wonderful face, and said "Too long" to myself—but off we went. . . . When we returned, the end was wildly funny; Mama would have enjoyed it enormously. We looked down through an opening in the floor. There we saw a roomy kitchen, with a big cement table and two cooks busy at it. They had little tongs in their hands, and they were deftly and busily picking nails and scraps of coffin handles out of Mama's dainty little heap of ashes and samples of bone. Mama herself being at the moment leaning over beside me, shaking with laughter. Then they swept her up into a sieve and shook her out; so that there was a heap of dust and a heap of bone scraps. And Mama said in my ear, "Which of the two heaps do you suppose is me?". . . and that merry episode was the end, except for making dust of the bone scraps and scattering them on a flower bed . . . grave, where is thy victory? And so goodnight, friends who understand about one's mother.

Analysis: "Untitled"

Now answer the questions that follow.

1. Summarize the piece in a few sentences.

   _____

   _____

   _____

   _____

   _____

2. What are the narrator's feelings toward his mother? Cite specific examples from the text to support your response.

   _____

   _____

   _____

   _____

   _____

3. List examples of unusual imagery and diction. Explain how they affect the meaning of the text.

_____

_____

_____

_____

4. Where is the humor? Find exemplary lines and name the technique used.

_____

_____

_____

_____

To see sample student responses to these questions, turn to page 117.

Multiple Choice: "Untitled"

Here are some multiple-choice questions based on the selection. Time yourself. Remember that on the actual test, you will have about 15 minutes to read a passage and to answer 12 to 15 questions on it.

1. Which statement best describes the central theme of the passage?
   (A) Death is a beautiful thing.
   (B) Loved ones live on in spirit and memory.
   (C) Death should not be viewed as a loss but rather as a passing.
   (D) The process of cremation is better than a traditional burial.
   (E) The memory of a loved one is sufficient for happiness.

2. The description of the cremation of Shaw's mother suggests a natural event that
   (A) greatly troubled Shaw; as his mother "sprang into flame," he realized how much he missed her
   (B) inspired an artistic desire within Shaw; the "garnet coloured flame" appealed to his senses
   (C) amused Shaw; he felt that it was a joy to watch his mother's streaming ribbons and he knew that she would feel the same
   (D) caused Shaw to admire the beauty in death; everything surrounding her cremation captivated him—the flame, the color, her peace
   (E) caused distress; Shaw regretted that his mother could not join him

3. Which of the following best conveys the author's central meaning in the passage?
   (A) "People are afraid to see it"
   (B) "earth to earth, ashes to ashes"
   (C) "Which of the two heaps do you suppose is me?"
   (D) "that merry episode was the end"
   (E) "grave, where is thy victory?"

4. The tone of the passage is one of
   (A) wondering amusement
   (B) comforting hope
   (C) unfathomable grief
   (D) ironic delight
   (E) cheerful glee

5. Which of the following best describes the organization of the passage?
   (A) connected stream of consciousness
   (B) unconnected stream of consciousness
   (C) chronological order
   (D) present time with flashbacks intermixed
   (E) both A and C

6. Shaw's description of his mother as a "wasted little figure with the wonderful face" can be best described as
   (A) sadly inaccurate
   (B) grimly disturbing
   (C) ironically respectful
   (D) lovingly nostalgic
   (E) sadly maudlin

7. All of the following display irony EXCEPT
   (A) "and the violet coffin mysteriously passed out through it and vanished as it closed"
   (B) "It looked cool, clean, sunny."
   (C) "and my mother became that beautiful fire"
   (D) "a big cement table and two cooks busy at it"
   (E) "And Mama said in my ear, 'Which of the two heaps do you suppose is me?'"

8. The first important shift in setting occurs in which sentence?
   (A) "I went behind the scenes at the end of the service and saw the real thing."
   (B) ". . . grave, where is thy victory?"
   (C) "There we saw a roomy kitchen . . ."
   (D) "the door fell . . ."
   (E) "A door opened in the wall . . ."

9. The phrase "You would have walked in or put your hand in without misgiving" is best understood to mean
   (A) the author has misgivings about his mother's death
   (B) the author sees the cremation process as ominous

      (C) the author considers the flame to be symbolic rather
           than actual
      (D) the author is accepting of his mother's death
      (E) The author wants to be cremated when he dies

10. The tone of "No heat, no noise. No roaring draught. No
    flame. No fuel" is one of
    (A) passive indifference
    (B) mild surprise
    (C) argumentative confusion
    (D) morbid fascination
    (E) flippant curiosity

11. "And mama said in my ear, 'Which of the two heaps do you
    suppose is me?'" This allows the reader to
    (A) understand the depressing undertone of the central
        purpose
    (B) understand Shaw's irreverent attitude toward his
        mother's death
    (C) experience the horror of the process
    (D) understand that the writer valued his mother's unique
        sense of humor
    (E) grasp the sadness Shaw felt at his mother's death

12. The "flame" and "fire" represent all of the following
    EXCEPT
    (A) ironic beauty
    (B) the fire of cremation
    (C) his mother's spirit
    (D) the beginning of life
    (E) a form of punishment

To see answers to these questions, turn to page 118.

Analyzing Prose for the Multiple-Choice Section: Activity 1

Practice writing your own multiple-choice questions. To do so:

- Find a piece that is brief yet rich in detail.
- Use two-word answers in some cases.
- Have a distracter—an answer that MIGHT, to the unwary,
  appear correct but is not as good or accurate as the correct
  one.
- Make sure all the answer choices you give for a specific
  question are about the same length and follow the same
  grammatical pattern.

- Try to model your questions on real ones. We've analyzed old AP exams and have found that they often ask for the following:

  Main idea
  Antecedent (when it does not clearly follow the noun)
  Shifts
  Point of view
  Organization
  Literary devices
  Allusions
  Tone

Try It Out

Now read the complete short story "Roselily" by Alice Walker. Then answer the questions that follow. These are somewhat generic questions that could apply to any piece of literature. They will help you to unlock the meaning of the piece.

Roselily

Dearly Beloved,

She dreams; dragging herself across the world. A small girl in her mother's white robe and veil, knee raised waist high through a bowl of quicksand soup. The man who stands beside her is against this standing on the front porch of her house, being married to the sound of cars whizzing by on highway 61.

we are gathered here

Like cotton to be weighed. Her fingers at the last minute busily removing dry leaves and twigs. Aware it is a superficial sweep. She knows he blames Mississippi for the respectful way the men turn their heads up in the yard, the women stand waiting and knowledgeable, their children held from mischief by teachings from the wrong God. He glares beyond them to the occupants of the cars, white faces glued to promises beyond a country wedding, noses thrust forward like dogs on a track. For him they usurp the wedding.

in the sight of God

Yes, open house. That is what country black folks like. She dreams she does not already have three children. A squeeze around the flowers in her hands chokes off three and four and five years of breath. Instantly she is ashamed and frightened in her superstition. She looks for the first time at the preacher, forces humility into her eyes, as if she believes he is, in fact, a man of God. She can imagine God, a small black boy, timidly pulling the preacher's coattail.

to join this man and this woman

She thinks of ropes, chains, handcuffs, his religion. His place of worship. Where she will be required to sit apart with covered head. In Chicago, a word she hears when thinking of smoke, from his description of what a cinder was, which they never had in Panther Burn. She sees hovering over the heads of the clean neighbors in her front yard black specks falling, clinging, from the sky. But in Chicago. Respect, a chance to build. Her children at last from underneath the detrimental wheel. A chance to be on top. What a relief, she thinks. What a vision, a view, from up so high.

in holy matrimony

Her fourth child she gave away to the child's father who had some money. Certainly a good job. Had gone to Harvard. Was a good man but weak because good language meant so much to him he could not live with Roselily. Could not abide TV in the living room, five beds in three rooms, no Bach except from four to six on Sunday afternoons. No chess at all. She does not forget to worry about her son among his father's people. She wonders if the New England climate will agree with him. If he will ever come down to Mississippi, as his father did, to try to right the country's wrongs. She wonders if he will be stronger than his father. His father cried off and on throughout her pregnancy. Went to skin and bones. Suffered nightmares, retching and falling out of bed. Tried to kill himself. Later told his wife he found the right baby through friends. Vouched for, the sterling qualities that would make up his character. It is not her nature to blame. Still, she is not entirely thankful. She supposes New England, the North, to be quite different from what she knows. It seems right somehow to her that people who move there to live return home completely changed. She thinks of the air, the smoke, the cinders. Imagines cinders big as hailstones; heavy, weighing on the people. Wonders how this pressure finds its way into the veins, roping the springs of laughter.

If there's anybody here that knows a reason why

But of course they know no reason why beyond what they daily have come to know. She thinks of the man who will be her husband, feels shut away from him because of the stiff severity of his plain black suit. His religion. A lifetime of black and white. Of veils. Covered head. It is as if her children are already gone from her. Not dead, but exalted on a pedestal, a stalk that has no roots. She wonders how to make new roots. It is beyond her. She wonders what one does with memories in a brand-new life. This had seemed easy, until she thought of it. "The reasons why . . . the people who" . . . she thinks, and does not wonder where the thought is from.

these two should not be joined

She thinks of her mother, who is dead. Dead, but still her mother. Joined. This is confusing. Of her father. A gray old man who sold wild mink, rabbit, fox skins to Sears, Roebuck. He stands in the yard, like a man waiting for a train. Her young sisters stand behind her in smooth green dresses, with flowers in their hands and hair. They giggle, she feels, at the absurdity of the wedding. They are ready for something new. She thinks the man beside her should marry one of them. She feels old. Yoked. An arm seems to reach out from behind her and snatch her backward. She thinks of cemeteries and the long sleep of grandparents mingling in the dirt. She believes that she believes in ghosts. In the soil giving back what it takes.

> *together,*

In the city. He sees her in a new way. This she knows, and is grateful. But is it new enough? She cannot always be a bride and virgin, wearing robes and veil. Even now her body itches to be free of satin and voile, organdy and lily of the valley. Memories crash against her. Memories of being bare to the sun. She wonders what it will be like. Not to have to go to a job. Not to work in a sewing plant. Not to worry about learning to sew straight seams in workingmen's overalls, jeans, and dress pants. Her place will be in the home, he has said, repeatedly, promising her rest she had prayed for. But now she wonders. When she is rested, what will she do? They will make babies—she thinks practically about her fine brown body, his strong black one. They will be inevitable. Her hands will be full. Full of what? Babies. She is not comforted.

> *let him speak*

She wishes she had asked him to explain more of what he meant. But she was impatient. Impatient to be done with sewing. With doing everything for three children, alone. Impatient to leave the girls she had known since childhood, their children growing up, their husbands hanging around her, already old, seedy. Nothing about them that she wanted, or needed. The fathers of her children driving by, waving, not waving; reminders of times she would just as soon forget. Impatient to see the South Side, where they would live and build and be respectable and respected and free. Her husband would free her. A romantic hush. Proposal. Promises. A new life! Respectable, reclaimed, renewed. Free! In robe and veil.

> *or forever hold*

She does not even know if she loves him. She loves his sobriety. His refusal to sing just because he knows the tune. She loves his pride. His blackness and his gray car. She loves his understanding of her *condition*. She thinks she loves the effort he will make to redo her into what he truly wants. His love of her makes her completely conscious of how unloved she was before. This is something; though it makes her unbearably sad. Melancholy. She blinks her eyes. Remembers she is finally being married, like other girls. Like other girls, women? Something strains upward behind her eyes. She thinks of the something as a rat trapped, cornered, scurrying to and fro in her head, peering through the windows of her eyes. She wants to live for once. But doesn't know quite what that means. Wonders if she has ever done it. If she ever will. The preacher is odious to her. She wants to strike him out of the way, out of her light, with the back of her hand. It seems to her he has always been standing in front of her, barring her way.

his peace.

The rest she does not hear. She feels a kiss, passionate, rousing, within the general pandemonium. Cars drive up blowing their horns. Firecrackers go off. Dogs come from under the house and begin to yelp and bark. Her husband's hand is like the clasp of an iron gate. People congratulate. Her children press against her. They look with awe and distaste mixed with hope at their new father. He stands curiously apart, in spite of the people crowding about to grasp his free hand. He smiles at them all but his eyes are as if turned inward. He knows they cannot understand that he is not a Christian. He will not explain himself. He feels different, he looks it. The old women thought he was like one of their sons except that he had somehow got away from them. Still a son, not a son. Changed.

She thinks how it will be later in the night in the silvery gray car. How they will spin through the darkness of Mississippi and in the morning be in Chicago, Illinois. She thinks of Lincoln, the president. That is all she knows about the place. She feels ignorant, *wrong,* backward. She presses her worried fingers into his palm. He is standing in front of her. In the crush of well-wishing people, he does not look back.

Analysis: "Roselily"

1. Briefly summarize the story.

   _____

   _____

   _____

   _____

2. What does the title tell you?

   _____

   _____

   _____

3. What is the purpose of the italicized text?

   _____

   _____

   _____

4. What do you think is the setting?

_____

_____

_____

5. What has been revealed about the characters? How has this been done?

Roselily: _____

_____

_____

_____

Roselily's betrothed (husband): _____

_____

_____

_____

6. What is the story really about?

_____

_____

_____

_____

Note: Compare your response to Question 6 with your summary above. Herein lies one of the keys to astute reading. Good literature seldom is just what it appears to be. Much meaning is submerged, and the critical reader must look for universal motifs and meanings. The beauty of good literature is that a piece can reveal more than one meaning or interpretation—as long as ideas are supported by the text.

To see sample student responses to these questions, turn to page 120.

Analyzing Prose for the Multiple-Choice Section: Activity 2

Now write your own multiple-choice questions to accompany the story "Roselily." Remember, it is the _process_ that is most important at this juncture. By imitating the types of questions you have encountered in this chapter, you will gain a better understanding of how AP questions are constructed. We've started you off with a few written by other students.

Which of the following best describes Roselily's feelings at her wedding?
(A) anticipation
(B) dread
(C) impatience
(D) resignation
(E) trepidation

The irony of the story is best manifested in which of the following statements?
(A) Although she is not a pure woman, she wears a white dress.
(B) Although she is trapped in marriage, she is freed from drudgery.
(C) Although the ceremony is Christian, she is marrying a Muslim.
(D) Although marriage is a passage to womanhood, she is renewing her youth.
(E) Although she is not in love, she is certain she will learn to love.

Lesson 6: Answers

Analysis: "Untitled"

Sample Student Responses

1. Shaw observes the cremation of his mother, which he finds to be beautiful and peaceful. He also finds it amusing and is certain that his mother would concur. Throughout the passage he senses his mother's presence and affirms his sense that her spirit will always be with him. He imagines his mother would be delighted by the process.

2.

Narrator's feeling	Quote/line/phrase/word supporting this assertion
"my mother became that beautiful fire"	respect and awe/admiration
"wasted little figure"	pity and love
"Mama would have enjoyed it enormously"	affection, closeness (note use of word <u>mama</u>)
"Mama herself . . . shaking with laughter"	friendly and close with his mother

3.

Imagery	Effect
"Pentecostal tongues"	Most Western religions don't advocate cremation, yet Shaw uses this allusion. Is it ironic?

"roomy kitchen . . . big cooks"	illustrates the absurd nature of the ceremony
"Mama would have enjoyed it"	makes funeral less depressing
"streaming ribbons of garnet coloured lovely flame"	makes the cremation magical, not disgusting at all
"violet coffin"	makes coffin seem beautiful, delicate, peaceful

4. <u>Quote</u>

<u>Quote</u>	<u>Technique/effect</u>
"Which of the two heaps do you suppose is me?"	Ironic—she is being separated as if she were the ingredients of a recipe, not a person. Also comments on the absurdity of ashes representing a person.
"behind the scenes"	metaphor—makes the funeral seem like a theatrical production
"deftly," "busily," "dainty," "samples of bone"	humorous description of grotesque task

Multiple Choice: "Untitled"

Answers

1. *B* The line "Grave, where is thy victory?" captures the essence of his meaning. Choice *A* is incorrect because passage does not state this. Choice *C* is a good distracter— although this statement reflects a truth in the passage, it is not the central theme. Choice *D* is incorrect because at no time does the speaker compare the cremation to a burial, and *E* is incorrect because Shaw is celebrating his mother, not discussing his personal happiness.

2. *D* Shaw admires the beauty within death. He realizes it is his mother's time to die, and that death is part of the natural cycle. Choice *A* is incorrect: Shaw is not greatly troubled by his mother's cremation. His language and tone—"the feet burst miraculously into streaming ribbons of garnet coloured lovely flame, smokeless and eager"—support his perception of the process as beautiful and celebratory. Choice *B* is incorrect because although Shaw sees beauty in his mother's cremation, he is not necessarily artistically inspired. Choice *C* is incorrect. Although Shaw is later amused by the odd procedures of the process of cremation, these lines do not convey this. (A caveat to remember: Respond specifically to the lines indicated in the question, not the entire passage.) Finally, *E* is also incorrect; this is your obvious throw-away choice.

3. *E* This is the most important statement. Quoting both the Bible and John Donne (especially since Shaw was a vocal atheist) underscores the author's belief that his mother's spirit cannot be vanquished by death. Note that there is a distinction between this question and the first one. (We're working on making you more discriminating readers!) Whereas Question 1 paraphrases possible meanings, this question refers to specific quotes within the passage. Choice *A* is incorrect because this phrase is not the central idea. Choice *B* describes the circumstances, not the meaning. Choice *C* is incorrect but a good distracter. Choice *D* is incorrect because the statement does not encompass the major theme.

4. *D* Although death and cremation are inherently sad, in the passage the speaker is ironically delighted. Choice *A* is incorrect because he is not exactly amused by cremation; rather, he is surprised and interested by the grace and beauty of this event. Choice *B* is wrong: the speaker is not looking for hope. Instead, he is glad because his mother has been relieved. Choice *C* is wrong because although it is evident that the son had a close relationship with his mother, he does not see her death as the cessation of her spirit. Therefore, he is not expressing bottomless grief. Finally, *E* is wrong because although Shaw recognizes the beauty of cremation and admires it, he is far from gleeful.

5. *C* The passage presents the events of the cremation in a sequential order. Choices *A*, *B*, *D*, and *E* are wrong because a stream of consciousness replicates the human thought process, which tends to produce unorganized, random thoughts in no particular order. This is in sharp contrast to the Shaw passage, in which ideas are expressed in logical order.

6. *D* Nostalgia can also mean fond remembrance, and this phrase captures Shaw's feelings. Note the word *maudlin* for future reference. It means "effusively or tearfully sentimental."

7. *A* Note the word *EXCEPT*. Our students often forget to do this as they look at the choices. Choice *B* is ironic, describing the fire as cool and the dark furnace as sunny. Choice *C* illustrates Shaw's idea that his mother is becoming part of the flame, rather than succumbing to it. Choice *D* is ironic because one does not usually associate cooks in the kitchen with the process of cremation. Choice *E* is also ironic; in Shaw's mind, his mother asks a delightfully incongruous question.

8. *A* Shaw literally moves from one place to another in the crematorium. Choice *B* is incorrect. Although the phrase

illustrates a change in attitude, there is no change in setting here. Choices *C* and *E* are incorrect as both refer to a continuation of the author's observation of the process from a fixed point.

9. *D* The passage illustrates the author's acceptance of his mother's death. Choice *A* is wrong since Shaw states just the opposite. Choice *B* is incorrect because the cremation is beautiful and no language supports the concept of ominous. Choice *C* is incorrect because the flame is real, not symbolic. Choice *E* is incorrect because the author does not address his own death in the passage.

10. *B* The speaker's description of the crematory is contrary to what he had initially expected. Choice *A* is incorrect because Shaw uses lively, animated language. Choice *C* is incorrect because the author is not angry or confused. Choice *D* is incorrect because *morbid* means "psychologically unhealthy," which the speaker is not. If part of an answer is wrong, the entire answer is wrong and you must move on. Finally, *E* is incorrect because the speaker is being serious.

11. *D* Although this is only a projection of what he *thinks* his mother would say in the situation, this phrase shows that the author knew her well and is anticipating her attitude. Choice *A* is not the best choice because the central purpose of the poem is not to depress. Choice *B* is not the best answer because Shaw's language indicates that he reveres his mother. Choice *C* is incorrect since it reflects a total misreading of the passage. Choice *E* is not the best answer because this line does not imply sadness.

12. *E* Here is *EXCEPT* again. The only thing the words do not represent is punitive action.

Analysis: "Roselily"

Sample Student Responses

1. This short story consists of the internal thoughts of a woman during her own wedding. A sense of isolation from the rest of the group is evident as the woman contemplates her life and what will probably be her future.

2. The title is probably the woman's name. I had a picture in my mind of the front porch of a house in Mississippi. I also thought about stones thrown in a still lake or little bombs, thoughts spreading rings, the mushroom cloud.

3. The italicized text is part of the traditional wedding ceremony. The words the minister speaks inspire Roselily's thoughts that follow.

4. The setting is the front porch of a house in Mississippi in modern times.

5.

Character	Quote	Technique	Effect
Roselily	"Her husband's hand is like the clasp of an iron gate."	simile	Her life will be tightly controlled.
	"God, a small black boy . . . coattail"	personification	preacher can even intimidate God
	"chokes off three and four . . . years of breath"	analogy	wishes she was virginal, childless
	"forces humility into her eyes"	pathos	She is powerless.
	"The fathers of her children . . . she would just as soon forget."	detail	They represent her old life, which she now regrets.
	"Imagines cinders as big as hailstones"	imagery	industrial North; crushes joy out of people
	". . . the detrimental wheel"	metaphor	racism
	"Proposal. Promises. A new life!"	climactic build-up	feels last chance to start
	"Lincoln"	allusion	symbol of freedom
	"She thinks of ropes, chains, handcuffs, his religion."	imagery/ analogy	His Muslim religion controls women.
	"a stalk that has no roots"	metaphor	worried about moving away from home; afraid kids will change
	"wearing robes and veil"	allusion/ analogy	reference to Muslim clothing; submission of women
	"The rest she does not hear."	detail	detachment

	". . . try to right the country's wrongs . . ."	exposition/ flashback	The father of her fourth child was a married civil rights worker.
	"Free! In robe and veil."	paradox	free, yet not free
Husband	"He smiles at them all . . . as if turned inward."	simile	holds self apart
	"teachings from the wrong God"	detail	He is Muslim; does not approve of their lifestyle.
	". . . stiff severity of his plain black suit"	connotation	serious, rigid, no-nonsense
	"A lifetime of black and white."	metaphor	strict rules
	"His place of worship. Where she . . . sit apart with covered head."	detail	She will be isolated.
	"He is standing in front of her . . . he does not look back."	analogy	He will always put himself first.

6. There's the obvious story about Roselily contemplating her life on her wedding day. More than that, though, she is a southern black woman, downtrodden and weary but still hoping for a better life. This may be her last chance, yet she fears that she may be moving from one kind of trap—southern racism—to another—a husband and religion that will engulf her.

PART 4

AP Essays

AP Prompts: A General Overview

Great chefs know that even when using the most basic ingredients it is possible to create a virtually infinite number of unique and interesting creations. Knowing the essentials and abiding by some strong basic rules do not preclude great individual products—and top AP essays are just that: great individual products.

As you have learned in your years at school, the first step in writing is to have a clear idea of your purpose. All writers write for a purpose, and that applies to students taking exams as well. On the essay portion of the AP, *your* purpose is simple: You must answer the three essay (also known as "free response") prompts as completely and coherently as possible. Study and respond to as many sample prompts as possible to develop facility in the process of writing an AP essay. Practice is particularly important because you will have 120 minutes—two hours—to write three essays.

Reading the AP Prompt

Your task on Section Two of the AP exam is to read the test passages, analyze them, and answer questions. However, your task is not *just* to analyze, but to respond to a specific prompt.

The prompt provides you with a *critical lens*; it requires you to analyze the passage with a specific *purpose* in mind. When you write your essay, you must show that you can adopt a specified critical lens.

Here are some sample AP prompts.

Sample Poetry Prompt

Prompt

The Canterbury Tales is a narrative poem; a combination of character sketches, conversations, and stories told by a group of pilgrims journeying to a religious site, the cathedral of Canterbury. The travelers entertain one another with stories, some ribald (off-color) and others sermonic.

In the following excerpt, one of the pilgrims, the Wife of Bath (who has had five husbands) tells her tale to the travelers. In a well-organized essay, analyze the literary devices (such as diction, tone, word choice, etc.) the Wife of Bath uses to convey her point of view.

Sample Prose Prompt

Prompt

What resources of language does Charlotte Brontë use to illustrate the characters of the narrator, nine-year-old Jane Eyre, and Helen Burns, the girl Jane Eyre is describing?

Sample Open Prompt

Prompt

"By their deeds shall ye know them." We often judge people by what they do; therefore, we consider people who commit cruel or reprehensible acts corrupt, base, or amoral. In literature, however, authors often introduce us to characters whom we learn to like or even respect, despite their deeds.

Write an essay about one such character for whom you developed admiration or compassion. Briefly explain why you felt his or her behavior to be condemnable or contemptible, and how the author's techniques influenced you to admire that person nonetheless. Do not summarize the plot. *(40 minutes)*

Great Expectations	*Richard III*	*Native Son*
Jane Eyre	*Moby-Dick*	*The Stranger*
Wuthering Heights	*Things Fall Apart*	*Antigone*
Medea	*Light in August*	*The Scarlet Letter*
Othello	*Beloved*	*Billy Budd*
Crime and Punishment		

A general plan for responding to each of the three types of prompts is basically the same:

Poetry Prompt	**Prose Prompt**	**Open Prompt**
Read the prompt	Read the prompt	Read the prompt
Read the poem	Read the prose passage	Choose a literary work
Analyze	Analyze	Analyze
Plan	Plan	Plan
Write	Write	Write

Although these prompts differ from one another in some key ways, they also have much in common. As a result, there are some general guidelines you may apply to all three.

Anatomy of a Prompt

To properly respond to a prompt, you must first be sure that you understand it. To fully understand it, you must analyze it. As you know, analyzing means breaking it into its parts. The prompts for poetry and prose questions are similarly constructed. Either type of prompt may take a complex form, as illustrated here by the poetry prompt, or a simpler form, as shown below in the prose example.

Poetry Prompt (complex type)

Prompt 1

The Canterbury Tales is a narrative poem; a combination of 2 character sketches, conversations, and stories told by a group of pilgrims journeying to a religious site, the cathedral of Canterbury. The travelers entertain one another with stories, some ribald (off-color) and others sermonic.

3   In the following excerpt, one of the pilgrims, the Wife of Bath (who has had five husbands) tells her tale to the travelers. In a well-organized essay, analyze the literary devices 4 (such as diction, tone, word choice, etc.) the Wife of Bath uses to convey her point of view.

Prose Prompt (simpler type)

Prompt 1

4 What resources of language does Charlotte Brontë use to illustrate the characters of the narrator, nine-year-old Jane 3 Eyre, and Helen Burns, the girl Jane Eyre is describing?

1. Label: This tells you that you are reading a prompt.

2. General Background Information About the Passage: Sometimes it is helpful to have a greater understanding of the historical or literary context of the passage. Not every prompt will provide this, but some will, ensuring that you will have the tools necessary to answer the question.

3. Specific Background Information About the Passage: Often, the passage is an excerpt from a larger work. This sets up the particular "scene" that you must read.

4. Writing Task: This tells you exactly what you must write about.

The open question takes a slightly different form:

Open Question

Prompt   1

2   "By their deeds shall ye know them." We often judge people by what they do; therefore, we consider people who commit cruel or reprehensible acts corrupt, base, or amoral. In literature, however, authors often introduce us to characters whom we learn to like or even respect, despite their deeds.

3   Write an essay about one such character for whom you developed admiration or compassion. Briefly explain why you felt his or her behavior to be condemnable or contemptible, and how the author's techniques influenced you to admire that person. Do not summarize the plot. *(40 minutes)*

Great Expectations	*Things Fall Apart*
Jane Eyre	*Light in August*
Wuthering Heights	*Beloved*
Medea	*Native Son* 4
Othello	*The Stranger*
Crime and Punishment	*Antigone*
Richard III	*The Scarlet Letter*
Moby-Dick	*Billy Budd*

1. Label: This tells you that you are reading a prompt.

2. General Theme: Usually, the open question will posit a universal truth or theme that is often echoed in literature.

3. Writing Task: This tells you exactly what you must write about.

4. Suggested Works: This lists some possible works on which you may base your answer.

It cannot be emphasized too much: Be sure to address the *specific* question. No matter how wonderful your writing, or how brilliant your essay, if it does not answer the question you have been asked, it will not earn a high score. An average essay with an adequate response to the question will outstrip a brilliant essay that is off-topic or that misses the point. In order to focus better, ask yourself the following questions:

1. What are some of the important words in the prompt? Underline them in the prompt.

_____   _____

_____   _____

2. What elements of the prompt do I need to explore? Note these in the prompt.

_____

_____

3. Is there more than one part to the prompt? List the parts below, and mark them in the prompt.

_____

_____

_____

Once you have thoroughly analyzed the prompt, you will understand your task.

Read and Analyze the Passage

Your second task is to read the passage itself. As you read, focus on the task specified in the prompt. Carefully note any literary techniques and devices that the author employs, especially if they are specifically mentioned in the prompt. For a review of literary elements, see Part 2.

A Case of Mnemonia

A mnemonic device is a catchy word or memorable expression that is often used to help students remember a series of steps in a given process. Many people find that it is easier to remember a clever word than a series of polysyllabic terms.

The mnemonic device *ppsssssttt* is one such tool that can come in handy when you are translating your literary analysis into writing. Each letter stands for a step in the process of examining a text:

Follow each of the steps when reading poetry or prose:

Paraphrase: This means putting the poem or story into your own words.

Purpose: The poetry and prose used on AP exams deal with universal issues. Good literature is specific and detailed in order to underscore more general concepts. The author's purpose may not necessarily be immediately clear, but an insightful reader will note related ideas.

Structure: If the piece is a poem, is it divided into stanzas? Is there any reason for these stanza breaks? Does a sentence begin in one stanza and then move to the next one (enjambment)? How does this affect meaning? If it is prose, how does the author develop the characters and the plot? How do the traditional story elements manifest themselves?

Shift: Are there changes in tone, point of view, language? Just as a car shifts to accelerate and accommodate hills, does the text move to reflect differences in attitude?

Speaker: Who is the speaker? Is there more than one? Is the speaker using first or third person? How does viewpoint affect meaning? Be careful not to confuse the speaker with the author; they are not necessarily the same.

Spelling/Grammar/Diction: Are there any unusual spellings, words, or capitalization? Is there inversion? Is the language unusual?

Tone: Is the tone positive or negative? What are the words that describe it most accurately?

Theme: Is a universal meaning offered, either explicitly or implicitly?

Title: Does the title give any hint as to the meaning?

Planning the Essay

Now that you have read and analyzed both the prompt and the literary passage, you are almost ready to write your essay. Before you actually start writing, however, you must complete one more step: You must *plan* your essay.

Just as you follow a systematic plan when you write a research paper or high school essay, so too must you approach the AP essay in an organized manner. Of course, you will not have the time to polish and revise your material as you would for other projects, and the AP readers understand this.

Your task in this exam is much narrower in scope: to develop a well-written first draft essay that clearly and completely answers the AP question.

Focused Brainstorming

Yeats' belief that a "line will take us hours . . ." is true of literature but not very practical when preparing for timed tests. You do not have hours to hone your words. In fact, you barely have enough time to write and quickly proofread the three essays you will be writing. The key to success may well lie in your ability to quickly brainstorm before writing your essay.

The difference between focused brainstorming and free association brainstorming is cohesion. In the latter, you allow your thoughts to take you in as many directions as possible; in fact, the more diverse or esoteric, the better. In focused brainstorming, however, you must concentrate on answering the prompt and not digressing.

In planning your AP essay, webs, clusters, outlines, annotations, or underlines are interchangeable. These are different terms that ultimately represent the same thing: *a system of rudimentary planning before committing yourself to writing a response.* Whichever method of brainstorming you select will help you clarify your thoughts. You will see if you have enough evidence to back up your assumptions, or if you need to rethink your original ideas. You will also be able to organize the material *before* you begin writing. Paradoxically, you will also save time. You may even have a few minutes left to proofread after you write.

Beware: An outline for a test is NOT the same as a formal outline. Do NOT worry about numbers (Arabic and Roman) and letters (capital and small). Indenting will do. Listing is fine. Avoid writing complete sentences. Brief phrases will suffice since you'll be writing the essay immediately after you do a preliminary plan. Remember that you will *first* jot down your ideas, *then* decide in what order you will use them. You will then write your first, and only, draft. The College Board recognizes this as a rough draft. That is all you will have time to write.

☞ *AP Tip*

The AP literature test NEVER calls for a summary. It usually asks for analysis, which demands a higher thinking level. Make sure your plan indicates this. Never answer a test question with a summary of the piece.

The most important task at this stage is to make sure that your outline (cluster, web, annotation, etc.) is a response to the prompt. As you have learned, an analysis of a poem or prose piece involves a *what* component and a *how* component (see pages 16–38).

To mirror this idea, AP prompts usually contain two parts, as well:

The *what* part is usually connected to the meaning of the piece.

Example:

> In *Lord of the Flies*, what does author William Golding imply about the twins?

The *how* part usually refers to the author's techniques. Your job is not only to list the techniques but also to indicate how they develop the ideas.

Example:

> How does Golding express this idea?

Sample Student Response

In Lord of the Flies, Golding refers to the twins as "samneric." Writing their names in this way symbolizes the symbiotic relationship they have with one another. They are not only twins; they are literally inseparable.

Brainstorming: Activity 1

Now read the following AP-style prompt and prose piece. Then examine the sample student essay plans that follow.

Prompt

Jonathan Edwards, a Puritan preacher (1703–1758), delivered the following sermon to his congregation. In it he describes the special relationship between God and "sinners." In a well-organized essay, discuss how Edwards develops his ideas. You might want to consider such elements as syntax, imagery, diction, and other rhetorical strategies.

SERMON:
Sinners in the Hands of an Angry God

The wrath of God is like great waters that are dammed for the present; they increase more and more and rise higher and higher, till an outlet is given; and the longer the stream is stopped, the more rapid and mighty is its course when once it is let loose. It is true that judgment against your evil works has not been executed hitherto: the floods of God's vengeance have been withheld; but your guilt in the meantime is constantly increasing, and you are every day treasuring up more wrath; the waters are continually rising and waxing more and more mighty; and there is nothing but the mere pleasure of God that holds the waters back, that are unwilling to be stopped, and press hard to go forward. If God should only withdraw his hand from the floodgate, it would immediately fly open, and the fiery floods of the fierceness and wrath of God would rush forth with inconceivable fury, and would come upon you with omnipotent power; and if your strength were ten thousand times greater than it is, yea, ten thousand times greater than the strength of the stoutest, sturdiest devil in Hell, it would be nothing to withstand or endure it.

The bow of God's wrath is bent, and the arrow made ready on the string, and the justice bends the arrow at your heart and strains the bow, and it is nothing but the mere pleasure of God, and that of an angry God, without any promise or obligation at all, that keeps the arrow one moment from being made drunk with your blood.

Thus are all you that never passed under a great change of heart by the mighty power of the Spirit of God upon your souls; all you that were never born again and made new creatures, and raised from being dead in sin to a state of new, and before altogether unexperienced light and life (however you may have reformed your life in many things, and may have had religious affections, and may keep up a form of religion in your families and closets, and in the house of God, and may be strict in it), you are thus in the hands of an angry God; 'tis nothing but his mere pleasure that keeps you from being this moment swallowed up in everlasting destruction.

However unconvinced you may now be of the truth of what you hear, by and by you will be fully convinced of it. Those that are gone from being in the like circumstances with you, see that it was so with them; for destruction came suddenly upon most of them; when they expected nothing of it, and while they were saying, *Peace and Safety:* Now they see that those things that they depended on for peace and safety were nothing but thin air and empty shadows.

The God that holds you over the pit of hell, much as one holds a spider or some loathsome insect over the fire, abhors you, and is dreadfully provoked: his wrath toward you burns like fire; he looks upon you as worthy of nothing else but to be cast into the fire; he is of purer eyes than to bear to have you in his sight; you are ten thousand times so abominable in his eyes as the most hateful venomous serpent is in ours. You have offended him infinitely more than ever a stubborn rebel did his prince; and yet 'tis nothing but his hand that holds you from falling into the fire every moment. 'Tis ascribed to nothing else, that you did not go to hell the last night; that you were suffered to awake again in this world after you closed your eyes to sleep: And there is no other reason to be given why you have not dropped into hell since you arose in the morning, but that God's hand has held you up. There is no other reason to be given why you have not gone to hell since you have sat here in the house of God, provoking his pure eyes by your sinful wicked manner of attending his solemn worship. Yea, there is nothing else that is to be given as a reason why you don't this very moment drop down into hell.

O sinner! Consider the fearful danger you are in. 'Tis a great furnace of wrath, a wide and bottomless pit, full of the fire of wrath, that you are held over in the hand of that God whose wrath is provoked and incensed as much against you as against many of the damned in hell. You hang by a slender thread, with the flames of divine wrath flashing about it, and ready every moment to singe it and burn it asunder; and you have no interest in any mediator, and nothing to lay hold of to save yourself, nothing to keep off the flames of wrath, nothing of your own, nothing that you ever have done, nothing that you can do, to induce God to spare you one moment. . . .

Sample Student Plans: "Sinners in the Hands of an Angry God"

Now examine two different kinds of plans developed by actual AP students. Both worked well. You need to determine which one you like. How you decide to organize depends on how you think.

From your preliminary outline or cluster, you can write a credible essay. You might eliminate some of the original points, add to others, and change the organization. You are at liberty to do this, because your points will not be lost or forgotten if they have been jotted down. The purpose of the outline (cluster/web/annotation, etc.) is to enable you to remain focused.

Student Sample #1: Jeff: Preliminary Outline

Extended Metaphors / Imagery
    floodwaters, floodgates, backed up
    bow of God's wrath
    held over hell like a spider over a flame

Repetition
    God
        nothing but God's will
        angry God
        "You have nothing without God"
    hell
        drop into hell at any moment
        pit of hell

go to hell
devil in hell
nothing, nothing, nothing in last paragraph
Rhetorical pauses
Uses commas and semicolons often to provide
dramatic pauses in his sermon

Student Sample #2: Janeen: Cluster

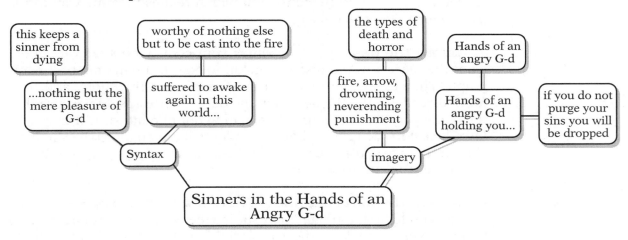

Which of the above methods works best for you? Sometimes it is best to try several different methods before deciding which one is right for you. You'll have plenty of opportunities in the chapters ahead!

Writing Your Essay

Starting Your Essay: The Hook

Did you ever pick up a book or magazine, read the first paragraph, say to yourself, "Oh, no!" then put the piece down? You don't want your reader to feel that way when grading your essay. Although your AP response is a rough draft, you will be rewarded if you can hook your reader. Try to avoid being mundane or simply repeating the prompt.

Hooks can take many forms, and not all work for every essay, or every writer. Here are some common hooks:

1. Unusual quote: It doesn't hurt to go into the AP exam with a few memorized quotes from the Bible, Shakespeare, and poetry. As you learned in Part 2, many writers choose to begin their works with epigraphs—brief quotes from other works that relate to their own. There's no reason why you shouldn't be able to do the same with your essay! *Important:* Make certain that you attribute the quote to its proper source. The reader is very familiar with classic literature, and you don't want to start off on the wrong foot by attributing a quote from Shakespeare to John Donne! Avoid quotes that have become overused or cliché—AP readers have grown tired of them. Also, if you are not certain of a quote's exact wording, you may paraphrase it, but be sure and mention that you are doing so.

2. Anecdote: A brief and interesting anecdote that relates to the piece you have just read, as well as to the point you are about to make, can serve to grab the reader's attention. The anecdote should be as short as possible, and should illustrate a universal theme that the reader will be able to relate to, and which relates in some way to the prompt or to the piece itself.

3. Quote the passage: Opening your essay with a relevant quote from the piece you are discussing can make for a dynamic first paragraph. The best way to handle this is to present the quote, and then move directly to the theme which the quote addresses. Make sure that the quote you choose retains its meaning out of context. If it does not, introduce it in such a way that the reader will understand why you have chosen that particular quote, and move quickly to make the point that the quote is meant to support.

4. Idea or thought that relates to question (universal): Some students prefer to jump right in by stating the point (or one of the points) that they wish to make at the very beginning of the essay. In order to do this well, you need to make sure that the idea is clearly stated. You must then go on to support your idea with examples from the piece you are discussing.

5. Rhetorical question: Although difficult to do well, a good way to arouse your audience's curiosity is to begin your essay with a series of questions relating to the prompt and/or piece. This does *not* mean simply restating the prompt as a question; rather, this is an opportunity to pose insightful questions about the piece that the prompt inspired. For example, a student responding to the open prompt on page 126, and choosing *Jane Eyre* as the work to discuss, might have opened his or her essay with the following questions: What makes a hero? Is it a person of great strength, intelligence, and physical beauty? Are heroes born, or are they made? Do heroes have weaknesses? Why is the flawed hero so inspiring? Important: if you begin your essay using this technique, make sure you address each of the questions raised in the body of your essay. If you don't intend to answer the question, don't ask it!

6. Shocker: Sometimes a shocking or controversial statement can provide a perfect opening for an essay. For example, a writer referring to the open prompt mentioned above, which asks students to describe the way in which an author elicited sympathy and respect for an outwardly reprehensible character, might begin his or her piece with the shocker "All people are bad." A student addressing the poetry prompt on page 126, which asks for a discussion of the literary devices used in the Wife of Bath's tale, might open the essay with the statement that "A woman can never marry too many times." Remember, though the shocker's main purpose is to get the reader's attention, it must be relevant to the prompt and/or the piece, and you must address it again at some point in your essay—even if only to refute it!

7. Tie-in with literary theory: A reference to a literary critic's comments on the author or the passage can be an impressive way to begin an essay, as long as you move quickly to presenting your *own* analysis. For example, a student writing about Jonathan Edwards' sermon might mention Perry Miller's assertion that Edwards "demolishes at tedious length all possible positions of his opponents," then proceed to argue that this establishes the tone of the piece. If you don't remember the critic's exact words, paraphrase. You may be able to use a more general connection between a passage and literary theory. Perhaps you can refer to Coleridge's belief that "works of imagination should be written in very plain language." You can also disagree with something a critic has said as long as you support your opinion and stay with the topic given in the prompt. For example, Poe remarked that *Paradise Lost* lacked unity due to its length.

Do not spend too much time thinking about an introduction. If you are desperate, you may use your thesis statement as the very first paragraph—and may expand the idea to be several sentences long. But this is generally not necessary; the readers understand that this is a timed test and that your papers are first drafts. Therefore, it's best to get to the point immediately and move on. *Tip:* You know you have a problem if the introduction is longer than the body of your essay.

Many students choose to write their introductions last. You should have a focus, your thesis, before you begin writing. But you may not know where exactly you are headed or what you are introducing. Some students plunge into the writing and hope to come up with a scintillating beginning later. Skip seven or eight lines, write your response, and then write your introduction. If this advice makes sense to you, practice with the exercises in this book and see if it works. Don't try this for the first time on the day of the test.

Below are the first paragraphs of Jeff's and Janeen's essays in response to "Sinners in the Hands of an Angry God," based on their outline and cluster. Can you tell which of the above devices each has chosen to use? How well do you think they work?

Student Sample #1, First Paragraph: Jeff

Religion is supposed to be uplifting, supporting, affirming. It's supposed to be a person's release, their last recourse, their sanctuary. Then again, people are supposed to take the Pope seriously when he wears that hat out in public, but we all know how well that works . . .

Student Sample #2, First Paragraph: Janeen

The rigid Puritan emphasis on devotion which is simply a page in history today originally stemmed from an ingrained fear of God's wrath, a fear probably heightened by such sermons as this one. In "Sinners in the Hands of an Angry God," Jonathan Edwards manipulates language with the effect of creating feelings of fear and guilt in the reader. Edwards achieves this primarily through use of metaphor, imagery, and diction.

Length

How long should the essay be? Long enough to cover the subject and short enough to be interesting. There is no magic formula for either length or how many examples and supporting details to use to develop the answer. Some people develop only one or two examples thoroughly; others develop more. Just be sure your essay is not a laundry list; explain how your details fit into the whole.

Students often wonder if the readers look for a magical number of paragraphs. They do not. Nowhere does the rubric address this issue directly—but you should certainly have more than one paragraph. Papers with three, five, seven, and even nine paragraphs have received 9s as well as 3s. It is *what* is said and *how* it is said that determine the score.

Diction

Just as you study diction to determine an author's purpose, your own diction needs to reflect your intelligence and perspicacity. Remember your audience: high school teachers and college professors. Therefore, you want your writing to reflect your facility with the English language and your ability to manipulate it.

The most important factor to remember when you write the essays is that the reader does not have to agree with your point of view. However, you must support your points with adequate examples and discussion, using logic and the text to support your contentions.

The Finished Product

When you have completed the above steps—reading the prompt, reading the piece, analyzing the prompt, brainstorming, writing the first paragraph (okay, you can save that until last if you want)—you will be ready to write your essay, and it'll be a lot easier than you think! You've already thought extensively about the piece and how it relates to the prompt, you've scanned the piece for literary devices and meaning, and you've organized your information. Now all that remains is to present your ideas and your supporting information in a clear, concise essay. You can do it!

Below are Jeff's and Janeen's essays on "Sinners in the Hands of an Angry God." Can you see how their earlier efforts at brainstorming and organization helped them to write upper-level essays?

Student Sample #1, Essay: Jeff

Religion is supposed to be uplifting, supporting, affirming. It's supposed to be a person's release, their last recourse, their sanctuary. Then again, people are supposed to take the Pope seriously when he wears that hat out in public, but we all know how well that works . . .

Jonathan Edwards, in his sermon entitled "Sinners in the Hands of an Angry God," paints a very different picture of religion. It is one alive with fiery imagery and intimidating rhetoric, one that scares dogma into its followers, one that castigates its own followers. In the sermon, he describes a furious deity, enraged at the sin and depravity that His followers have engaged in, and one who holds complete control over their destinies. The sermon is an attempt to frighten his parishioners into a righteous life by convincing them that their God could drop them into the depths of hell in an instant, and only by His grace do they remain alive. He does a pretty convincing job of it through his use of imagery, repetition, and writing for oral emphasis.

Edwards' imagery is simply amazing. His sermon begins with an extended metaphor describing the great waters that are dammed for the present. His description of the rising waters of sin summons images of the Great Flood. The image of water is one of the most powerful in nature, and Edwards manipulates it beautifully. Towards the end of that paragraph, he describes the unfathomable power of the coming flood. The next paragraph develops a metaphor surrounding a bow and arrow, the bow of God's wrath and the arrow of justice and righteousness. Again, Edwards summons up fantastic, violent imagery to frighten his audience and enrapture them with God's strength. Finally, the second to last paragraph draws parallels between the way God views us and the way we view spiders or serpents. The sense of disgust and loathing that he conjures up makes us feel lower than low, and fully expresses God's indignity at having to protect us. All of these images succeed in fully expressing the sense of angry distaste that God feels towards us, and makes us repent for having made Him feel so.

Student Sample #2: Essay: Janeen

The rigid Puritan emphasis on devotion which is simply a page in history today originally stemmed from an ingrained fear of God's wrath, a fear probably heightened by such sermons as this one. In "Sinners in the Hands of an Angry God," Jonathan Edwards manipulates language with the effect of creating feelings of fear and guilt in the reader. Edwards achieves this primarily through use of metaphor, imagery, and diction.

Edwards stirs strong feelings in the reader through the words he chooses to describe sinners, God, and hell. The fact that Edwards always uses the word "sinners," and never simply "people" makes the reader feel as if they don't want to be placed in this horrible category. The sinners are further described as "hateful, "venomous," and "abominable" in the fifth paragraph. These words make the sinners sound repulsive even in God's eyes, a fearful notion for any religious person.

By describing the severity of God's feelings toward the sinners, one gets a sense of the true power of the wrath of God. Words like "offended" and "abhors" let us know that God is not only angry, but disgusted and hateful. The purpose of using such strong language is to push the reader to be more pious in the future, and to feel guilt for the sins he has committed in the past. If there was any doubt, words like "flames," "singe," and "burn," describing hell, assure the reader that this is not a desired fate.

Writing Effective Essays About Poetry

Sometimes a rose is a rose is a rose, and sometimes . . . a rose is just a rose. This is what makes poetry difficult—when are the words to be taken literally and when figuratively? Much depends on the entire piece, not just one section of it. When listening to a song, we try to hear the lyrics as well as the music itself in order to understand the song's mood and meaning. Poetry is best understood when it is read aloud, which is a little difficult to do at the AP exam. But it's a good idea to read it out loud while studying for the test; hearing the words can help you more easily determine a poem's rhythm, mood, and meaning.

Since poets often try to share their innermost feelings and thoughts —without expecting others to have identical feelings—poems tend to be more figurative than works of prose. John Ciardi believed that reading a poem was similar to throwing a stone in a pond: Ripples would appear, which in turn would create other ripples. What the poem means to you often depends on which ripple catches your fancy.

Poets themselves have found it difficult to define the elusive qualities of their craft. Here are a few of their attempts.

"Poetry is not a turning loose of emotion, but an escape from emotion."
—T. S. Eliot

". . . prose—words in their best order; poetry—the best words in their best order."
—Samuel Taylor Coleridge

"Poetry is the spontaneous overflow of powerful feelings: it takes its origin from emotion recollected in tranquillity."
—William Wordsworth

"I would define, in brief, the poetry of words as rhythmical creation of beauty. Its sole arbiter is taste."
—Edgar Allan Poe

"Poetry is the record of the best and happiest moments of the happiest and best minds."
—Percy Bysshe Shelley

"[Poetry] has the virtue of being able to say twice as much as prose in half the time, and the drawback, if you do not give it your full attention, of seeming to say half as much in twice the time."
—Christopher Fry

Poets select their words carefully. They are frugal with them, often to the point of being parsimonious. Every word counts. The challenge—and the fun—for the reader is to try to understand the whole by examining the parts.

Try It Out

Let's look at a poem by e. e. cummings.

[l(a]

l(a

le
af
fa

ll

s)
one
l

iness

Taking It Apart: "[l(a]"

Cummings pushed the poetic envelope in a direction it had not gone before. He turned nouns into verbs, eliminated capitalization, and used punctuation marks to express ideas. But the power unleashed by this deceptively simple poem is amazing. Who has not at least once felt alone and unprotected in our universe? The poignancy of that feeling comes through in the appearance of the poem as one long column. One. Solitary. Then, if we read between the parentheses, we see that *a leaf falls*. Does anyone hear the leaf? Does anyone care?

Poets are not necessarily didactic and do not presume to answer questions. They help us see the world in a new way. Sometimes they show us the paradoxes and ironies of life.

At best, we can only guess at the poet's purpose, thoughts, feelings, motif, or ideas. This is the challenge and the beauty of this particular art form. Poets are deliberately elliptical, ambiguous, unclear. They think and write in metaphors and other figurative language, which, by definition, are inexact comparisons. But the game is exhilarating and the rewards numerous.

On the AP test, you have only a brief time in which to acquaint yourself with a poem. The readers are aware of this and will read your essays accordingly. Here are some exercises that will help you to recognize the various literary elements as they appear in poetry.

Poetry: Activity 1

The following poems have words missing. Fill in the blanks, using the Word Banks provided beneath each selection. Why did you select certain words? How does your choice of words fit the author's purpose?

Sonnet 116

by William Shakespeare

Let me not to the marriage of true minds
Admit (1)_____. Love is not love
Which (2)_____ when it alteration finds,
Or bends with the remover to remove.
O, no! it is an ever-fixèd mark
That looks on tempests and is never shaken;
It is the star to every wand'ring (3)_____,
Whose worth's unknown, although his height be taken.
Love's not Time's (4)_____, though rosy lips and cheeks
Within his bending sickle's compass come;
Love alters not with his (5)_____ hours and weeks,
But bears it out even to the edge of doom.
        If this be error, and upon me proved,
        I never writ, nor no man ever loved.

Word Bank

1. impediments, obstacle, much hindrance

2. changes, alters, modifies

3. ship, boat, bark

4. tool, work, fool

5. brief, short, few

If We Must Die

by Claude McKay

If we must die, let it not be like hogs
Hunted and penned in an inglorious spot,
While round us (1)_____ the mad and hungry dogs,
Making their mock at our accursed lot.
If we must die, O let us (2)_____ die,
So that our precious blood may not be shed
In vain; then even the monsters we defy
Shall be constrained to honor us though dead!
O kinsmen! We must meet the common (3)_____!
Though far outnumbered let us show us brave,
And for their thousand blows deal one deathblow!
What though before us lies the open grave?
Like (4)_____ we'll face the murderous, (5)_____ pack,
Pressed to the wall, dying, but fighting back!

Word Bank

1. bark, growl, snap

2. sadly, gloriously, nobly

3. enemy, foe, assailant

4. soldiers, knights, men

5. cowardly, vainglorious, vicious

It's not important if you chose the right word (although you may turn to page 155 if you wish to see the answers). Instead, try to analyze what makes one word more effective than another. Study the way in which words affect meaning.

Carefully selecting correct words is important for writers. For readers, discerning how the words are used is the key to understanding the poem and to writing an effective essay about it. Understanding the implications of language, diction, and word choice is therefore quite important in understanding a poem.

☞ *AP Tip*

When you read a poetry selection on the AP exam, check first to see if the poem is an extended metaphor. If you recognize this common poetry technique, it can be the key that unlocks the poem's meaning.

Try It Out

Now try your hand at analyzing a poem—actually the lyrics to a song—written by the 1960s rock group The Beatles.

Eleanor Rigby

By John Lennon and Paul McCartney

Ah, look at all the lonely people!
Ah, look at all the lonely people!

Eleanor Rigby
Picks up the rice in the church where a wedding has been,
5   Lives in a dream.
Waits at the window
Wearing the face that she keeps in a jar by the door.
Who is it for?

All the lonely people,
10   Where do they all come from?
All the lonely people,
Where do they all belong?

Father McKenzie,
Writing the words of a sermon that no one will hear,
15   No one comes near.
Look at him working,
Darning his socks in the night when there's nobody there.
What does he care?

All the lonely people
20   Where do they all come from?
All the lonely people
Where do they all belong?

Eleanor Rigby
Died in the church and was buried along with her name.
25   Nobody came.
Father McKenzie,
Wiping the dirt from his hands as he walks from the grave,
No one was saved.

All the lonely people,
30   Where do they all come from?
All the lonely people,
Where do they all belong?

Ah, look at all the lonely people!
Ah, look at all the lonely people!

Analysis: "Eleanor Rigby"

Now apply the mnemonic *ppsssssttt*.

Paraphrase _____

_____

_____

Purpose _____

_____

_____

Structure _____

_____

_____

Shift _____

_____

_____

Speaker _____

_____

_____

Spelling/grammar/diction _____

_____

_____

Tone _____

_____

_____

Theme _____

_____

_____

Title _____

_____

_____

To see a sample student response to the above worksheet, turn to page 156.

Try It Out

Now apply what you have learned to an AP-style prompt followed by an excerpt from Geoffrey Chaucer's *The Canterbury Tales*, written between 1386 and 1400. You will recognize this prompt from Lesson 7.

Prompt

The Canterbury Tales is a narrative poem; a combination of character sketches, conversations, and stories told by a group of pilgrims journeying to a religious site, the cathedral of Canterbury. The travelers entertain one another with stories, some ribald (off-color) and others sermonic.

In the following excerpt, one of the pilgrims, the Wife of Bath (who has had five husbands) tells her tale to the travelers. In a well-organized essay, analyze the literary devices (such as diction, tone, and word choice) the Wife of Bath uses to convey her point of view.

From The Canterbury Tales

Take wise King Solomon of long ago;
We hear he had a thousand wives or so.
And would to God it were allowed to me
To be refreshed, aye, half so much as he!
5　He must have had a gift of God for wives,
No one to match him in a world of lives!
This noble king, one may as well admit,
On the first night threw many a merry fit
With each of them, he was so much alive.
10　Blessed be God that I have wedded five!
Welcome the sixth, whenever he appears,
I can't keep continent for years and years.
No sooner than one husband's dead and gone
Some other Christian man shall take me on,
15　For then, so says the Apostle, I am free
To wed, o' God's name, where it pleases me.
Wedding's no sin, so far as I can learn.
Better it is to marry than to burn.
Virginity is perfect, unforsaken,
20　Continence too, devoutly undertaken.
But Christ, who of perfection is the Well,
Bade not that everyone should go and sell
All that he had and give it to the poor

To follow in His footsteps, that is sure.
25   He spoke to those that would live perfectly,
And by your leave, my lords, that's not for me.
I will bestow the flower of life, the honey,
Upon the acts and fruit of matrimony.

Now follow the steps below to analyze the poem.

Analysis: Excerpt from *The Canterbury Tales*

Step 1: Read the Prompt

What are some of the important words in the prompt?

_____   _____

_____   _____

What elements of the prompt do you need to explore?

_____

_____

Is there more than one part to the prompt? _____

_____

_____

Step 2: Read the Poem
As you read, use the *ppsssssttt* mnemonic device to unlock the poem's meaning.

Paraphrase _____

Purpose _____

Structure _____

Shift _____

Speaker _____

Spelling/grammar/diction _____

Tone _____

Theme _____

Title _____

Step 3: Brainstorm
Develop a cluster or an outline.

Step 4: Write Your Essay
On a separate piece of paper, write an essay responding to the prompt. At the end of this lesson, we have included student samples: responses to the worksheet, an outline (annotation) of the poem, and several of the first two paragraphs of a response to the prompt.

 **Try It Out**

The best way to score well on a rigorous test is to practice with difficult passages. Read this excerpt from Milton at least three times, but keep in mind that on exam day you may only have time for one or two readings.

Prompt

The following excerpt from John Milton's *Paradise Lost* recounts Satan's most persuasive temptation of Eve in the Garden of Eden. In a well-developed essay, explain what the speech reveals about both Satan and Eve and how the author achieves this. Be sure to include in your discussion such techniques as diction, imagery, and any other devices you identify in the piece. Do not summarize the passage.

From Paradise Lost

     He ended; and his words, replete with guile,
Into her heart too easy entrance won:
Fixed on the fruit she gazed, which to behold
Might tempt alone; and in her ears the sound
5   Yet rung of his persuasive words, impregnated
With reason, to her seeming, and with truth:
Meanwhile the hour of noon drew on, and waked
An eager appetite, raised by the smell
So savory of that fruit, which with desire,
10   Inclinable now grown to touch or taste,
Solicited her longing eye; yet first
Pausing awhile, thus to herself she mused.
    "Great are thy virtues, doubtless, best of fruits,
Though kept from man, and worthy to be admired;
15   Whose taste, too long forborne, at first assay
Gave elocution to the mute, and taught

The tongue not made for speech to speak thy praise:
Thy praise he also, who forbids thy use,
Conceals not from us, naming thee the Tree
20   Of Knowledge, knowledge both of good and evil;
Forbids us then to taste! but his forbidding
Commends thee more, while it infers the good
By thee communicated, and our want:
For good unknown sure is not had; or, had
25   And yet unknown, is as not had at all.
In plain then, what forbids he but to know,
Forbids us good, forbids us to be wise?
Such prohibitions bind not. But, if Death
Binds us with after-bands, what profits then
30   Our inward freedom? In the day we eat
Of this fair fruit, our doom is, we shall die!
How dies the Serpent? he hath eaten and lives,
And knows, and speaks, and reasons, and discerns,
Was death invented? or to us denied
35   This intellectual food, for beasts reserved?
For beasts it seems: yet that one beast which first
Hath tasted envies not, but brings with joy
The good befallen him, author unsuspect,
Friendly to man, far from deceit or guile.
40   What fear I then? rather, what know to fear
Under this ignorance of good and evil,
Of God or death, of law or penalty?
Here grows the cure of all, this fruit divine,
Fair to the eye, inviting to the taste,
45   Of virtue to make wise: what hinders then
To reach, and feed at once both body and mind?"
    So saying, her rash hand in evil hour
Forth reaching to the fruit, she plucked, she eat!
Earth felt the wound; and Nature from her seat,
50   Sighing through all her works, gave signs of woe,
That all was lost. Back to the thicket slunk
The guilty Serpent. . . .

Now follow the steps below to analyze the poem.

Analysis: Excerpt from *Paradise Lost*

Step 1: Read the Prompt

What are some of the important words in the prompt?

_____   _____

_____   _____

What elements of the prompt do you need to explore?

_____

_____

Is there more than one part to the prompt? _____

_____

_____

Step 2: Read the Poem

As you read, use the *ppssssttt* mnemonic device to unlock the poem's meaning.

Paraphrase _____

Purpose _____

Structure _____

Shift _____

Speaker _____

Spelling/grammar/diction _____

Tone _____

Theme _____

Title _____

Step 3: Brainstorm

Develop a cluster or an outline.

Step 4: Write Your Essay

On a separate piece of paper, write an essay responding to the prompt. Then look at the sample student essays on pages 159–166.

Try It Out

Read the following prompt carefully and fill out the worksheet that follows. Then make an outline or cluster of the poem, and answer the prompt in a clear, concise essay.

Prompt

Although John Donne eventually became one of the great religious orators and poets of the 17th century, he was a brilliant, complex, and frequently irreverent man-about-town in
his youth. In his early secular (worldly) poetry, his attitude toward women was nearly always cynical.

Read "The Indifferent" carefully. Then, in a well-constructed essay, discuss how the speaker presents his view of
women using wit, a wide range of knowledge, and a variety of
unusual poetic devices.

The Indifferent

I can love both fair and brown;
Her whom abundance melts, and her whom want betrays;
Her who loves loneness best, and her who masks and plays;
Her whom the country form'd, and whom the town;
5   Her who believes, and her who tries;
Her who still weeps with spongy eyes,
And her who is dry cork, and never cries.
I can love her, and her, and you, and you;
I can love any, so she be not true.

10   Will no other vice content you?
Will it not serve your turn to do as did your mothers?
Or have you all old vices spent and now would find out others?
Or doth a fear that men are true torment you?
O we are not, be not you so;
15   Let me—and do you—twenty know;
Rob me, but bind me not, and let me go.
Must I, who came to travel thorough you,
Grow your fix'd subject, because you are true?

Venus heard me sigh this song;
20 And by love's sweetest part, variety, she swore,
She heard not this till now, and that it should be so no more.
She went, examin'd, and return'd ere long,
And said, "Alas! some two or three
Poor heretics in love there be,
25   Which think to stablish dangerous constancy.
But I told them, 'Since you will be true,
You shall be true to them who are false to you.'"

Analysis: "The Indifferent"

This worksheet differs slightly from those presented previously. You
can decide which method of brainstorming works best for you.

Mnemonic device _____

1. What qualities would you want your lover/significant other to have?

   Friendship, Kindness, _____

   _____

2. How do these differ from those of the speaker in this poem?

   He likes both whose ^^ roddnt bad _____

3. Paraphrase the poem.

   _____

4. The *what* (theme):

   _____

5. The *how:*

   Tone: _____

   Purpose: _____

   Title: _____

   Figurative language:

   _____   _____

   _____   _____

   _____   _____

   _____   _____

   Diction: _____

   Shifts? Irony? Paradox? Hyperbole? Understatement?

   _____

   _____

   _____

   _____

When you have finished writing your essay, turn to page 166 to see sample student responses to the prompt. How does your essay compare? Did other students raise points that you had not previously noticed? Do you agree with the readers' analysis of the student essays? A scoring rubric for "The Indifferent" is shown below. What score do you think your essay has earned?

RUBRIC: "The Indifferent"

9–8	Writers of these outstanding essays clearly understand the text. These essays accurately recognize the irony in the description of a "virtuous" and desirable lover. They will point out that the speaker's cynical attitude calls for inconstancy rather than the usually desirable virtue of fidelity from his ideal love. These essays will specify SEVERAL of the poetic devices (for example: tone, irony, paradox, overstatement, allusion, exaggeration, rhyme scheme, puns) which Donne uses, and they will demonstrate clearly and with strong support how these devices function to achieve their effects. Writers of these essays demonstrate an exceptional mastery of the elements of sentence structure, diction, and organization. While not necessarily flawless, these essays address the prompt with exceptional flair.
7–6	These essays accurately identify the wit and irony in the poem, but they do so with less insight. These essays specify appropriate poetic devices, but they do so less completely or less effectively than the best papers. They may misinterpret one part of the poem, but they recognize the tone and attitude of the speaker correctly. They are well written, and they accomplish the task of the prompt with sufficient specific support.
5	These essays are adequately written, yet superficial. They do not demonstrate stylistic maturity or confident control over the elements of composition. These essays discuss the text vaguely, or they inadequately analyze the author's techniques. They may cite stylistic techniques without sufficiently supporting how they work in developing the author's purpose.
4–3	These essays are adequately written but either summarize or misinterpret the work. Even a well-written summary will receive no higher than a four. These essays may simply list stylistic techniques and provide little or no discussion, evidence, or support. The writing may also be significantly flawed with syntactical errors and a lack of organization.
2–1	These essays are poorly written and replete with errors in diction, spelling, or syntax. They may use the passage merely as a springboard for an essay on a general topic. There may also be serious misinterpretation of the text. They are often too short.
0	These essays are nothing more than a restatement of the prompt.
–	This is for the response that has nothing to do with the question.

Lesson 8: Answers

Poetry, Activity 1

Answers
"Sonnet 116"

1. impediments

2. alters

3. bark

4. fool

5. brief

"If We Must Die"

1. bark

2. nobly

3. foe

4. men

5. cowardly

Analysis: "Eleanor Rigby"

Sample Student Response

<u>Paraphrase:</u> Rigby and McKenzie are both lonely people. Rigby cleans the church and, although she performs useful tasks, is unknown by the congregants. She puts on a mask, a disguise, for the world. No one attends her funeral. Father McKenzie writes sermons; no one listens to them. He, too, is lonely, sitting alone mending his socks in the evening. Ironic that these two do not seem to connect, although they both probably work in the same church. When they do meet, it is too late. She is dead and being buried by the priest.

<u>Purpose:</u> These two represent nameless people in society who are ignored. What can we do to identify and help those people without anyone? Is the purpose to open our eyes and think about others around us?

<u>Structure:</u> Narrative poem with refrain/chorus. Rhyme scheme: 6 lines—2, 3 rhyme; 5, 6 rhyme

<u>Shift:</u> Moves back and forth between Rigby and McKenzie

<u>Speaker:</u> Omniscient 3rd person

<u>Spelling, diction:</u> Many rhetorical questions. Simple, unadorned, plain language.

<u>Tone:</u> Serious, lamenting, sad, haunting thoughtful, depressing, sympathetic

<u>Theme:</u> Loneliness. Is this a symptom of a larger problem: people are egotistical? Is Rigby always the bridesmaid but never the bride? Does McKenzie represent God—who ignores those who do not believe in Him? We see people but really don't know what they feel.

<u>Title:</u> Why Rigby and not McKenzie? Does he have the church while she has nothing? Title, by focusing on one lonely person, calls attention to all others who are lonely.

Analysis: Excerpt from *The Canterbury Tales*

Sample Student Response

<u>Paraphrase:</u> In this excerpt from Chaucer's <u>The Canterbury Tales</u>, a woman speaks of her opinions on sex and marriage. The Wife of Bath is the perfect example of a woman thinking as she pleases rather than as society deems fit. She does act in accordance with her society however. She doesn't have affairs; she simply marries frequently. She marries out of sexual desire, but marries Christian men to justify her deed. She says herself in lines 22–27 that they were not all perfection nor are we ourselves expected to be. She's very blunt in her words: "Blessed be God that I have wedded five." Not every housewife would wish to be caught saying this. She compares herself to a king, and manipulates the word of God and Jesus Christ so that her actions are permissible.

Part of her allure is her "take me as I am" challenging attitude. We see from her admiration of King Solomon that she really has no shame for her behavior. In the first ten lines of the poem, the speaker tells the story of wise King Solomon. It is clear she was sure to mention the word "wise" in an attempt to persuade the reader to see his sexual escapades as permissible. She uses hyperbole ("we hear he had a thousand wives or so") to make her actions seen less sinful. She praises God for her having "wedded" five husbands. As soon as one is dead, she knows she will marry another Christian and "bestow the fruits of matrimony." She quotes the Apostle as saying she is free to marry again as one husband is "dead and gone," thereby using the word of God to justify her actions. However, in lines 21–25, she frees herself from the laws (and therefore the punishments) of Christ by stating that Christ only intended those who lived perfectly to follow his footsteps (demonstrating her hypocrisy). She's doing it the proper way, according to her rules, and so she will not "burn" for having an affair. She is going to heaven.

Author's note: *As we can see, paraphrasing or summarizing may begin to help us understand what is said, but tone, meaning, and purpose—very important elements—are missing.*

<u>Purpose:</u> This poem serves the purpose of illustrating the mentality of a woman who has married numerous times. It shows her philosophy on how the "ideal" is not meant for everyone. Highly important values such as virginity and abstinence may be a chosen lifestyle for some, but not her, and certainly not many others as well. The poem is thoughtful and insightful. It is somewhat upbeat in its style (exclamation marks and cheerful diction). At the same time, however, it is serious in its religious references. Overall, the writer seeks to give the reader a new outlook toward marriage. She spends each day living it fully for herself and no one else. She believes that life is meant to be enjoyed, and one way that she can do that is by not limiting herself to just one man.

<u>Structure:</u> Narrative poem, rhyme scheme: 2 lines

<u>Shift</u>: No shifts in tone, points of view, or language. At the end of line nine, however, the speaker shifts from biblical allusion to personal experience. On line 21 is another shift—references to Christ.

<u>Speaker</u>: The speaker is the Wife of Bath who has had five husbands and relates her story to her fellow travelers to Canterbury. She is the only speaker in the poem, and the first person device is used. Using her as the viewpoint makes her story more personal and more dramatic.

<u>Spelling/grammar/diction</u>: First line: "Take wise King Solomon of long ago"—historical allusion

<u>Fourth line</u>: "refreshed"—euphemism for sex

<u>Fifth Line</u>: "a gift of God"—hyperbole

<u>Eighth line</u>: "many a merry fit"—euphemism for sex

<u>Fourteenth line</u>: "take me on"—euphemism for sex, figurative language for matrimony

<u>Fifteenth line</u>: "For then, so says the Apostle, I am free"—unusual syntax

<u>Eighteenth line</u>: "Better it is to marry than to burn"—inversion, figurative language

<u>Line 21</u>: "who of perfection is the Well"—capitalization of "well"

<u>Line 27</u>: "the flower of life, the honey"—figurative language, metaphors

<u>Tone</u>: The tone of this piece can be described as carefree. She expresses her views as bluntly as she can while realizing that they happen to be the opposite views that Christ possessed. Words such as "refreshed," "gift," "merry," "free," and "perfect" help give this poem a positive tone.

<u>Theme</u>: Sex is part of human nature; certainly not a sin if one is married. The reference to King Solomon is proof that some of the greatest religious leaders in human history were not exactly celibate, yet they managed their sexual affairs in the proper, correct religious way. Therefore, according to the Wife of Bath, having another spouse after the previous one is dead and having sex with the new spouse is not a sin and she will not go to hell, even though she admits that abstaining from sex and upholding celibacy and virginity are more perfect and holy.

<u>Title</u>: The term "wife" has certain moral connotations; it turns out that the Wife of Bath has a different set of morals from those that the term connotes.

Excerpt from <u>The Canterbury Tales</u>: Outline

Biblical justification
  King Solomon
  Apostle says it's okay
  Jesus says you don't have to be perfect

Justifies imperfection
>   lines 17/18: "Better to marry than to burn"
>   lines 25/26: "by your leave that's not for me"
>   ". . . can't keep continent for years and years"
>   lines 3–16 suggest God's will for her to be married
>   quotes Bible lines 15, 21–22

Double meaning, sexual references
>   "to be refreshed"
>   "the flavor of life, the honey"
>   "threw many a merry fit"

<u>Excerpt from The Canterbury Tales: Opening Paragraphs</u>

Since WWII, adults have begun to pursue their own interests more than ever. As people have grown more independent, our sense of family has suffered severely. Not surprisingly, divorce rates have skyrocketed. Marriage is increasingly considered a means to personal happiness, not a sacred institution. Part of this philosophy is humorously expressed by the Wife of Bath, a character in Chaucer's <u>Canterbury Tales</u>. In the above excerpt, the Wife of Bath uses biblical justifications, selfish rationalizations, and suggestive double meanings to convey her point of view.

The Wife of Bath begins her speech by referencing King Solomon, who had a thousand wives. This "Gift of God" is one she wishes would be lavished upon her. She continues to call upon God as her inspiration for marriage by thanking him for her five husbands. Then, she uses the Bible and its point of view on divorce and widows to justify her earthly attitude. When talking about Christ, she points out that he did not expect everyone to be as perfect as he. All of these things combine to suggest that the Wife of Bath truly feels as if God wants her to continue to get married. Her beliefs, in a sense, come from God, and therefore God mustn't disapprove of her actions.

Analysis: Excerpt from *Paradise Lost*

Sample Student Essays

Here are three essays written by students. Read them carefully and then refer to the generic rubric on page 155. Then look at the reader's comments concerning the essays. Note that this particular poem once again illustrates the importance of developing a diversified vocabulary and a working knowledge of allusions. Knowing the story of Adam and Eve, the snake, and the apple will enable you to grasp the poem's meaning more readily.

Jessie (Score: 6)

Reason, the very quality that separates us from the chimpanzees and gorillas, also appears to separate us from purity and godliness. Eve rationalizes, with the assistance of Satan, that there exists no reason not to sample the fruit of knowledge. Milton's shifts in point of view, the rhetorical questions, and logos each bring us closer to Eve, allowing us to empathize with her. Satan is referred to less in this excerpt, and although Milton compels us to accept Satan's logic, through Eve, the Devil retains his less-than-savory status.

The first ten lines and the last six lines are written from the point of view of an omniscient narrator. However, it is after the shift to first person narration through the eyes of Eve, in line 13, that most of the characterization of Eve occurs. By "zooming in" (and later zooming back out) Milton draws us closer to Eve and allows us to feel a greater sense of immediacy. We experience first-hand the temptation that Eve suffers. Sharing her temptation, which is developed through vivid imagery on Milton's behalf, prevents us from condemning her, and actually starts us empathizing with her.

"What . . . forbids us to be wise?" Eve is appealing (albeit rhetorically) to the audience. We feel as if we are being asked, "Was death invented?" was "this intellectual food, for beasts reserved?" These questions further draw us in with Eve. We are experiencing together Satan's temptations and thus we are empathetic.

The logos with which Satan speaks to Eve shows his premeditated villainy, but it also makes sense to both Eve and ourselves. By the end of the poem we have shared the experience of temptation, together questioned the Lord's decree, and logically agreed to taste the apple together. We cannot condemn Eve and thus accept her for what she is. Human.

Satan, on the other hand, remains shady and surreal. He never speaks. He is never spoken of directly, only through vague pronouns and "Serpent." In the end he is "guilty" as he slides back into the dark shadows of the thicket.

Milton has developed Eve as a human and Satan remains evil. We empathize with Eve and only "see" Satan in the poem as "Serpent" "tempting" with "guile" the innocent.

Reader Analysis: Jessie (6)
Positive

- begins well; good focus; good hook
- generally good first paragraph—solid, clear
- keen understanding of passage
- answered question
- sentence variety
- decent vocabulary
- integrates quotes well

Negative

- awkward phraseology ("Satan is referred to less")
- needs to integrate words like *logos* more smoothly and display clearer understanding of words used—slight imprecision
- minor grammatical errors—"draws . . . allowing"
- seems unfinished
- lack of elegance in writing—sentence balancing awkward
- needs to develop ideas (mentions only imagery) more thoroughly

Elana (Score: 7)

Many years ago, Eve made a decision that revolutionized the human perception. While in the Garden of Eden, a serpent convinced her to feast on the forbidden apple. In *Paradise Lost*, the author John Milton describes this critical decision. The conniving serpent, an extension of Satan, convinces the desirous, naive Eve to bite the apple. Through the diction, imagery, and rhetorical strategies, the characters of Eve and Satan are revealed.

The serpent approaches Eve with an array of cogent arguments. His argument begins with flattery, an easy entrance to her heart. He follows with persuasive words "replete with guile" and "impregnated with reason." Ultimately, he is attempting to appeal to Eve and her desires. His primary objective is to swindle her. His timing is perfect, instigating her when she is vulnerable. The Satan serpent has provoked her appetite as the "hour of noon drew on." Additionally, the description of the serpent is representative of his character. He is described with disgust as he "slunk" back to the thicket as a "guilty Serpent."

The reader can recognize the extent of his lies, as Eve seriously considers her decision. Eve is impressed by his ability to speak. He evidently has convinced her that his verbal skills are attributed to the taste of the apple. Such a lie is an appropriate representation of his mischievous nature.

The Serpent greatly affects Eve, and truly reveals her character. Her reactions display her desirous and eager spirit, as well as her flawed characteristic of being easily duped.

In the beginning, she is taken in by his flattery, as he is easily invited "into her heart." As his argument proceeds, we see her almost youthful spirit appear. She is captured by his speech, and her excitement intensifies. She "gazes" with her "longing eyes" and recognizes the "savory." She "muses" about the possibilities of the apple. Undoubtedly, she is drawn into Satan's scheme of temptation. Yet we see her desire and excitability intensifying with her "eager appetite."

She begins to ask questions, as a function of the argument. These questions, instigated by the Serpent, validate her inevitable decision to bite the apple. "How dies the Serpent," she asks with curiosity. Through these questions she becomes a greater proponent of the decision to taste the apple. She is tempted and desires to know more.

By the end of the passage, Eve has convinced herself of the wonders of the apple. She accentuates this great apple because of the effects on the serpent. He "knows and speaks and reasons and discerns." As well, she proclaims that this once "fair fruit" is now the "cure of all" and a "fruit divine."

Her final action is when she reaches her "rash hand" and "plucked" the fruit. This final action reflects all the excitement and intensity of her desire. However, she "plucked" the fruit, which is an intimation of the destruction, impetuousness, and lack of reason.

While in the Garden of Eden, the Satan Serpent effectively convinced Eve to take the bite that would change the human race. Through the diction, imagery, and numerous rhetorical devices, the conniving character of Satan and the desiring and excitable character of Eve are revealed.

Reader Analysis: Elana (7)
Positive

- sophisticated vocabulary
- understanding of the passage
- cites appropriately and correctly

- blends quotes elegantly and effortlessly
- analysis implied and subtle, not a listing
- good opening sentence
- organization conducive to reader's understanding, flows logically
- complexity of expression

Negative

- pedestrian beginning and ending
- choppy paragraphing structure
- needs to develop fewer thoughts more fully
- summarizes

Michelle (Score: 8)

In his epic poem Paradise Lost, John Milton retells the biblical story of Eve's succumbing to the appealing arguments of Satan. As the story is slowly recounted, the speech of both Eve and Satan reveal their underlying characters through a variety of literary techniques. Through diction, imagery, and tense shift, Eve is exposed as a morally weak individual and Satan is exposed as a manipulator "repute with guile."

From the beginning of the passage Milton employs formal diction and ornate vocabulary for all of his characters' speeches. As she muses to herself, Eve ponders the taste of the apple, which would "give eloquence to the mute." Such language reveals that Eve is ignorant—not stupid. If she is capable of using extensive vocabulary and pontificating moral quandaries concerning why "was death invented," she clearly knows what she is doing. She instead gives into temptation against logic. Unfortunately, as Milton notes in line two, "into her heart too easy entrance." Although Eve knows better, she is unable to rigidly keep to what she knows to be right. Satan on the other hand, that "guilty serpent" uses enticing language to convince Eve to sin. Although we did not actually hear his argument, his suggestive diction was "replete with guile" and tricky, and "persuasive," "impregnated with reason and to her with truth." He is obviously a very smooth character, able to successfully move the opinions of innocent girls with his enticing rhetoric. His intelligence is also demonstrated through his logical argument to Eve. The overall formality of the language clearly contributes to the seriousness of the piece.

The characters of Eve and Satan are also demonstrated through Milton's skillful employment of tense shift. The Serpent/Satan, "he hath eaten and lives." Eve, "she plucked, she eat!" By changing the verb tense from past to present mid-sentence, Milton emphasizes the present tense verb. The Serpent "lives" because he is able to endure. He has no shame in his deceitful act and remains. Eve follows suit, to her destruction. There is yet another shift at line 12/13, as Eve "to herself . . . muses." As we enter Eve's thoughts we enter the present tense of her thought and begin to more fully understand her reasoning. As she ponders rhetorical questions such as "what profits our freedom?" and "For us alone/was death invented" and "What fear I then?", she reveals herself to be truly seduced by the options presented before her, and ultimately acts to satisfy temptation.

The images created by Milton's formal diction also contribute toward characterizing Eve and Satan. The figurative language employed is particularly effective. Through such examples as personification or "words impregnated with reason" and "appetites raised by the smell so savory of that fruit," the audience is able to fully comprehend what Eve is. We begin to understand her dilemma.

Reader Analysis: Michelle (8)

Positive

- effective beginning and conclusion
- accurate analysis of both meaning and methods
- insightful
- real appreciation of complex language
- fresh thinking
- clear sense of voice
- confident writing—not tentative
- flows
- integrates quotations naturally and persuasively and effectively
- smooth and subtle transitions, but they're there
- notice verb tense shift—perspicacious reading
- responded well to all parts of the question
- sentence structure varied and sophisticated
- universality and simplicity of her final statement

Negative

- some awkwardness of phrasing and misused words
- some misuse of words, i.e., "repute" for "replete" and "into" for "in to"

Analysis: "The Indifferent"

Sample Student Responses

Below are three student essays on John Donne's "The Indifferent," followed by a reader analysis comparing the three responses.

Student Essays: "The Indifferent"

Nazia (Score: 9)

what than restated

In his poem, "The Indifferent," John Donne employs a sense of both wit and cynicism, breadth of wisdom, and several poetic devices to reveal his view of women as temporary objects in his life whose qualities are unimportant. Donne's wittiness is evident throughout the poem; his wit adds a bit of surprise to his words. This sense emerges in line 9, when he writes, "I can love any, so she be not true." He admits that he can love any type of woman, except one that is faithful to only him. His sense of wittiness arises from his twist of words and the outrageous concept he presents. The reader does not expect the sudden shift of ideas in the poem or Donne's recommendation of unfaithfulness. He further employs witty puns in the first stanza of the poem. He uses the phrases "abundance melts" and "want betrays" to represent both the physical appearance and the financial status of the women. These puns clearly display his view of women; he is classifying them as though they are possessions, and their characteristics hold no importance for him.

Donne seems to draw his wit from unexpectedness. In line 20, he claims that "love's sweetest part" is "variety." These words further reflect his missing sense of loyalty toward women; he never speaks lovingly of them. He says here that women are temporary—he enjoys drifting from one to another. Clearly, the author's sense of wit is apparent even in the subject of the poem. It is a love poem about unfaithfulness.

In "The Indifferent," Donne also expresses cynicism toward women and those who remain in a "true" relationship. He uses the phrase "poor heretics" to describe individuals who believe in lasting, faithful love; he identifies them as "non-believers" and naïve. His cynicism can also be detected in line 11, where he claims that the women's mothers were unfaithful so they should behave similarly; he is implying that women do not posses a high sense of morality. The author also reveals a slight cynicism toward men. He asks the women in the second stanza if a "fear that men are true torment(s)" them. He tells women that most men are not true to their beloved.

Secondly, John Donne displays his breadth of wisdom in "The Indifferent" to further solidify his belief that women are material objects with unmemorable qualities. He uses his knowledge to persuade his audience that he is indeed credible. Donne is suggesting quite an uncommon idea; he wants to capture his readers' attention and coerce them to consider his point of view. Donne effectively accomplishes this through two different manners. The first is by citing his vast experience with women. In the first stanza, he identifies what he believes are all types of women and expresses a sense of familiarity with each one. In line 15, he claims that he has been with "twenty" women. By revealing these details, Donne suggests that he does not possess any loyalty and associates no sense of importance with women. He views them as objects, obtaining one after another.

Another manner that he uses to reflect his range of wisdom is by presenting his own intelligence. In the last stanza of the poem, he utilizes the mythological allusion of the goddess of sexual love and physical beauty, Venus. The symbolism he uses here makes his view clear. Venus does not represent faithfulness; she is receptive to Donne's idea—she regards it as revolutionary ("she heard not this till now"). This allusion enhances his credibility and sets up a defense for his argument. Donne refers to religion in his poem to again represent his intelligence. He uses the image of the "heretics" in the last stanza and, in the first stanza, the depiction of one woman whose belief in God is strong and another who questions God.

Finally, John Donne uses several poetic devices to strengthen his view that women are objects. In the first stanza, Donne juxtaposes opposing types of women; this classification of qualities into extremes signifies Donne's attitudes toward women. He writes of their characteristics without expressing any affection for them, revealing that their inner traits are unimportant; he "can love any." Donne's use of the objective pronoun "her" in the first stanza further emphasizes that he is objectifying women, regarding them as material possessions. The pronoun "her" also evokes a sense of distance. He is speaking as though he has no human affection or closeness with them.

Donne's simple diction, including his use of adjectives, provides the poem with a subtlety that makes his idea more valid and, in a way, less disagreeable to the reader. His words are simple, but full of meaning; his adjectives reinforce and add to them. He uses simple diction in the phrase "rob me, but bind me not" to express that he does not wish to be loyal to one woman. He goes on to modify the word "constancy" with the adjective "dangerous"—this seems to be an oxymoron, but it is truly suggestive of Donne's belief in unfaithfulness. He warns against being "true" to one. He employs a revealing adjective in the phrase "poor heretic" to display his sympathy toward those that believe in a faithful relationship.

The author uses rhetorical questions in the second stanza. He seems to be speaking to both women and himself—it appears that he is defending his argument to a level that is universal. Donne uses the metaphors in the phrases "spongy eyes" and "dry cork" when referring to women, thus further associating them with inanimate objects. His repetition in line 8, "I can love her, and her, and you, and you," again signifies his "indifference." He sees women as an array of objects to be chosen from.

The author adds complexity to his poem through several other poetic devices. He consistently employs connotative words, such as "masks and plays" and "her whom the country formed," to provide the reader with images rather than bluntly stating the women's traits. Donne again adds subtle complexity in line 20, by inserting the words of his song, "Love's sweetest part, variety." Although this is almost unnoticeable at first glance, these words are essential to the central meaning of the poem. They serve to explain his desire to never be faithful to one; he does not wish to be settled within a relationship. Donne peculiarly ends three of the lines in his poem with the word "true," though he is advising not to be so—this serves to add further complexity to the poem.

In brief, John Donne clearly expresses that women are objects that he does not wish to be bound to. He is witty and cynical and expresses his broad range of knowledge in his poem, "The Indifferent." He advocates unfaithfulness and variety in love. Donne manipulates various poetic devices, including rhetorical questions, connotative words, symbolism, and metaphors, in order to solidify his view. He is a man who is "indifferent" toward women and does not want to be in love with the same woman for long.

Michelle (Score: 8)

In his evolution from libertine to religious poet, John Donne similarly altered his view of women. In his poem, "The

Indifferent," the speaker presents his view of women with wit, a wide range of knowledge, and a variety of poetic devices.

Oddly, the speaker clearly feels that faithful women are unlovable, while the unfaithful are to be desired. Vice and virtue have switched roles. And variety in love has become the spice of life. He skillfully reveals his paradoxical viewpoint of women through wit. By combining verbal cleverness with keen perception, the speaker is able to focus his opinions through various techniques of humor such as puns and hyperbole. In the first stanza, as he contrasts the type of women he is able to love, he employs a great deal of play on words. One particular female is "her who masks and plays." A masked woman can either be a masked participant of a masquerade ball or a woman who wears a figurative mask to disguise her true personality. Another woman stirs the sexual pun of being a "dry cork," while others are those "the country form'd, and whom the town." The puns are often used in the service of truth; they emphasize the essential nature of something, in this case, the reversal of vice and virtue as beneficent traits for women to possess. Within the same stanza, as the speaker utilizes hyperbole. This exaggeration of the number of women he has loved expresses strong emotion and creates that witty, comic effect.

Through his narration, the speaker demonstrates his wide range of knowledge, especially with regard to the female gender. The fact that he is able to so readily name a long list of women it is possible for him to love clearly suggests that he has had first-hand experience with the subject, or else thought about it at great length. The woman who is "fair and brown," the woman who "believes" or "tries," both are discussed in order to provide the ambivalent speaker with a sense of authority and lend merit to his idea of fidelity being a vice. His knowledge of mothers further adds to the argument at hand. In asking "Will it not serve your turn to do as did your mothers?", he ponders and poses the question of why daughters should be faithful if their mothers are not. The speaker is also able to present his view of women through his gamut of general knowledge concerning mythology. His support from Venus, the goddess of love, develops his case and provides structure for his presentation of women.

The speaker also utilizes a variety of poetic devices to fully convey his paradoxical view concerning women. In the first stanza, antithesis is constantly used to contrast the multifarious women that are deserving of the speaker's love, essentially because they are not faithful. By contrasting the "fair" and "brown," the loner "who loves loneliness best" and the social butterfly who "masks and plays," and the country and city girls, the speaker emphasizes his points that there are a lot of different types of women who he can love and consequently do not possess a deep sense of fidelity. Beginning in the second stanza, he employs rhetorical questions such as "Will no other vice content you? Will it not serve your turn to do as did your mothers?" to address women's fears and ultimately delve into their mind sets to demonstrate his own. In the third stanza, the speaker shifts to Venus the goddess of love's comment in his favor and promises to punish the "two or three" faithful lovers by making them "true to them who are false to [them]." He is able to have another knowledgeable source support his views, giving them more credibility. The two juxtaposed words represent the paradox of the reversal of vice and virtue as a desirable trait in a woman. Additionally, in all three stanzas the speaker illustrates his points with imagery and figurative language such as "spongy eyes . . . dry cork" that "never cries."

In the three stanzas of John Donne's poem "The Indifferent," the male speaker paradoxically believes that a woman's greatest vice is in fact fidelity and he is only able to love women that are untrue. His view of women is skillfully presented with wit, a wide range of knowledge, and a variety of poetic devices.

Greg (Score: 8)

Fidelity. A word one will never hear on the modern-day Jerry Springer show for both its ludicrous definition and polysyllabic nature. Certain less-than-reputable areas of the media will have people believe that faithfulness and monogamy mean nothing, and everyone falls "victim" to cheating on his or her loved "one." John Donne, however, was apparently centuries ahead of his time then, endorsing such practices in "The Indifferent." The narrator rallies for multiple partners for all, while expressing his views on women—that one is no different than any other (with the exception between the naïve faithful and the realistic unfaithful) and men should therefore love indiscriminately. Donne develops his arguments using clever wit, a wide range of knowledge, and figurative language.

First, well known for his wit, Donne does not disappoint his audience in "The Indifferent." He begins immediately employing pun after pun, naming a multitude of characteristics women can possess, but each with a unique, suggestive connotation. Does "Her whom abundance melts . . ." indicate a wealthy, material woman or one who simply is large size? Both images come to mind regardless. "Her who believes, and her who tries" is in reference to religion, while "her who is dry cork" both means apathetic and unloving while also having sexual undertones. His wit continues on into the third stanza, where he speaks of the myth of "heretics" who honestly believe in fidelity. He uses litote to discuss the "two or three" heretics out there, for whom he pities for their unending, unreturned devotion and naiveté. To use the word "heretic" in such a way is itself bizarre and unexpected. In fact, the entire argument is clearly unorthodox, best exemplified by the final line of the first stanza: "I can love any, so she be not true." Therein lies the twist of the poem, allowing wit to introduce his point.

Additionally, Donne creates ethos by demonstrating his knowledge, using allusion, and utilizing general devices of argumentation. In the first stanza, as said before, he lists all characteristics he has witnessed in the opposite sex, thereby portraying him as a "man-about-town," knowledgeable in what he has to say. The audience acknowledge all the "hers" he lists, while successfully establishing his authority. Later the mythological allusion again expresses his intelligence, making an unusual parallel between Venus and what he is advocating. He actually brings in a god to justify his argument, and it works; Venus is by far the symbol for fidelity, and she does in fact reinforce "variety."

Serving both to display his wide range of knowledge and as a poetic device, Donne exercises the power of argumentative devices to serve his purpose. He introduces with anaphora which again reinforces ethos by its nature. He then ironically and unexpectedly twists what he has said to call for infidelity by the end of the first stanza. Addressing the opposing viewpoint, he dismisses fidelity by frankly stating that no one practices it other than a few eccentrics, thereby justifying his own desires. He uses reason to ask if women are truly justified themselves in applying their backward thinking to non-monogamists, followed by a clever allusion and litote to strengthen his point. He concludes by pointing out that these "heretics" are only doomed to love those who are not faithful to them, a cruel punishment for the over-idealistic. It is this placing of certain aspects of his argument and the progression itself that intensify his point.

Figurative language is also efficient in "The Indifferent." In addition to the aforementioned wit, litote, allusion, and anaphora, Donne recruits rhetorical questions, polysyndeton, and appropriate diction to express his view on women and relationships. Theatrical questions permeate the entire second stanza, where he is justifying his argument. He asks, "Will it not serve your turn to do as did your mothers?" (again related to ethos) and "Must I . . . / Grow your fix'd subject, because you are true?" This technique serves to invoke more audience involvement as if he were truly speaking to all women, while making his language more poignant. Polysyndeton is utilized in line 8, where the speaker claims, "I can love her, and her, and you, and you . . ." This serves to place all women on the same level for the speaker and therefore this carries over psychologically to his audience. Since they are all equal and the same to the speaker, he is advocating arbitrary choosing of mates, and is indifferent to the women specifically. This relates to the title—applicable to all of his lovers and thus all of his lovers' lovers.

Moreover, Donne's diction is refined and appropriate. "Dry cork" has a sexual connotation, as does "travel thorough [through] you." There are religious undertones throughout the poem as expressed in the diction, such as "believers and heretics." Heretics is more associated with religious dissidents, most often those from the Roman Catholic Church. In addition, the adjectives used in "The Indifferent" are well chosen and stand out as a result. All words associated with fidelity are negative and infidelity positive, as expected in an argument. "Rob," "Bind," "travail," "fixed," and "torment" all have less than positive connotations, and all are employed when discussing foolish, "dangerous constancy" (another adjective). Furthermore, infidelity is described using more positive words such as "sweetest" and "variety" making the speaker's opinion clear.

Thus, "The Indifferent" by John Donne rejects loyalty and faithfulness for the more realistic (not to mention fun) idea of infidelity. He develops his arguments coherently while expressing his view on relationships and women in general. He views them as inseparable from each other in his mind, and therefore advises to love as many as "twenty" of them at the same time indiscriminately. He views those women that are devoted to their loved ones as naïve, unrealistic, and smothering of their beliefs onto their *more liberal loved ones. He successfully expresses his point through the use of wit, knowledge, and poetic devices, and leaves the reader ironically entertained by such an unorthodox proposition.*

Reader Analysis, Student Essays: "The Indifferent"

The three students whose work appears above understood the poem and answered the question, which asked them to discuss how the speaker presents his view of women with wit, a wide range of knowledge, and a variety of unusual poetic devices. Many of our students found this poem puzzling. It upset their expectations—which may be one reason why many scholars think so highly of it. The top essay-writer's conclusion that the speaker "advocates unfaithfulness and variety in love" is a perceptive and sophisticated interpretation of an unorthodox stance. Understanding the *what* automatically begins to place her as a writer of an upper-half paper.

She also addresses the *how* with depth, thus demonstrating a commanding knowledge of rhetorical strategies. Not only does she recognize these strategies, but she also supports her assertions with perception, insight, and striking appropriateness.

This student incorporates quotes smoothly, with flair and elegance, throughout the essay. Please note her verbs: *reflect, persuade, utilizes, enhances, coerce, juxtaposes, solidify, defends, advocates, manipulates.* Her evocative adjectives—*slight, revealing, universal, inanimate, connotative*—highlight the accurate points she is presenting. Her prose blends unobtrusively with the language of the poem—no mean task.

Note also the essay's organization. There is no one "right" way to organize, but whatever method you use, it should be apparent to the reader. The student used the prompt itself, not a bad idea when properly utilized as it is here. To facilitate her organization, she used transitions clearly.

The student's textual evidence is pertinent. To exemplify the speaker's wit, she cites the phrases "abundance melts," "want betrays," and "love's sweetest part is variety." To underline his cynicism, she uses "fear that men are true torment(s) them." To support the assertion that the speaker displays a breadth of knowledge, the student presents mythological allusions, symbolism, illustrative religious references, and the student's own experiences. Furthermore, she presents a thorough analysis of the speaker's diction.

The other two students' essays show a firm grasp of Donne's meaning and intent. They effectively analyze the poem, but their writing does not exhibit the confidence and maturity of the 9 essay.

Writing Effective Essays About Prose

We are analysts by nature. Every moment of our lives requires some sort of studying, as we are constantly determining the essence of all we encounter. The same is true for what we read. Then how do you go about separating prose into themes and ideas, with the ultimate goal of synthesis? This is the *what* part of an analysis.

A careful reading of both the prompt and the prose passage is necessary in order to be able to write an insightful and sensitive essay in response to the prompt. In addition, it is essential that you possess a comprehensive vocabulary, as well as an understanding of the many literary devices through which authors express themselves. This is the *how* part of an analysis.

Finally, developing your ability to internalize, to speculate, and to trust your instincts will result in an upper-level essay, one that will satisfy you and delight your readers. With this in mind, carefully read John Cheever's short story "Reunion."

 ## Taking It Apart

Reunion

The last time I saw my father was in Grand Central Station. I was going from my grandmother's in the Adirondacks to a cottage on the Cape that my mother had rented, and I wrote my father that I would be in New York between trains for an hour and a half, and asked if we could have lunch together. His secretary wrote to say that he would meet me at the information booth at noon, and at twelve o'clock sharp I saw him coming through the crowd. He was a stranger to me—my mother divorced him three years ago and I hadn't been with him since—but as soon as I saw him I felt that he was my father, my flesh and blood, my future and my doom. I knew that when I was grown I would be something like him; I would have to plan my campaigns within his limitations. He was a big, good-looking man, and I was terribly happy to see him again. He struck me on the back and shook my hand. "Hi, Charlie," he said. "Hi, boy. I'd like to take you up to my club, but it's in the Sixties, and if you have to catch an early train I guess we'd better get something to eat around here." He put his arm around me, and I smelled my father the way my mother sniffs a rose. It was a rich compound of whiskey, after-shave lotion, shoe polish, woolens, and the rankness of a mature male. I hoped that someone would see us together. I wished that we could be photographed. I wanted some record of our having been together.

We went out of the station and up a side street to a restaurant. It was still early, and the place was empty. The bartender was quarreling with a delivery boy, and there was one very old waiter in a red coat down by the kitchen door. We sat down, and my father hailed the waiter in a loud voice. *"Kellner!"* he shouted. *"Garçon! Cameriere! You!"* His boisterousness in the empty restaurant seemed out of place. "Could we have a little service here!" he shouted. "Chop-chop." Then he clapped his hands. This caught the waiter's attention, and he shuffled over to our table.

"Were you clapping your hands at me?" he asked.

"Calm down, calm down, *sommelier*," my father said. "If it isn't too much to ask of you—if it wouldn't be too much above and beyond the call of duty, we would like a couple of Beefeater Gibsons."

"I don't like to be clapped at," the waiter said.

"I should have brought my whistle," my father said. "I have a whistle that is audible only to the ears of old waiters. Now, take out your little pad and your little pencil and see if you can get this straight: two Beefeater Gibsons. Repeat after me: two Beefeater Gibsons."

"I think you'd better go somewhere else," the waiter said quietly.

"That," said my father "is one of the most brilliant suggestions I have ever heard. Come on, Charlie, let's get the hell out of here."

I followed my father out of that restaurant into another. He was not so boisterous this time. Our drinks came, and he cross-questioned me about the baseball season. He then struck the edge of his empty glass with his knife and began shouting again *"Garçon! Kellner! Cameriere! You!* Could we trouble you to bring us two more of the same."

"How old is the boy?" the waiter asked.

"That," my father said, "is none of your God-damned business."

"I'm sorry, sir," the waiter said, "but I won't serve the boy another drink."

"Well, I have some news for you," my father said. "I have some very interesting news for you. This doesn't happen to be the only restaurant in New York. They've opened another on the corner. Come on, Charlie."

He paid the bill, and I followed him out of that restaurant into another. Here the waiters wore pink jackets like hunting coats, and there was a lot of horse tack on the walls. We sat down, and my father began to shout again. "Master of the hounds! Tallyhoo and all that sort of thing. We'd like a little something in the way of a stirrup cup. Namely, two Bibson Geefeaters."

"Two Bibson Geefeaters?" the waiter asked, smiling.

"You know damned well what I want," my father said angrily. "I want two Beefeater Gibsons, and make it snappy. Things have changed in jolly old England. So my friend the duke tells me. Let's see what England can produce in the way of a cocktail."

"This isn't England," the waiter said.

"Don't argue with me," my father said. "Just do as you're told."

"I just thought you might like to know where you are," the waiter said.

"If there is one thing I cannot tolerate," my father said, "it is an impudent domestic. Come on, Charlie."

The fourth place we went to was Italian. *"Buon giorno,"* my father said. *"Per favore, possiamo avere due cocktail americani, forti, forti. Molto gin, poco vermut."*

"I don't understand Italian," the waiter said.

"Oh, come off it," my father said. "You understand Italian, and you know damned well you do. *Vogliamo due cocktail americani. Subito."*

The waiter left us and spoke with the captain, who came over to our table and said, "I'm sorry, sir, but this table is reserved."

"All right," my father said. "Get us another table."

"All the tables are reserved," the captain said.

"I get it," my father said. "You don't desire our patronage. Is that it? Well, the hell with you. *Vada all'inferno.* Let's go, Charlie."

"I have to get my train," I said.

"I'm sorry, sonny," my father said. "I'm terribly sorry." He put his arm around me and pressed me against him. "I'll walk you back to the station. If there had only been time to go up to my club."

"That's all right, Daddy," I said.

"I'll get you a paper," he said. "I'll get you a paper to read on the train."

Then he went up to a newsstand and said, "Kind sir, will you be good enough to favor me with one of your God-damned, no-good, ten-cent afternoon papers?" The clerk turned away from him and stared at a magazine cover. "Is it asking too much, kind sir," my father said, "is it asking too much for you to sell me one of your disgusting specimens of yellow journalism?"

"I have to go, Daddy." I said. "It's late."

"Now, just wait a second, sonny," he said. "Just wait a second. I want to get a rise out of this chap."

"Goodbye, Daddy," I said, and I went down the stairs and got my train, and that was the last time I saw my father.

Analysis: "Reunion"

Now answer the questions below. This will give you a sense of the types of questions you should ask yourself when analyzing a complex piece of prose.

1. What is your impression of Charlie? What is the father-son relationship like at the beginning of the story? At the end?

   _____

   _____

   _____

2. List some of the stylistic devices you discovered.

   _____

   _____

   _____

   _____

3. Let's backtrack. Consider the title. What does the word *reunion* conjure up for you? Close your eyes and imagine a reunion you would be eager to have with family, friends, schoolmates, etc. Or think of a reunion you might anticipate with dread. What are your immediate feelings about the reunion you chose?

   Reunion would be with _____

   I would be feeling _____

   because _____

4. Analyze the story. First, consider the title. What is ironic about it? Could you think of another title that would capture the experience as well? What is it?

   Title's irony _____

   Your title _____

   After the completion of these preliminary ponderings, we are now ready to undertake an in-depth analysis of "Reunion."

Section 1

Consider the setting. What is ironic about the meeting taking place in Grand Central Station? Discuss the fact that Charlie's father's secretary arranged their meeting. What comment do you think Cheever is making by including this detail?

Setting _____

Comments _____

Look at such devices as the diction, imagery, tone, and the dialogue in this first paragraph. Do you see the complexity of the short story beginning to emerge?

While you might not want to use all of these devices, choose a few from the list below, or add your own, already chosen, and begin to dissect the paragraph. How would the story differ if the point of view were the father's instead of Charlie's?

Tone: the writer's attitude toward his subject _____

Diction: word choice _____

Imagery: that which appeals to the senses _____

Syntax: sentence structure _____

Dialogue: words spoken by characters _____

Different points of view _____

You might want to continue this exercise through the entire story to sharpen your skills. You don't need to answer every question, but try to think critically about each one.

Section 2

Consider every detail as you read. The skilled and sensitive Cheever has included much in this seemingly simple account. How is the father portrayed here (his actions, words, appearance)?

Father's portrayal _____

For example, what do you think is ironic about the father's having command, albeit limited command, of several languages? His boisterousness in the empty restaurant is unnecessary and rude. How do you think Charlie is reacting to this? Can you recall a similar situation when one of your parents embarrassed you? Why is an occurrence such as this particularly painful?

Consider the contrast of the quiet dignity of the very old waiter with the father's obnoxious behavior. In addition to a consideration of the *what* of the story, always delve into the *how*. You may use any of the following elements, or add your own.

Tone _____

_____

_____

Imagery _____

_____

_____

Diction _____

_____

_____

Dialogue _____

_____

_____

Repetition _____

_____

_____

Section 3

What role does alcohol play in "Reunion"? Notice that once again there is interaction between the father and a waiter in the second restaurant. Why do you suppose Charlie's father was not so boisterous this time? Choose a line that is particularly memorable and discuss it below.

_____

_____

_____

_____

_____

Section 4

Paragraph four begins, "He paid the bill, and I followed him out of that restaurant into another." The precious time is waning. What is revealing about the fact that the father has not concerned himself with his son's lunch but is instead on a quest for a drink? Could the term "Master of the hounds" be an allusion to Hades and the father's descent into the abyss? To what else might it allude? Is there anything at all humorous about this encounter? Consider, also, the repetition of "Beefeater Gibsons." What could this signify?

_____

_____

_____

_____

_____

_____

Section 5

Charlie's father displays a command of yet another language, Italian. And again, there is a reference to hell when the father says, *"Vada all'inferno."* Is Cheever alluding to Dante's Inferno here? What could this mean?

_____

_____

_____

_____

Section 6

The sad reunion is ending, yet the father is still committed to his path of self-destruction. Why does he make a scene at the newsstand? What does this reveal about him? Now reread the first and last lines: "The last time I saw my father was in Grand Central Station." " 'Goodbye, Daddy,' I said, and I went down the stairs and got my train, and that was the last time I saw my father." Why are they especially poignant?

_____

_____

_____

☞ *AP Tips for Writing Essays About Prose*

1. Read the passage carefully, always keeping the question or prompt you have just read in mind.

2. Underline, circle, make notes in the margin, or use any other method that works for you to focus on key words, phrases, symbols, etc., that you feel contribute to the meaning of the piece.

3. Label or list literary devices and elements you wish to mention in your essay, such as figurative language, point of view, shifts, tone, style, syntax, flashback, etc. (For a review of literary devices and elements, see Part 2.)

Try It Out

Below is a prompt and a passage from Charlotte Brontë's *Jane Eyre*. Read them carefully.

Prompt

What resources of language does Charlotte Brontë use to illustrate the characters of the narrator, nine-year-old Jane Eyre, and Helen Burns, the girl Jane Eyre is describing?

---

from *Jane Eyre*

The only marked event of the afternoon was that I saw the girl with whom I had conversed in the verandah dismissed in disgrace by Miss Scatcherd from a history class, and sent to stand in the middle of the large school-room. The punishment seemed to me in a high degree ignominious, especially for so great a girl—she looked thirteen or upwards. I expected she would show signs of great distress and shame; but to my surprise she neither wept nor blushed: composed, though grave, she stood, the central mark of all eyes. "How can she bear it so quietly—so firmly?" I asked of myself. "Were I in her place, it seems to me I should wish the earth to open and swallow me up. She looks as if she were thinking of something beyond her punishment—beyond her situation: of something not round her nor before her. I have heard of day-dreams—is she in a day-dream now? Her eyes are fixed on the floor, but I am sure they do not see it—her sight seems turned in, gone down into her heart: she is looking at what she can remember, I believe; not at what is really present. I wonder what sort of a girl she is—whether good or naughty."

Analysis: Excerpt from *Jane Eyre*

Step 1: Read the Prompt

What are some of the important words in the prompt?

_____   _____

_____   _____

What elements of the prompt do you need to explore?

_____

_____

Is there more than one part to the prompt?

_____

_____

_____

Step 2: Read the Passage

As you read, use the *ppssssttt* mnemonic device to unlock the passage's meaning.

Paraphrase _____

Purpose _____

Structure _____

Shift _____

Speaker _____

Spelling/grammar/diction _____

Tone _____

Theme _____

Title _____

Step 3: Brainstorm

Develop a cluster or outline. Be sure to consider both the *what* (the meaning) and the *how* (technique). Referring to one but not the other will result in a lower-scoring essay.

Step 4: Write Your Essay

On a separate piece of paper, write an essay responding to the prompt. At the end of the chapter, we have included a sample student outline, as well as the opening paragraph of the student's essay.

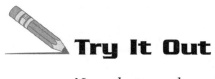

Try It Out

Now that you have honed your essay-writing skills, reread the John Cheever story on page 178. Then read the following prompt and complete the exercises that follow.

Prompt

In a well-planned essay, show how Cheever, through stylistic devices, including tone, reveals the complex relationship between Charlie and his father during their reunion.

Analysis: "Reunion"

Step 1: Read the Prompt

What are some of the important words in the prompt?

_____   _____

_____   _____

What elements of the prompt do you need to explore?

_____

_____

Is there more than one part to the prompt?

_____

_____

_____

Step 2: Read the Story
As you read, use the *ppssssttt* mnemonic device to unlock the story's meaning.

Paraphrase _____

Purpose _____

Structure _____

Shift _____

Speaker _____

Spelling/grammar/diction _____

Tone _____

Theme _____

Title _____

Step 3: Brainstorm
Develop a cluster or an outline.

Step 4: Write Your Essay
Take the next 30 minutes to write your own response to "Reunion." Remember that the prompt is as follows: Show how Cheever, through stylistic devices, including tone, reveals the complex relationship between Charlie and his father during their reunion. Then give yourself a score on your essay using the rubric below. When you are finished, turn to page 190 to see sample student responses to "Reunion."

RUBRIC: "Reunion"

9–8   Writers of these eloquent essays clearly understand the story, as well as both the father's and the son's characters, and they correctly interpret the complexity of the father-son relationship. In their discussion of this complexity, they accurately analyze the story and the methods through which the author achieves its tone, such as irony, structure, point of view, or contrast. Writers of these essays demonstrate a sophisticated mastery of sentence structure, word choice, and organization. While the writing need not be flawless, it must reveal the writer's ability to address the prompt with flair and efficiency.

7–6   These essays also accurately discuss the complex relationship between Charlie and his father as presented in the story, as well as the different elements that create its tone, but they do so with less insight than do the essays in the 9–8 range. They may misinterpret a minor part of the father's or son's characterization. Their discussion of the *how,* or techniques employed, is well developed. While these essays are well written with a strong sense of audience, they are less sophisticated than the top-range essays. Lucid and insightful, these essays fulfill the task, although with less originality and/or conciseness than those at the higher level.

5   These essays discuss the conflict between the father and the son and the complex relationship between the two, as well as tone, but they do so on a more simplistic level than do those in the 7–6 range. Their discussion of the *how* may be somewhat superficial and too general. The writer of a 5 may even misunderstand the complexity of this relationship. While these essays are adequately written, they may lack organization and demonstrate gaps in the elements of writing.

4–3   These essays address the major theme of the story but they do so in a cursory manner or present major inaccuracies in interpretation. The discussion of relationship, the overall tone, or the author's techniques may be poorly developed or may focus on only one aspect. Misunderstandings of either the *why* or the *how* are significant, or the essays are merely plot summaries. Writing also is significantly flawed with grammatical errors and misspellings.

2–1   These essays either entirely misrepresent the relationship between father and son, or they miss or misinterpret the story's tone. Even though there may be some correct commentary, proofs will be sketchy and poorly proven. In addition, they may be unacceptably brief and replete with errors.

Focus!

This story evokes many emotional responses from our students. A caveat: This is not the time to get off-topic by denouncing alcoholism (or bad parenting, absent fathers, etc.). A response that is off-topic will result in a failing essay. Furthermore, while it is acceptable to give your reader (whether it is your English teacher, peer editor, or the actual AP readers) a sense of yourself as the writer, this is also not the time to reveal personal anecdotal information, or to relate similar experiences you have had. Answer the question with honesty and passion, but *answer the question*.

Lesson 9: Student Responses

Analysis: Excerpt from *Jane Eyre*

Sample Student Responses

Below are a sample outline based on the *Jane Eyre* prompt, and the first paragraph of an essay written in response to the prompt. Is this student's outline similar to yours? How does your first paragraph compare to the one below?

Annotation

Jane

      Sympathetic, timid, innocent, naïve toward punishment

      Word Choice

            "Is she in a day-dream now"—reveals interest and concern for others; her compassion

            Strong words like "ignominious," "distress," "shame" express Jane's deep sympathy

      Style

            Questions Jane asks (punctuation) show she's thoughtful and analytic Irony that Jane feels the pain that should only be felt by the one who's being punished

Helen Burns

      Diction

            "Composed" and "grave" describe strength in a demeaning experience

            Her eyes are fixed on the floor. She endures the punishment solemnly

Style
> Figurative language: "her eyes . . . her sight seems turned in, gone down into her heart"

Setting
> She is being punished like a child in a setting of older students—patience and composure

First Paragraph

Charlotte Brontë's Jane Eyre describes two young girls: Jane Eyre and Helen Burns. Brontë expresses how strongly sympathetic Jane is by her use of highly effective diction. Jane is also portrayed as intelligent through her insightful and analytical thoughts. Through her use of questioning, her figurative language, and her sensitivity, Brontë gives us a sense of both Jane, a child, and Helen, the object of her admiration.

Analysis: "Reunion"

Sample Student Responses

Below are two upper-level essays and a midlevel essay on John Cheever's "Reunion." Read them and determine their strong points. Which opening line do you like better? Which essay has the better closing paragraph? Remember that the essays do not have to be perfect, and that the readers are told to "reward the student for what they do well." How does your own essay compare with these? Do you think these essays were scored fairly according to the rubric on page 188?

Student Essays: "Reunion"

Jennifer (Score: 8)

Eager to please, submissive, intimidated, proud, and embarrassed, Charlie recedes as his father dominates and leads. This reunion is hardly a meeting of mutual interest, for Charlie's youthful expectations are muted by his father's lack of control. Their encounter is a monopolized exchange orchestrated by his father. As Charlie observes, Charlie reveals to the reader the absence of a relationship. Utilizing tone, diction and perspective, Cheever conveys the intricacy of their reunion.

Interestingly, Charlie confirms their meeting through his father's secretary. One could mistake their reunion for a formal business luncheon. They are both pressed for time. Charlie admits that he would be in New York between trains for an hour and a half. One wonders if the hastiness of their encounter is intentional.

Upon discovering his father, Charlie experiences a mixture of pride and fear. He sizes up his father, "my flesh and blood, my future and my doom, a stranger." The use of the first person here engages the reader. Charlie anticipates his father's expectations. Initially, he seeks his father's approval, recognizing that he would, "have to plan his campaigns within his father's limitations." Charlie predicts that he will probably be something like his father. He aches for his father's companionship. This is indicated by his unspoken wish that "someone would see them together." Charlie wants to experience, to etch, to soak in, his father. He sniffs his father as his "mother sniffs a rose." This metaphor and the description that follows establish Charlie's identity of masculinity, realized in his first impressions of his father. Appealing to the senses, Cheever describes the father's BO as a "compound of whiskey and a mature male." Even his father's abrupt, slap-on-the-back greeting embodies the tough guy persona of a "big, good-looking man." Charlie is overwhelmed by his father's boisterousness, his pungent odor and his big, good-looking frame.

However, Charlie grows increasingly uneasy and embarrassed in his father's presence. As they enter an empty restaurant, his father hails the waiter with a "boisterousness that seemed out of place." So begins Charlie's silent judgment. He is the withdrawn spectator.

With obnoxious commands and caustic language, Charlie's father tries to control and intimidate. He cross-questions Charlie, and orders the waiter like a trained animal. His impatience leads to derisive commands—"Get us another table," sarcastic condescension—"Chop-chop," and false ingratiation—"If it wouldn't be above and beyond the call of duty." Throughout this spree, Charlie follows his father from restaurant to restaurant. As his father threatens and throws tantrums, one wonders who is the adult?

Charlie's father expects the worst service with his premature, sizzling criticism. He rudely demands and he receives the response he expects: curtness instead of courtesy. He embraces retaliation with a smugness that screams, "I could've told you," for he is determined to be right.

Sparring with the waiters, he affirms his arrogant, false superiority. His boisterousness is further agitated by "Gibson Beefeaters" or "Bibson Geefeaters." Using the language of a typical hot-shot megalomaniac, Charlie's father order his waiters to "make it snappy" or to come off it.

Despite his crudeness, Charlie's father is an intelligent man. His comments sting with the acuity of a strategically placed mine. Shrapnel. He can even communicate his acerbic comments in multiple languages, making prejudiced, cultural judgments. He wants Charlie to know that he's the man. With this argumentative attitude, he affirms his feigned authority. For his finale, Charlie's father unnecessarily instigates a clerk by insulting his merchandise. However, Charlie must leave before the act is over. His father orders him to "just wait a second. I want to get a rise out of this chap." Charlie leaves and never looks back.

By altering the setting, Cheever creates multiple opportunities to convey the boisterous arrogance of Charlie's father. Additionally, the use of interior monologue conveys Charlie's retreat from his father's abrasiveness.

Ultimately, Charlie's image is reduced to reality. Their relationship is left at the station, like a penny caught between the rails.

Reader Analysis: Jennifer (8)

While this student wrote an outstanding essay, the essay demonstrates what may well be a strength can also undermine a superbly written piece. In this case, the student demonstrates originality and an individual voice by opening with four accurate descriptive phrases before mentioning the subject's name or his situation. But what begins as a dynamic and effective sentence limps somewhat before the close because the words *recedes* and *dominates* do not convey precisely what the writer means. At least one reader felt that the jarring notes prevented the immersion necessary for the very top score.

The student presents a clear and accurate assessment of the situation, perceives the complexity of the father-son relationship, and addresses three specific elements—tone, diction, and perspective—in the development of the essay. Interesting phrasing, varied sentence structure, and a fairly impressive vocabulary range enhance the essay ("sarcastic condescension," "false ingratiation," "feigned authority," and "caustic language"). The near misses, however, are distracting and prevented the reader from assigning the highest score ("recedes," father's "tough guy persona," "typical hot-shot megalomaniac"). The easy, informal structure and style of the essay works in some instances, but works against itself in others. At times the student seems to lose a sense of audience.

Several ideas are well-developed and well-supported. The relationship between father and son is clearly defined and amply supported, but the essay would have benefited from reorganization and consolidation of the short paragraphs which illustrate Charlie's growing embarrassment. The reader perceives a lack of coherent support for all the components addressed, specifically the element of tone. However, tone is implied throughout.

This is a very strong essay that meets most of the requirements for a high score, but leaves room for improvement. The student exhibits a command of a wide range of the elements of good writing.

Scott (Score: 6)

How complex can a father-son relationship be? Depending on the personality of the father and the son, a relationship develops that functions on many levels. In Cheever's short story "Reunion," Charlie is upset. After a divorce, it had been three years since Charlie had last seen his father, and he was looking forward to this meeting. In this short story, Cheever displays the complex relationship between Charlie and his father through his use of tone, dialogue, and ironic humor.

Cheever narrates the story through Charlie after the so-called reunion occurred. By using this style, Cheever achieves two different tones that intertwine in the passage. The Charlie reflecting back is regretful that the reunion was not as successful as he would have liked; the Charlie partaking in the reunion is resentful of his father's attitude and behavior.

Reflecting on his father, he chooses to describe his "rankness of a mature male," which shows Charlie resents his father because he describes this smell. He also realizes that his father is "his future and his doom," which demonstrates he is fearful as well as resentful that he may also behave like this in his own future. Cheever repeats the word "boisterous" to describe his father, which portrays the negative tone that Charlie felt toward his father. On the other hand, Charlie seems regretful because he begins and ends the story with "last time I saw my father." Charlie also says "Goodbye, Daddy" to bring a type of closure to this relationship that he regrets he could never fulfill. Finally, Cheever describes the father as "a stranger . . . but my flesh and blood," thus demonstrating that Charlie recognizes how the relationship is and how he would like it to be. In each case, whether Charlie is resentful of his father, or regretful about his behavior, Cheever uses a tone which shows the complex relationship that Charlie and his father shared.

Cheever also characterizes Charlie's father through his dialogue, thus illustrating why the relationship between Charlie and his father is so complex. In every restaurant they attend, Charlie's father is shouting something at the waiter to get them thrown out. Cheever demonstrates through the dialogue between Charlie's father and the waiters how rude and inconsiderate the father is, and thus why Charlie has such a complex relationship with him. Also through the dialogue, Cheever displays that Charlie's father is only concerned with obtaining a drink. He repeatedly orders a "Beefeater Gibson" rather than concerning himself with obtaining food for Charlie. By portraying Charlie's father as a man who cares more about a drink than his son, Cheever demonstrates why Charlie is so resentful of his father. Finally in the father's dialogue, he mentions "master of the hounds" and "Vada inferno" both of which are allusions to hell and Dante's Inferno. By alluding to hell, Cheever shows that Charlie's father is basically descending into hell, and so is the complex relationship between Charlie and his father. Thus the dialogue that Charlie's father uses characterizes him and highlights the complexity of his relationship with his son.

Cheever finally illustrates the relationship between the two through his use of ironic humor. Right away, this irony is prevalent when after three years of being apart from his son, Charlie's father has his secretary make the appointment to meet him. This demonstrates that his father doesn't care enough about Charlie to speak to him personally. Also, in the restaurants, it is ironic that for a boisterous, and seemingly uneducated man, he is able to speak the different languages. These scenes not only cause laughs, but as Charlie reflects on them, he displays that his father is a competent man, and Charlie is regretful that his father doesn't act like one. Finally, the title is the greatest source of humorous irony in the story. The connotation of a reunion is a happy, cheerful coming together of family members, usually out of love. However, Charlie and his father's reunion is almost the complete opposite. They don't unite on any emotional or mental level, and most importantly, it is the last time they see each other. Once the story is completed, it is obvious that this title is definitely ironic, and combined with the other irony in the story, causes rueful laughter.

Therefore, the relationship between Charlie and his father is obviously complex. Cheever amplifies the complexity through his use of tone, dialogue, and ironic humor by showing the type of man Charlie's father really is. Once his character is established, it is no wonder that Charlie and his father never spoke again.

Reader Analysis: Scott (6)

This essay is a strong 6. Beginning with a question, the opening paragraph gives evidence of the writer's insight and analytical ability. Unlike many others, this essay reflects upon the two implicit narrators: Charlie the child, and Charlie the adult looking back. Complexity of tone is addressed with words such as *regretful, resentful* and *negative*. With specific and apt examples, the writer supports the premise. The use of dialogue to explore the father-son relationship is also addressed, although the writer's fluency is not as sophisticated as it would be in an 8 or a 9 paper. Awkwardness in phrases, such as "restaurants they attend" and "cause laughs," as well as repetitiveness in restating the prompt detracts from what could be more specific and appropriate support. Transitions ("also," "on the other hand," "in each case," "most importantly," "finally," and "thus") are well-placed and serve to connect intricate thoughts and combine to further the essay. Insight continues to be apparent throughout: The writer notes that Charlie's father is basically descending into hell, and so is the complex relationship. The writer also addresses irony, but doesn't provide sufficient support. He addresses the title, although not as completely or as much in depth as would an 8 or a 9 essay. While the ending merely restates the prompt, it does manage to tie the essay together. The writer is clearly skilled and intelligent: a more thorough analysis and a few more examples supporting the writer's points would have earned this essay a higher score.

Kristen (Score: 5)

"The last time I saw my father," introduces and concludes the story. After a disappointing reunion, Charlie does not see his father again. Whether the reason is death, choice, or inconvenience, Charlie regrets that his last visit had no positive effect on their relationship.

The detached tone indicates Charlie's distance from his father. The secretary confirmed the meeting as if they were business associates. The mother divorced him implying he had some kind of problem. The phrases "my flesh and blood" and "my future and my doom" are parallel structures. The genetic disease of alcoholism is within Charlie, and he fears it may find a way to control him the way it has controlled his father. The use of dialogue further describes the gap between Charlie and his father. Charlie speaks only to say he must go. He speaks to his father directly, following his short statements with "Daddy." Whereas he explains the actions of his father, "Daddy" expresses a childlike innocence of a son that looks up to his dad. The rude, ranting speech of the father indicates his lack of clear thinking. During his bar-hopping, he speaks to Charlie only to "cross-question" and order him to "Come on." He calls Charlie by his name, except for the times he referred to him as "sonny." "Sonny" is usually used by an older person toward a non-related younger one.

The contrast between Charlie's initial feelings toward his father and his feelings when he left shows how Charlie gave his father an honest chance and was disappointed. At first he was "happy to see him." The analogy of how he smelled his father demonstrated that he treated him as if he were delicate and beautiful. While he fears dependence of alcohol, Charlie is helpless around his father. He does not react to his cruel words, and he submits to his *demands. His father repeatedly commands him to come, and he repeatedly "follows him out."*

"I wanted some record of us being together." Charlie wanted to have a connection with his father that he could remember. Twice he told him he had to go. He ended the reunion in order to save the good parts. The longer he stayed, the more he did not want to see. Perhaps that is why it was the last time he saw his father.

Reader Analysis: Kristen (5)

This essay, while insightful, is much thinner than the upper-level essays; hence it is a 5. The interpretation is expressed tentatively and somewhat unconvincingly. The rubric states that a 5 essay discusses the conflict between the father and the son and addresses the complexity of their relationship, but does so with less insight than essays in the 7–6 range.

Much more is needed to develop the opening paragraph. The student could have mentioned Cheever's rhetorical strategies and could have given more specific information about the complexity of the relationship between father and son. In the second paragraph, although the student introduces tone, there is no support given for it. The writer might have traced the story's complexity of tone to better illustrate its poignancy. For example, the story begins with an enthusiastic and hopeful Charlie, and then evolves into what is clearly a description given from memory by a somewhat bitter and disillusioned young man. Instead of introducing the issue of alcoholism in the second paragraph, the writer should have addressed the tonal changes throughout the story.

The organization of the essay is not as controlled or logical as it might be; however, the discussion of the short story's dialogue is apt and insightful ("Sonny is usually used by an older person toward a non-related younger one"). Diction is addressed—"Daddy," "Sonny," "my flesh and blood"—with accurate connotations assigned to those terms, but the student does not develop these ideas fully or fruitfully. While the student covers the surface aspects of the relationship, and mentions tone, contrast, and dialogue, limited evidence is provided in a sporadic way with no evident direction, and without the support of compelling logical arguments. In another instance the writer discusses the analogy of "how he smelled his father." This also could have been developed further. Why "delicate and beautiful"? At this point the essay lapses into paraphrase and borders perilously close on the merely narrative, with no new analysis or support. Some awkward phrasing ("He ended the reunion in order to save the good parts.") displays the writer's lack of sophistication and understanding of the piece, but the positive aspects of the essay ultimately outweigh the negative, thus making this a true 5.

The Open Literature Question

The AP exam always includes one open question. This enables students to choose a piece of literature that they have already read and studied, and discuss it as it pertains to the prompt.

The question may be accompanied by a list of suggested titles or authors from which you may draw. You should certainly consider this list, which will provide good choices and possibly lead you to alternate ideas. Remember that these are only suggestions, and that you are not limited to the list; you are allowed to choose a work or an author of *comparable quality* to those mentioned. Remember that some authors whom you deem comparable may be frowned upon by AP readers. When in doubt, check with your AP English teacher well before the exam. Write about a work you know well and feel very comfortable discussing.

Sometimes it is hard to decide which work or author you would like to choose. In such cases, it is helpful to brainstorm about a few different ideas—list, outline, web, cluster—using whatever system you feel most comfortable with. Do not simply go with the first work, author, or character in the work. Halfway through the essay you may regret your choice and you will not have time to change your mind!

Taking It Apart: The Open Question

Now read a sample open question and a step-by-step example of how to respond.

Prompt A

"By their deeds shall ye know them." We often judge people by what they do; therefore, we consider people who commit cruel or reprehensible acts corrupt, base, or amoral. In literature, however, authors often introduce us to characters whom we learn to like or even respect, despite their deeds.

Write an essay about one such character for whom you developed admiration or compassion. Briefly explain why you felt his or her behavior to be condemnable or contemptible, and how the author's techniques influenced you to admire that person. Do not summarize the plot. *(40 minutes)*

Great Expectations	*Things Fall Apart*
Jane Eyre	*Light in August*
Wuthering Heights	*Beloved*
Medea	*Native Son*
Othello	*The Stranger*
Crime and Punishment	*Antigone*
Richard III	*The Scarlet Letter*
Moby-Dick	*Billy Budd*

Step 1: Read the Prompt Carefully

What are some of the important words in the prompt?

_____   _____

_____   _____

What elements of the prompt do you need to explore?

_____

_____

Note that the key to the question is its second part: Why does the reader feel admiration for that person? How has the author encouraged respect for the character?

Step 2: Plan

Once you dissect the question, you can then move on to brainstorming a list of characters that would be suitable for discussion. The best way to select a character is to brainstorm/cluster/outline until you have several good possibilities. Limit your choices to works you have read and are familiar with. Too often, movies are quite different from the books upon which they're based, and your reader knows that. So do not choose *Moby-Dick*, for example, if you have only seen the movie.

Remember that you are NOT limited to the list provided by the College Board. (As readers, we remember being relieved when a student selected a book not on the list. Taking risks and being different can reap benefits.) However, make sure your selection is relevant. Try not to select too arcane a book. Look over the books suggested, circle the ones you know, and add any titles that you think are appropriate and that you know well. Or you might begin by thinking of characters rather than book titles.

Characters:

_____   _____   _____

_____   _____   _____

_____   _____   _____

After you have created your list, consider the reasons why you feel sympathetic toward one of the characters. You can make a serious error here if you did not read the prompt carefully. You must choose a character you liked _despite some bad or cruel things he or she did_. This is the time to limit your choice and begin your cluster. Did the character's background or personal experiences elicit empathy? Was the authorial voice intrusive and judgmental? Did the author's language and diction evoke positive feelings? Were the character's evil actions justifiable? Were there mitigating circumstances?

Since your reader is already very familiar with the work, and since you have been instructed not to summarize the plot, you need not dwell on the character's dark side—his or her immorality or evil or selfishness. Briefly mention the reasons why he or she is considered evil; then discuss the events or characteristics that elicited your compassion.

This is the time to select one character and quickly jot down the reasons you feel sympathy toward that person. _____

_____

_____

_____

_____

From your cluster, write the first paragraph of your essay responding to the prompt. Remember to remain focused. _____

_____

_____

_____

_____

_____

_____

_____

Prompt A: Sample Student Responses

Here are a couple of sample first paragraphs written by students.

Student A

Anxiety, vengeance, fear. As the infamous "schoolteacher" approached 124, Sethe experienced all these emotions. In an attempt to "save" her children from the clutches of slavery, she killed one, her infant daughter, seemingly having no regard for the sanctity of human life. Yet Morrison proves that what she did was an act of love and for this we come to admire her.

Student B

It has been said that one in ten Americans has lied or stolen once in their lives. By this account, can anyone be trusted? Are people honest? Is it fair to conclude that "By their deeds ye shall know them?" In Shakespeare's <u>King Lear</u>, the character of Edmund is, in fact, very different from how he first appears and it is necessary to know all that he experiences before passing judgment on him. Therefore, by analyzing all of Edmund's deeds, his true character can be determined.

Note: At first, it may take you up to 20 minutes to complete all of the above tasks. As you practice, aim to complete all of these steps in about 10 minutes, leaving the remaining 30 for completing the essay and proofreading.

Step 3: Write Your Essay

Remember that after you have practiced these steps a few times, you will be able to do them quickly. The rubric nowhere specifies length, thesis statement, or the number of points that should be covered. You need to make sure you answer the question as accurately and as completely as possible. Although this is not meant to be a persuasive essay, you do want to convince the reader that your perspective is sound.

Score Yourself

Below is a rubric for Prompt A. Read the rubric carefully, and then read your essay. What score would you award yourself? What points do you need to work on? Swap papers with a friend and score each other's essays. Did the score your friend gave you match your own? Was it close? To see student essays responding to this prompt, turn to page 211.

RUBRIC: "By their deeds ye shall know them"
9–8 Writers of these essays will convincingly analyze and appropriately support specific techniques—such as characterization, contrast, point of view, and tone—which led them to admire the character. These essays are well organized, demonstrate an exceptional command of the elements of the composition, and display evidence of stylistic maturity. They explain with precision why the character's deeds are worthy of condemnation.

7–6	For essays that are somewhat less well written: they may show occasional lapses in syntax, diction, or organization. These essays explain with less precision why the character's deeds are contemptible. They then analyze specific techniques used by the author that led the students to admire the character created, despite cruel or reprehensible deeds. The analysis also has less clarity or precision than the top essays.
5	For essays that are adequately writtten yet superficial. They do not demonstrate stylistic maturity or confident control over the elements of composition. These essays discuss the character's deeds vaguely or inadequately analyze the author's techniques. They may cite stylistic techniques without sufficiently supporting how they work in developing admiration for the character.
4–3	For essays that are adequately written but either summarize or misinterpret the work. These essays may simply list stylistic techniques providing no discussion, evidence, or support. There may be syntactical errors and a lack of organization. They may select a character so evil that one cannot admire that person.
2–1	For essays that are poorly written and show consistent errors in diction, spelling, or syntax. These essays provide little explanation of the character's deeds and no explicit analysis of the author's techniques. They may use the passage merely as a springboard for an essay on a general topic.
0	For essays that contain no explanation of the character's deed.

Try It Out

Now try responding to another open question. Remember to read and analyze the whole prompt before formulating your answer.

Prompt B

"No one has come forward in defense of laughter. No, laughter is more meaningful and more profound than [most think]. . . . Those who say that laughter incites are unjust. Only the dismal incites, while laughter gives light. Many things would incite man if presented in their nakedness; but illuminated by the power of laughter, they bring reconciliation to the soul." (Gogol)

Choose a novel, play, or long poem that illuminates the human condition through the power of laughter. In a well-constructed essay, explain how the work expresses one or more profound truths about human beings and discuss the specific techniques the author uses to convey these ideas.

You may select a work by one of the following authors or another author of comparable merit. *(40 minutes)*

Aristophanes	Molière
Margaret Atwood	Vladimir Nabokov
Jane Austen	Gloria Naylor
Samuel Beckett	Walker Percy
Lord Byron	Harold Pinter
Geoffrey Chaucer	Alexander Pope
Charles Dickens	Barbara Pym
T. S. Eliot	Mordecai Richler
William Faulkner	William Shakespeare
Henry Fielding	George Bernard Shaw
Zora Neale Hurston	Tom Stoppard
Aldous Huxley	Jonathan Swift
Henry James	Anthony Trollope
Ben Jonson	Mark Twain
Franz Kafka	Voltaire
Margaret Laurence	Evelyn Waugh
Bobbie Ann Mason	Oscar Wilde

Step 1: Read the Prompt

Again, read the prompt carefully and decide what you need to do. You may wish to underline or circle key words or phrases. Remember that for most essays you need to explain *what* and *how*.

Which words do you consider important? Are any of them unclear or ambiguous? Can you work out their meaning from the context? Do you have any questions about the prompt?

Note these key elements in the prompt:

- How is laughter meaningful?
- How is it profound?
- How can the dismal incite?
- How can laughter give light?
- What is reconciliation to the soul?
- Why does the soul need to be reconciled?

Step 2: Plan

It is helpful to again think in terms of *what* and *how*. The *what* in this prompt is the truth about humans that is illuminated through laughter. The *how* refers to the techniques (figurative language, details, anecdotes, examples, development of character, rhetorical strategies, etc.) employed by the author to develop truths about humans which are edifying, not stultifying; uplifting, rather than trivial and pedestrian.

Make sure you understand what we learn about human nature through laughter. Do not define, rephrase, or explain the question in your essay: you don't have time. Nor do you want to insult your reader. Your well-supported discussion of the prompt will indicate that you understand the question(s) it posed.

Keep in mind the fact that literary works have multiple meanings; there is no one "right" meaning. If you select a work you have studied in class, you have a better chance of interpreting the work's major ideas. You certainly don't want to simplify or totally misconstrue the author's intent ("*Macbeth* is about hospitality" or "Hawthorne ridicules the Ten Commandments"). Some books lend themselves to contradictory interpretations ("Twain was a racist" or "Twain ridiculed racism"). Scholars have argued with one another about which is accurate. Therefore, you may interpret the work as you wish, but your examples *must* prove your point.

Scholars also disagree on the definition of "literary merit." You might want to take a risk and select an esoteric work; however, you don't want to waste time explaining why you chose a certain work, so it is best to make a judicious selection. Once again, the list that often accompanies the question is merely a list of suggested works, meant to help you begin brainstorming. If you are confident about your knowledge of one of the authors listed, you can skip this step. If not, review the list carefully: which of the suggested books struck you as being particularly humorous? Do you remember a particularly cathartic passage by one of the authors? Whose work made you laugh and cry simultaneously? Apply these questions to books that are not on the list, but which you may wish to discuss in your essay.

Brainstorm other authors and works of literary merit in which laughter was enlightening.

Title: **Author:**

_____   _____

_____   _____

_____   _____

_____   _____

Students added the following authors to the above list: Frank McCourt, Neil Simon, and Woody Allen. Remember that the question calls for a novel, play, or long poem. Woody Allen and Neil Simon have written both screenplays and regular stage plays. Screenplays are very often collaborations, and are subject to change by the director, so you would have to be very sure you had chosen a stage play, or your choice would be unacceptable. Frank McCourt's *Angela's Ashes* is problematic because it is an autobiography. In other words, remember to follow the instructions carefully and choose a work in one of the specified genres.

You now need to quickly brainstorm all the examples of laughter that brought about enlightenment that you remember in a particular work.

_____   _____   _____

_____   _____   _____

_____   _____   _____

_____   _____   _____

Many students chose to discuss Kafka's *Metamorphosis* for this question. Their lists included:

Samsa trying to get out of bed

The manager racing downstairs

Gregor's father throwing apples

The first maid's fears

Gregor covering the picture on the wall

The boarders' reaction to seeing Gregor

Others selected Voltaire's *Candide* with the following examples from the book:

The old woman with one buttock

Finding Pangloss with syphilis

The red sheep in the Eldorado coming back

The gold and gems in Eldorado being regarded as valueless

The crook who fooled Candide in Paris

Religious ceremonies to ward off earthquakes

The writer who bashed everything he wrote

Idea that every woman Candide met had been raped, brutalized, or sold into slavery

Man of church, the grand Inquisitor having Cunégonde for a mistress

The description of Cunégonde at the end

☞ *AP Tip*

As you go through the exercises presented here, don't worry about time. With practice, you will be doing much of this work quickly and automatically. The process is important, and you should walk slowly through the steps that you will eventually be taking independently and rapidly.

Before you begin writing, you still need to deal with the question of the work's meaning. What is it? This is one time that you might want to write a sentence that you can later use in your essay. Remember that there needs to be a connection between thought-provoking humor and the meaning of the work. This is why brainstorming is so important: it gives you time to think through and eliminate the irrelevant, the trivial, and the nonsequiturs.

Now, make a cluster or outline for your essay.

There is still time to change your author or your book. If you find that the examples you used cannot adequately answer the prompt, change the book. Just think how far ahead of the game you are since you have not yet begun writing the essay. You have brainstormed other works; try them now.

_____

_____

_____

_____

Step 3: Write Your Essay

It is now time to write your essay. Remember, long introductions are not necessary—the important thing is to have a clear, unifying thesis. You may write the first paragraph last; skip some lines if this method appeals to you. Be sure to watch your time, but don't become obsessive about it. Just make sure you leave time to proofread and eliminate egregious errors. This paper is treated as a rough draft, but you need to show facility and control of the language in your writing. You want to use sophisticated, not pedantic, language; you also should vary your sentence lengths and beginnings.

Compare what you have written with the student responses below. You will see three students' first lines, followed by concluding paragraphs. This may give you an idea of the variety of possibilities—and will enable you to see what seems to work, as well as what does not work. In order to make it easier for you to compare techniques, we've used essays by students who all chose to discuss Voltaire's *Candide*.

Student Sample #1: Ross

Modern psychology points to the existence of the belief perseverance phenomenon—we are extremely unwilling to alter or modify our basic beliefs even when they have been ridiculed; sometimes, we hold them more dear . . .

There is something ironic in a satire of optimism, because in writing with the goal of changing society, Voltaire presupposes a large degree of hope. If we can laugh at a character who holds one of our tenets, we can more easily admit our errors. To pretend that one's beliefs are perfect is the ultimate arrogance.

Student Sample #2: Flowers

All Candide's antagonists, exaggerated and caricatured though they may be, are real . . .

Candide's failing is his trust of Leibnizian philosophy. He deigns to understand the world, and thusly fears nothing and trusts everything. Afterwards, he shows not hatred, but confusion at the apparent breach of his belief in this being "the best of all possible worlds." The reader is left to conclude the above truth, that this is not the best of all possible worlds, and Voltaire makes handy several deserving contributors to this state. Again, however, Voltaire does not advocate their abolition by blood and iron, or by any means whatsoever. What his ridicule creates is not an eruption, but an erosion of the base of faith on which all societal institutions lie.

Student Sample #3: Angie

For Candide, the world was in a bubble . . .
Wild characters and exaggerated pasts of unbelievable moral degradation are the instruments that make us laugh. However, they also make us think.

Which student's beginning is the best? Which conclusive paragraph did you find to be the strongest? To see the students' complete essays and how they scored, turn to page 217.

Improving Your Essay-Writing Skills

Excellent writing can improve your overall score by almost ten points. Even one point can make a difference in the overall final score. How is this possible? Readers are advised that if a paper falls, for example, into a 6–7 range, they can reward the writer by awarding the higher of the two scores. This additional point, when tabulated at the end, translates into a raw score differential of 3.3333. Write well on three essays and you have gained almost ten extra points.

Read the following do's and don'ts carefully and incorporate the directions into your essays until they feel easy and natural.

1. Develop your opening paragraph fully. A good analytical essay usually has paragraphs that are more than one or two sentences long. There isn't a specified number of sentences: four or five are good, but there is no magic number. An AP essay does differ, however, from other essays in one significant way: since this is a timed writing, you must get to the point quickly. Focus directly on the point(s) you wish to make. Do not take a roundabout route.

2. Do not say, "This essay will . . ." Never announce that you are going to do something; instead, DO IT. A strong thesis statement addressing the heart of the essay prompt will make clear your intent. The readers are trained to make a rather rapid determination as to whether your essay begins as an upper- or a lower-half response, and even though they will read with an open mind to the very end, remember how important first impressions always are. You want to make a good first impression, and you can do so by demonstrating your understanding of the question, the passage, and your confidence in attacking the task. Do not repeat the prompt word-for-word. The reader is quite familiar with it, and will almost certainly skip over an opening that is totally formulaic.

3. Do not waste time, ink, space, or effort with a fluffy introductory paragraph. The tired old practice of leading with a general statement and following with a specific tripartite thesis sentence at the end of a cookie-cutter paragraph sends the reader's eye zooming down the page to find out where the essay *really* begins. This is not to say that a dynamite introductory sentence, a good hook, or an apt short quotation is out of place in the opening lines. In fact, a strong opening sentence is heartily recommended. But your essay is meant to make a point, and it's best to get to that point as quickly as possible, as you have a limited time in which to make it!

4. Remember your audience: high school English teachers and college English professors. Cute and clever do not fare well here, nor do abbreviations, symbols or signs, personal notes, or climbing upon soapboxes. You should instead engage in a scholarly, thoughtful, and insightful response.

5. Write in active voice rather than passive. This will help your ideas come through with clarity and confidence, and it will

show that you understand the subject, or the doer. Active voice also forces a writer to be *specific*, which is *crucial* on the AP exam. Example: "The baby is killed," or "Sethe kills her baby."

6. Analyze, don't praise. The readers know that the work at hand is of literary merit. Do not waste time reiterating that. Instead, write about the ways in which the passage works to further the writer's intent. Think about the last movie you saw. If a friend asked your opinion of it, how much time would you spend telling him or her how good it was before you started to explain why it was good? What details would you focus on to prove your point? The acting? The plot? The sets? The music? The costumes? Wouldn't you eventually get around to describing what the movie meant and how important the meaning of it was to you?

7. Use your paragraphs to guide the reader's thought process (and, obviously, to convey your own). Without being arbitrary (no set number of sentences is ideal), divide your essay into compact thought-packages that flow naturally from one to the next. The best essays will lead the reader to an inevitable conclusion. There will be a sense of closure, of completion, that will leave the reader more than satisfied. Here are some helpful tips that will work for beginnings or endings:

   a. Remember the concept of the "audience." How would your essay differ if you were writing for your English teacher? For your best friend? Would your vocabulary change? Would your tone change? Would your opinion change to suit the audience?

   b. Next, write a brief description of the last bad book you read. Analyze, don't condemn, but relate your experience in such a way as to prevent others from wasting their time.   *no emotion*

8. Use transitions to assist in the logical progress of your essay. Transitions will efficiently reveal connections between ideas that are alike, or different, or between ideas that illustrate cause and effect. They can also be used to denote the passage of time. We have found the following transitions to be particularly useful:

after	doubtless	on the other hand
also	eventually	perhaps
although	finally	similarly
as a result	furthermore	therefore
before	hence	yet
but	however	
consequently	next	

9. Finally, and perhaps most importantly, don't be afraid to take risks. You will be rewarded for thinking on your own and for writing with confidence. The safe path will probably

result in an upper-level score, but it is only the strikingly original and intuitive paper that will earn an 8 or a 9. Think of class discussions. Isn't it always the comment that stops you cold, makes you think and understand in a new way that you find memorable and noteworthy? Strive for the same in your own response.

Ready, Steady, Go!

You've studied hard, learned about literary devices and allusions, written your own multiple-choice questions, and analyzed many pieces of poetry and prose. Now you're ready to take the sample AP tests that follow!

You know it's important to be relaxed and well rested when you take the exam, so be sure to get a good night's sleep and eat a decent breakfast before you take the practice test. Try to replicate as nearly as possible the conditions under which you'll be taking the real exam.

Taking the practice exam will not only help you to learn what areas you need to concentrate on; it will also help you feel more comfortable when you eventually take the real test, because you'll have a better idea of what to expect.

So . . . sharpen a few Number 2 pencils, find your favorite pens, and assign yourself a time to report for your first practice test.

Good luck!

Lesson 10: Student Responses

Sample Student Responses and Reader Analysis: Prompt A

Read the student essays below. Do you think the reader scored them appropriately according to the rubric? How do these essays compare to your own response to the prompt?

Diane (Score: 8)

Hummingbirds flutter in her ears. She sees him. She needs to act. Quick. Run. Hide. Now. Without a moment's hesitation, she sweeps her four children under her broad wings and carries them into a hidden shed. He is coming, he will hurt them, capture them, take them to that Hell. She must save them, whatever the cost may be.

I developed a great sense of admiration for the heroic character of Sethe. In Toni Morrison's

Beloved, she demonstrates great courage, devotion, and a deep love for her children as she battles the evils threatening to capture them to the horrific institution of slavery. Morrison utilizes techniques such as anecdotes, supporting characters, and understatement to gain my respect for Sethe.

First and foremost, Morrison's Beloved is cleverly structured into multiple stories within a main storyline. As each anecdote interjects, it reveals a great deal about the institution of slavery and provides ramifications for Sethe's lethal act. For instance, Sethe's escape from Sweet Home reveals her courage and devotion. With a "chokecherry tree" etched in her aching back, Sethe runs. She runs since she needs to reach her awaiting baby and her two other sons. She runs because she must never subject the child kicking within her to the pain and toil she has experienced. When Baby Suggs discusses her own eight children moved like checkers on a gameboard, she also epitomizes the brutality of slavery and the attachment many slaves longed to have with their distant children.

Supporting characters also emphasize Sethe's heroic qualities and the severity of the conditions in which she lived. Stamp Paid, guide and helper to Sethe as she crosses the Ohio River, looks at her with awe. He is struck with intense joy as he watches her coddle her children, not allowing them to escape from her sight. His pain in providing berries for a feast attests to this. When Sethe "rescues" the crawling already? Baby from the horrors of slavery, Stamp Paid is in shock. But he understands.

Paul D also illustrates Sethe's unique personality and devotion. As he traces with his fingers the chokecherry tree on her back, he feels and understands her pain. He sympathizes with her for her beating; yet, silently, congratulates her for her courage and her unwavering strength. Paul D's positive perspective and attachment to Sethe influenced me to admire her even more. He does not see her as a brutal woman who killed her child. He finally comes to understand her deed of love.

Finally, Morrison's use of litote develops the sense that slavery is worse than one can possibly imagine. The impact of her simple statements at crucial moments underscore the horror underneath. Her unspoken words resound. When Stamp Paid picks up a red ribbon tied to wet woolly hair and asks, "What are these people?", she quietly makes one of the most valid, effective comments about slavery in the entire novel. Other examples include the wide-mouthed black boy statue at the Bodwin's house, Baby Suggs' realization that she has a self, someone and something to love, and the mark Sethe's mother had on her breast. Each of these examples verify why Sethe's act of murder—done for love—make her a heroine, not a villain.

Sethe is a woman of great strength, courage, and love, and I admire her.

Reader Analysis: Diane (8)

This strong 8 is characterized by its insight, fluency, and risk-taking. The student has clearly answered the question. *Beloved* is an appropriate choice for this prompt, and Sethe does inspire admiration despite committing horrific acts. Specificity is abundant, precise, and accurate ("crawling already," "Baby," "chokecherry tree," Paul D's actions, the "black boy statue"). These serve to reinforce the thesis and to show the student's deep awareness of the novel's intent.

The student's opening is unique and invites the reader to continue. It is not a typical opening, but it displays the writer's ability to synthesize in the time given. Her use of fragments is deliberate and effective, revealing her command of the English language. She uses the personal "I" effectively, not intrusively, and thus establishes a sense of the writer. (As a general rule, it is best to avoid first person when writing an AP essay.)

Analysis is perceptive and knowledge of literary techniques is evident: anecdotes, supporting characters, litotes. Transitions are smooth and unobtrusive and propel the essay. The ending is brief yet moving. Only the best writers can get away with single-sentence paragraphs. This student is one of them.

Ana-Laura (Score: 6)

To the casual observer, Edna Pontellier, from Kate Chopin's The Awakening, is an ungrateful woman; she cheats on her husband, neglects her children and, in the end, kills herself. Yet somehow, she is the novel's heroine, providing something for everyone to aspire to and admire. It is Chopin's use of language and events in the story that manipulates the reader's perception of the character, molding Edna into an admired character.

At the start of the novel, Mr. Pontellier is introduced to the reader. Although he worships Edna and gives her anything her heart desires, he is cold and distant. Chopin's use of language in describing him makes it clear that he is more concerned with her appearance socially than with her happiness. The perfect example is when Mr. Pontellier gets mad at Edna for being gone on her "visiting" day, and his dislike for her art. It is these restraints he has on her that make Edna rebel. The reader finds himself siding with Edna as Mr. Pontellier becomes more and more restraining. Edna's rebellion is justified.

The other way Chopin manipulates the reader to cheer for Edna is by making her strong. In the time period the *book takes place, women were to "be seen, but not heard," they were trophies, good only for bearing children. To contrast this, Chopin makes Edna a cold mother. Edna sends her children away so she can be free. She frees herself from any monetary ties she has with her husband, and partakes in traditionally male activities, such as going to the track. By making Edna flawed in her time period, Chopin creates a strong heroine in the present.*

Even Edna's affair is justified by Chopin. The reader finds out that there is no love, nor was there ever any love, in Edna's relationship with her husband. It is no wonder that she has an affair in a relationship where there is passion. The reader can side with Edna when she finds love and passion—even if it is outside her marriage.

Reader Analysis: Ana-Laura (6)

While not as thorough, insightful, or specific as the 8, this essay fulfills the rubric for a typical 6. The student answers the question, provides support for her points, and displays competent writing skills. The choice of *The Awakening* is appropriate, as is the character, Edna. Transitions also propel and illuminate the writer's points.

However, there is much more to Kate Chopin's complex novel than is indicated in this essay. A better and more thorough analysis, including supporting details, would have raised this student's score. Given the time constraints, the writer did a competent job.

Karl (Score: 4)

In the book Beloved by Toni Morrison, the character of Sethe murders her baby and tries to kill her other children. By most people's terms, such an act is completely evil. Sethe should be hung immediately for her crime. But the reader of Beloved would disagree. By being vague, evoking pity, and manifesting evil, Toni Morrison convinces the reader that murdering her children was the right thing to do, even though it was wrong.

Throughout the beginning of the book, Morrison is extremely cryptic in her references toward the actual act. With only vague, occasional references to "oily blood," the reader really has no idea what the circumstances were surrounding the murder. Instead, Morrison focuses on the life of Sethe, the hardships and pains, allowing the reader the chance to get to know Sethe before they learn the truth. This tends to get the reader on her side.

Sethe's life before and after her infanticide was completely unlivable. Forced to flee slavery, fully pregnant; beaten; leaving her husband behind; not knowing if she'd make it, or if her children were alive waiting for her; only to be pursued by her former master empowered by fugitive slave laws. Afterward, she is completely cut off from society. Needless to say, the reader comes to pity poor Sethe, and even empathize with her rage and she kills her children so they won't be killed.

In addition to evoking pity, Morrison manifests true evil and pits it against Sethe: a schoolteacher comparing her to an animal for his pupils, friends and family lost, burned, beaten, and killed, the master's nephew who opens her back, and a master seeking to double his profits by selling her children. Faced with this, the reader understands Sethe's rage, even admires her courage and unselfishness at being able to ruin her life to save her children's from being ruined.

By utilizing vagueness, evoking pity, and manifesting evil, Toni Morrison manages to convince the reader that the murderous Sethe is not evil. The reader is left trying to understand this sharp conflict of ethos and pathos. How could what is wrong be right?

Reader Analysis: Karl (4)

This 4 does not indicate a complete and accurate understanding of the text. Errors become distracting and hinder the analysis. The writer twice states that Sethe killed her children, but in the book she murdered only one. Nor did her master seek to "double his profits by selling her children," nor is Morrison "cryptic" in her references to the deed. Poetic she is. Inaccuracies such as these create doubt in the reader's mind.

Furthermore, the writing (syntax, sentence structure, and word choice) is uneven, choppy, and confusing. The lack of fluency and the simplistic writing fail to adequately develop the thesis. Throwing out terms such as "ethos" and "pathos" without analyzing and explaining their relevance to the text does not work.

Sample Student Responses and Reader Analysis: Prompt B

Read the essays below. How do they compare to the first lines/last paragraphs you read earlier? Did the students flesh out their ideas as you thought they would? What score would you have awarded each essay after reading its first line/last paragraph? Did that score change after you read the entire essay? Why or why not?

Ross (Score: 9)

Modern psychology points to the existence of the belief perseverance phenomenon—we are extremely unwilling to alter or modify our basic beliefs even when they have been ridiculed; sometimes, we hold them more dear. Through laughter, this tendency is mitigated. We more easily reject an idea when it is reduced to such an absurdity that we cannot help but to laugh.

While Candide is foolish by some assessments and an innocent victim of misteachings by others, his behavior produces laughter regardless. It is how he explains misfortune after misfortune that we find so ludicrous. It is beneficial, he reasons, that Pangloss was executed, for if he had not been, he would never have escaped and they would never have been reunited. After receiving thousands of lashings from the Bulgars, who he naively follows, Candide is grateful for the leniency in punishment. Candide, as a result of Pangloss's tutelage, believes that the world is perfect—what is, is right. The problem is that his conception of the good is wholly unformed and ambiguous—whatever happens need not fit a pattern or principle because whatever happens _is_ the pattern or principle.

By extending the (anti-?) philosophy of optimism to its logically necessary conclusion, Voltaire reveals its unreasonableness. First we laugh, then we contemplate. However silly Candide is made to be, we all know there is some optimism deep down in all of our hearts. Were there not, it would seem the only consistent action would be to resign oneself to a life of apathy. Voltaire does not want us to abandon all hope in our capacity for goodness, but by creating laughter, he forces the reader to reexamine his / her own beliefs and temper them with a dose of realism.

Pococurante is a man of extraordinary wealth but he remains unsatisfied. Candide has trouble understanding the discontent—are not material possessions the source of salvation? Of course not, we realize. We might even laugh at _both_ characters—Pococurante for his failed attempt at happiness and Candide for his flawed vision of the good life.

But this laughter, once again, is simultaneously sobering. Are we not all guilty of both characters' shortcomings? This is the thoughtful laughter Voltaire realizes is necessary to challenge existing value systems. We (hopefully) recognize the inconsistency in condemning greedy corporate tycoons and cheating on our taxes and consider that the root of that particular animosity might be jealousy, rather than a carefully reasoned belief.

Eldorado is the perfect city—streets of gold, unlimited food supply, hordes of genius—but it is free of monks to "burn at the stake all who disagree with them." Here, Voltaire's criticism is much less subtle. It seems (and it is) patently absurd to kill another human being because of a disagreement, but devout believers—ostensible paragons of virtue—have done so for centuries. We laugh, then lament irrationality and its disastrous consequences.

There is something ironic in a satire of optimism, because in writing with the goal of changing society, Voltaire presupposes a large degree of hope. If we can laugh at a character who holds one of our tenets, we can more easily admit our errors. To pretend that one's beliefs are perfect is the ultimate arrogance.

Reader Analysis: Ross (9)

This essay responds to a challenging prompt with elegance, insight, and fluency. The first paragraph philosophizes, "Modern psychology points to the existence of the belief perseverance phenomenon." This is followed by a clear, concise focus and is supported throughout the paper with appropriate textual details, reasoning, and great depth. The rich vocabulary (*mitigated, ludicrous, simultaneously sobering, animosity*) propels the thought process and analysis. This, together with syntactical sophistication ("We laugh, then lament irrationality and its disastrous consequences"), immediately elevates this essay.

It is the logic and the support that are extraordinary. The writer knows the work well, citing numerous examples such as the lashings Pangloss received, Candide's beliefs, and Pococurante's dissatisfaction. By selectively enumerating aspects of the work which support the thesis (how laughter illuminates profound truths), the writer proves his organizational skills. Note that he does not summarize, hoping that some of what he writes will hit the mark. There is nothing superfluous or repetitive here.

The conclusion is powerful. Surely this is a 9 paper.

Flowers (Score: 7)

All Candide's antagonists, exaggerated and caricatured though they may be, are real. Church and state alike are corrupt; thieves, liars and hypocrites abound; and injustice flourishes in any climate. Had Voltaire attacked them directly, he would have become a victim as surely as his protagonist did. Inflammatory speeches and the revolutions they create may bring villains to the wall, but there can be found a position to battle back from. Satire and ridicule, however, sap strength and bring the largest malignancy to its knees.

Candide's misadventures are no vehicles of plot; indeed, the very existence of a plot is debatable. Rather, the scope of his experiences is as large as it is due to Voltaire's grapeshot attack; Candide is made to travel anywhere that his author has a gripe. These disjointed anecdotes, when conjoined (albeit jarringly), comprise the novel.

Interestingly, Voltaire predates Hegel in his use of the dialectic. Each thesis (Christian religion, Pangloss, the Baron) has its antithesis (Doradoan religion, Martin, Cacambo); the synthesis is left to the reader. Generally, Voltaire makes his theses so ridiculous as to render debate unnecessary. He accomplishes this by use of a sardonic understatement. Improbable, illogical, and impossible events and persons are described plainly and matter-of-factly. By these humorous comparisons, Voltaire proves one truth of life: conflict is inevitable, and justice doesn't always win out.

Candide's failing is his trust of Leibnizian philosophy. He deigns to understand the world, and thusly fears nothing and trusts everything. Afterwards, he shows not hatred, but confusion at the apparent breach of his belief in this being "the best of all possible worlds." The reader is left to conclude the above truth, that this is not the best of all possible worlds, and Voltaire makes handy several *deserving contributors to this state. Again, however, Voltaire does not advocate their abolition by blood and iron, or by any means whatsoever. What his ridicule creates is not an eruption, but an erosion of the base of faith on which all societal institutions lie.*

Reader Analysis: Flowers (7)

This is not a conventional essay. For that reason, perhaps, it would be appealing to any reader. Intelligently written, the essay displays a wide base of knowledge and includes that unobtrusively to support its thesis. The writer, who is in total command, apparently knows *Candide* well and certainly understands the concepts of laughter and satire as tools for illumination.

However, it would behoove even this writer to make the examples more text-specific. There are references to the characters, but no mention of the specific situations in which they find themselves.

The student's mastery of vocabulary and syntax is exceptional. Even though one is not required to have outside knowledge, this essay provides a perfect example of the reason why being well read is advantageous. This student seamlessly incorporates history and philosophy into the discussion—and does so economically and logically.

Angie (Score: 5)

For Candide, the world was in a bubble. A bubble that was strengthened by the knowledge that his world, this bubble of innocence, was the best of all possible worlds. In the words of esteemed scholar / teacher / philosopher / friend, Pangloss, this world was indeed the best of all possibilities. In every adventure Candide embarks on, this philosophy is proven flawed. Human suffering is rampant and Candide suffers as he searches for his love. The truths Voltaire expresses through Candide are simple enough: there is much human suffering brought on through greed, selfishness, violence, abuse, war, and want. Criticizing this through satire is something that Voltaire does with great ease. He exaggerates Candide's adventures–creating characters laden with hyperbolical past, situations of the absurd, settings of great importance, with men of low moral worth—all for the purpose of bringing attention to the state that the world is in. Greed, violence, abuses of people, and war constitute Candide's world.

His world begins with war. This war, he soon finds out, kills mother, father, brother, and sister. They are not his family, but close enough to it. In addition he loses his only love, Cunégonde. The Franco-Prussian war is brutal and savage, and all the world suffers when war is waged. But Candide finds his love and his scholar, Pangloss. Pangloss has become grotesque and suffers from syphilis (another human folly—lust). The irony of this is firmly apparent because as Candide found his friend, Pangloss is promptly hanged by the Inquisition. The situation is humorous, though, because the mass execution was after an awful earthquake which Pangloss and Candide had been rejoicing over, in that they survived in this best of all possible worlds. Is this dark humor? The human suffering and sinful nature of man is obvious and yet Voltaire treats it lightly so that we may laugh now but hopefully notice and change.

Every woman Candide meets thereafter has been raped, brutalized, beaten, eaten, sold as a prostitute or slave, and some have endured a combination of the abominations. The women have either been victims, or willing victims in some cases, but Candide still believes that this is the best of all possible worlds. The stories of these women are repugnant and unbelievable. Although horror upon horror are heaped on helpless women, we laugh because the situations are so unbelievable: for example, a woman with one buttock and even better several women, each with one buttock, sold into slavery and prostitution but able to ride horses.

Greed contributes to human suffering. A Dutch pirate steals Candide's wealth. A sailor will help Candide go to Venice for ten, then twenty, and finally thirty thousand piastres. A lady in Paris succumbs to her greed by sleeping with Candide and taking the two diamonds off his fingers.

Wild characters and exaggerated pasts of unbelievable moral degradation are the instruments that make us laugh. However, they also make us think.

Reader Analysis: Angie (5)

This essay is a midlevel paper. It does support its thesis with numerous examples, indicating the student's familiarity with the chosen work and understanding of the prompt. Sentence structure and syntax indicate a reasonably well-trained writer, but the text overall lacks fluency.

The student's understanding of the concept of laughter and how it contributes to a work's meaning is apparent in her sentence: "Man's sinful nature is obvious, yet Voltaire treats it lightly so that we may laugh now, but hopefully notice and change." However, the opening paragraph meanders. It occasionally loses focus. In addition, the paper lapses into plot summary too frequently. Not until the second paragraph does the writer mention laughter (even though she alludes to it with the words "hyperbolic" and "absurd" in her opening). Too often she mentions a point but does not bother to analyze it.

PART 5
Practice Tests

Practice Tests: Be Prepared!

To do your best on these tests, you should find a place where you can work without distractions or interruptions for three hours. Our students have found that taking the tests in this manner helps to prepare them for the actual test.

Part One of each test consists of a total of four or five poetry and prose selections, with approximately fifty-two questions. You will be taking the real test on a scantron sheet. In order to approximate the amount of time it would take to fill out a scantron sheet, number a blank piece of paper before you begin timing yourself. When you are taking the practice test, write the letter of the answer you believe is correct next to each number.

When you are finished with Part One, you may take a five-minute break. Then turn to Section Two and look at the three essay prompts. (*Note:* It is important to begin timing yourself *before* you look at the prompts, as this is how the real test will be conducted.) You may answer the prompts in any order you wish, making sure to label your essays clearly. Make sure to watch your time. You have a total of two hours in which to answer all three prompts: we suggest that you allot yourself roughly forty minutes per prompt. Make sure you leave yourself enough time to quickly proofread each essay.

Practice Test 1

Section One
60 minutes

Part One: Multiple-Choice Questions

QUESTIONS 1–15: Carefully read the following passage from Bell's "Something About the Family." Then answer the questions that follow.

I must now attempt to say something about the family. Here is a good deal of uncertainty, of legend, and of scandal.

According to H.A.L. Fisher, the historian, there was at the Court of Versailles during the last years of the old régime a certain
5   Chevalier Antoine de l'Etang; his person was pleasing, his manners courtly, his tastes extravagant and his horsemanship admirable. He was attached to the household of Marie Antoinette—too much attached it is said, and for this he was exiled to Pondicherry where, in 1788, he married a Mlle. Blin de Grincourt.
10   M. de l'Etang entered and died in the service of the Nawab of Oudh; he left three daughters. Adeline, the one with whom we are concerned, married a James Pattle who was, we are told, a quite extravagantly wicked man. He was known as the greatest liar in India; he drank himself to death; he was packed off home in a cask of
15   spirits, which cask, exploding, ejected his unbottled corpse before his widow's eyes, drove her out of her wits, set the ship on fire, and left it stranded in the Hooghly.

The story has been told many times. Some parts of it may be true. It is certainly true that Mrs. Pattle came to London in 1840 with
20   a bevy of daughters and that these ladies had a reputation for beauty. Four of them should be mentioned in these pages: Virginia, Sarah, Julia, and Maria.

Virginia Pattle, the most beautiful of the sisters, married Charles Somers-Cocks and became Countess Somers; she was a dashing,
25   worldly woman, impulsive, rather eccentric, who lived in great style. Of her daughters, one became Duchess of Bedford; the other, Isabel, married Lord Henry Somerset. This alliance, though grand, was by no means happy. Lord Henry, a charming man it seems, delighted Victorian drawing rooms with his ballads. He was, I believe, the
30   author of *One More Passionate Kiss*; this embrace was reserved, however, not for his beautiful wife but for the second footman. Lady Henry endured his infidelities for a time but presently she could stand no more. She confided in her mother who, allowing her indignation to master her prudence, made a public scandal. The
35   sequel is interesting in as much as it gives a notion of the ethos of the Victorian age and its system of morality.

Lord Henry fled to Italy and there lived happily ever after. His wife discovered that she had been guilty of an unformulated, but very heinous, crime: her name was connected with a scandal. Good society
40   would have nothing more to do with her. She was obliged to retire from the world and decided to devote herself to the reclamation of inebriate women, a task which she undertook with so much good sense and good humor that she won the affection and admiration, not only of men of charity and good will, but even of the women she assisted.

1. The narrator's attitude toward society can best be described as
   a. derisive cynicism
   b. mocking criticism
   c. dignified respect
   d. scornful arrogance
   e. personal attachment

2. The purpose of the passage is most likely to
   a. relate a piece of significant history
   b. relate the narrator's family history
   c. criticize the hypocrisy of high society
   d. show how scandal hurts aristocrats
   e. demonstrate that most tragic stories are resolved happily

3. All of the following are techniques used in the passage EXCEPT
   a. modified sentences
   b. parenthetical interruptions
   c. exaggeration
   d. dramatization
   e. metaphors

4. The phrase "too much attached" (lines 7–8) implies that Monsieur de l'Etang's relationship to the household of Marie Antoinette was one of
   a. unyielding scorn
   b. mild disdain
   c. intimate involvement
   d. friendly acquaintanceship
   e. political alliance

5. In this passage, the narrator reflects on all of the following EXCEPT
   a. ethical standards
   b. the historical background of the Victorian Age
   c. high society
   d. the ironies of life
   e. others' misfortunes

6. The narrator in the passage is a(n)
   a. sympathetic observer
   b. awed admirer
   c. critical commentator
   d. scornful informer
   e. regretful reporter

7. The passage contains all of the following EXCEPT
   a. understatement
   b. hyperbole
   c. allusion
   d. apostrophe
   e. humor

8. Which of the following phrases best depicts the narrator's use of hyperbole?
    a. ". . . happily ever after"
    b. ". . . very heinous crime"
    c. ". . . dashing, worldly woman"
    d. ". . . reclamation of inebriate women"
    e. ". . . a charming man it seems"

9. In the following sentence, "It is certainly true that Mrs. Pattle came to London in 1840 with a bevy of daughters . . . ," the word "bevy" most nearly means
    a. abundance
    b. gang
    c. pack
    d. plethora
    e. group

10. The list of events in lines 13–17 ("He was known as . . . stranded in the Hooghly") serves mainly to
    a. make the reader feel apathetic towards the characters
    b. convey the surreal tone of the passage
    c. give a detailed history of the character
    d. change the reader's feelings about lying
    e. accurately recount the information given

11. The last paragraph of the passage does all of the following EXCEPT
    a. ridicule admiration for society's standards
    b. show narrator's admiration for the good deeds of Isabel
    c. affirm Lord Henry's happiness
    d. exaggerate the scandal
    e. describe Isabel's life after the scandal

12. The structuring of the sentence starting with "He was known as the greatest liar in India," serves mainly to
    a. establish a feeling of tragedy
    b. show the weakness of the characters involved
    c. trivialize a very serious matter
    d. discuss the role of fate
    e. illustrate the consequences of dishonesty

13. In which of the following phrases does the narrator use a pun?
    a. ". . . he drank himself to death"
    b. ". . . extravagantly wicked man"
    c. ". . . worldly woman"
    d. ". . . the second footman"
    e. ". . . cask of spirits, which cask . . . ejected his unbottled corpse"

14. Which of the following describes the purpose of "Lord Henry fled to Italy and there lived happily ever after"?
    a. to create sympathy for Lord Henry
    b. to poke fun at Isabel's resolution of the conflict

      c. to show Lord Henry's resolve to correct the situation
      d. to create sympathy for Isabel
      e. to question Isabel's motives in the scandal

15. The narrator of the passage is
      a. H.A.L. Fisher
      b. a helpful participant
      c. a noble relative
      d. an enthusiastic observer
      e. a well-informed historian

QUESTIONS 16–28. The following poem is by Seamus Heaney, contemporary Irish poet and Nobel prize winner. It reflects his thoughts and feelings upon seeing a photograph of a woman's body retrieved from a bog (wet, spongy ground with soil composed mainly of decayed vegetable matter). Scientists believe that the body can be traced back to the Iron Age. Heaney sees a parallel between what he perceives as the woman's sacrificial ritual murder and the violence in today's world.

Punishment

       I can feel the tug
       of the halter at the nape
       of her neck, the wind
       on her naked front.

5   It blows her nipples
       to amber beads,
       it shakes the frail rigging
       of her ribs.

       I can see her drowned
10   body in the bog,
       the weighing stone,
       the floating rods and boughs.

       Under which at first
       she was a barked sapling
15   that is dug up
       oak-bone, brain-firkin:

       her shaved head
       like a stubble of black corn,
       her blindfold a soiled bandage,
20   her noose a ring

       to store
       the memories of love.

Little adulteress,
before they punished you

25   you were flaxen-haired,
undernourished, and your
tar-black face was beautiful.
My poor scapegoat,

I almost love you
30   but would have cast, I know
the stones of silence.
I am the artful voyeur

of your brain's exposed
and darkened combs,
35   your muscles' webbing
and all your numbered bones:

I who have stood dumb
when your betraying sisters,
cauled in tar,
40   wept by the railings,

who would connive
in civilized outrage
yet understand the exact
and tribal, intimate revenge.

16. In the poem, the speaker maintains a tone most accurately
described as
    a. melancholy and reproachful
    b. ironic grimness
    c. sorrowful participant
    d. remote and disinterested
    e. elevated and authoritative

17. The quality of the "little adulteress" that the narrator seeks
to evoke in the poem is most probably her
    a. fragile vulnerability
    b. cool, unflagging courage
    c. reputation for seducing men
    d. ethical laxity
    e. unfortunate transgression

18. The poem contains all of the following EXCEPT
    a. enjambment
    b. metaphors
    c. assonance
    d. aphorism
    e. alliteration

19. The effect of the use of the first person in the poem
    a. expresses the narrator's physical pain
    b. expresses outrage at hypocrisy
    c. creates an informal tone
    d. evokes compassion for the victim
    e. creates a chasm between the speaker and the reader

20. The "stubble of black corn" (line 18) most nearly represents
    a. remaining kernels of burnt corn
    b. short hair of an African woman
    c. shaved head of a criminal
    d. ritual tribal sacrifice
    e. rejected chaff

21. The "stones of silence" (line 31) most likely represent
    a. weighing stones
    b. stones thrown at the woman
    c. a scapegoat
    d. deception
    e. silent assenters

22. The purpose of the third stanza is to
    a. give a detailed description of the woman's appearance
    b. shift from the past to the present
    c. reveal the nature of the woman's punishment
    d. establish the poem's ascetic mood
    e. reveal the quality of the woman's life

23. In the final line of the poem the word "tribal" connotes
    a. ritualistic ceremony
    b. barbaric action
    c. oriented toward the masses
    d. induced by society
    e. small, factious community

24. The tense shift in line 29 functions also as a shift from
    a. criticism to empathy
    b. objectivity to criticism
    c. cause to effect
    d. physical to affective
    e. present to past

25. All of the following images suggest punishment except
    a. "her noose a ring"
    b. "her drowned body in the bog"
    c. "a stubble of black corn"
    d. "undernourished"
    e. "her naked front"

26. The speaker's relationship to the woman in the bog is that of a
    a. mourning brother
    b. voyeuristic hedonist

    c. nostalgic lover
    d. dispassionate observer
    e. anguished spectator

27. "Civilized outrage" in the last stanza is an example of
    a. oxymoron
    b. simile
    c. synecdoche
    d. apostrophe
    e. personification

28. Heaney's use of "tar-black face" (line 27) and "darkened combs" (line 34)
    a. illustrates the length of time the woman's body has lain in the bog
    b. suggests the African heritage of the tortured woman
    c. portrays the blackness of the woman's act
    d. alludes to women's evil nature
    e. refers to the burns she has sustained

QUESTIONS 29–41. Read the following short story by Sandra Cisneros carefully. Then answer the questions that follow.

Eleven

What they don't understand about birthdays and what they never tell you is that when you're eleven, you're also ten, and nine, and eight, and seven, and six, and five, and four, and three, and two, and one. And when you wake up on your eleventh birthday you expect to feel
5 eleven, but you don't. You open your eyes and everything's just like yesterday, only it's today. And you don't feel eleven at all. You feel like you're still ten. And you are—underneath the year that makes you eleven.

    Like some days you might say something stupid, and that's the
10 part of you that's still ten. Or maybe some days you might need to sit on your mama's lap because you're scared, and that's the part of you that's five. And maybe one day when you're all grown up maybe you will need to cry like if you're three, and that's okay. That's what I tell Mama when she's sad and needs to cry. Maybe she's feeling three.
15   Because the way you grow old is kind of like an onion or like the rings inside a tree trunk or like my little wooden dolls that fit one inside the other, each year inside the next one. That's how being eleven years old is.

    You don't feel eleven. Not right away. It takes a few days, weeks
20 even, sometimes even months before you say Eleven when they ask you. And you don't feel smart eleven, not until you're almost twelve. That's the way it is.

    Only today I wish I didn't have only eleven years rattling inside me like pennies in a tin Band-Aid box. Today I wish I was one

25   hundred and two instead of eleven because if I was one hundred and
two I'd have known what to say when Mrs. Price put the red sweater
on my desk. I would've known how to tell her it wasn't mine instead
of just sitting there with that look on my face and nothing coming out
of my mouth.

30   "Whose is this?" Mrs. Price says, and she holds the red sweater
up in the air for all the class to see. "Whose? It's been sitting in the
coatroom for a month."

       "Not mine," says everybody, "Not me."

       "It has to belong to somebody," Mrs. Price keeps saying, but
35   nobody can remember. It's an ugly sweater with red plastic buttons
and a collar and sleeves all stretched out like you could use it for a
jump rope. It's maybe a thousand years old and even if it belonged to
me I wouldn't say so.

       Maybe because I'm skinny, maybe because she doesn't like me,
40   that stupid Sylvia Saldívar says, "I think it belongs to Rachel." An
ugly sweater like that, all raggedy and old, but Mrs. Price believes her.
Mrs. Price takes the sweater and puts it right on my desk, but when I
open my mouth, nothing comes out.

       "That's not, I don't, you're not . . . Not mine," I finally say in a
little voice that was maybe me when I was four.

45   "Of course it's yours," Mrs. Price says. "I remember you wearing
it once." Because she's older and the teacher, she's right and I'm not.

       Not mine, not mine, not mine, but Mrs. Price is already turning
to page thirty-two, and math problem number four. I don't know why
but all of a sudden I'm feeling sick inside, like the part of me that's
50   three wants to come out of my eyes, only I squeeze them shut tight
and bite down on my teeth real hard and try to remember today I am
eleven, eleven. Mama is making a cake for me for tonight, and when
Papa comes home everybody will sing Happy birthday, happy
birthday to you.

55   But when the sick feeling goes away and I open my eyes, the red
sweater's still sitting there like a big red mountain. I move the red
sweater to the corner of my desk with my ruler. I move my pencil and
books and eraser as far from it as possible. I even move my chair a
little to the right. Not mine, not mine, not mine.

60   In my head I'm thinking how long till lunchtime, how long till I
can take the red sweater and throw it over the schoolyard fence, or
leave it hanging on a parking meter, or bunch it up into a little ball
and toss it in the alley. Except when math period ends Mrs. Price says
loud and in front of everybody, "Now, Rachel, that's enough," because
65   she sees I've shoved the red sweater to the tippy-tip corner of my desk
and it's hanging all over the edge like a waterfall, but I don't care.

       "Rachel," Mrs. Price says. She says it like she's getting mad. "You
put that sweater on right now and no more nonsense."

       "But it's not—"

70   "Now!" Mrs. Price says.

       This is when I wish I wasn't eleven because all the years inside of
me—ten, nine, eight, seven, six, five, four, three, two, and one—are

75 pushing at the back of my eyes when I put one arm through one
sleeve of the sweater that smells like cottage cheese, and then the
other arm through the other and stand there with my arms apart like
if the sweater hurts me and it does, all itchy and full of germs that
aren't even mine.

That's when everything I've been holding in since this morning,
since when Mrs. Price put the sweater on my desk, finally lets go, and
80 all of a sudden I'm crying in front of everybody. I wish I was invisible
but I'm not. I'm eleven and it's my birthday today and I'm crying like
I'm three in front of everybody. I put my head down on the desk and
bury my face in my stupid clown-sweater arms. My face all hot and
spit coming out of my mouth because I can't stop the little animal
85 noises from coming out of me, until there aren't any more tears left in
my eyes, and it's just my body shaking like when you have the
hiccups, and my whole head hurts like when you drink milk too fast.

But the worst part is right before the bell rings for lunch. That
stupid Phyllis Lopez, who is even dumber than Sylvia Saldívar, says
90 she remembers the red sweater is hers! I take it off right away and
give it to her, only Mrs. Price pretends like everything's okay.

Today I'm eleven. There's a cake Mama's making for tonight, and
when Papa comes home from work we'll eat it. There'll be candles
and presents and everybody will sing Happy birthday, happy birthday
95 to you, Rachel, only it's too late.

I'm eleven today. I'm eleven, ten, nine, eight, seven, six, five, four,
three, two, and one, but I wish I was one hundred and two. I wish I
was anything but eleven, because I want today to be far away already,
far away like a runaway balloon, like a tiny o in the sky, so tiny-tiny
100 you have to close your eyes to see it.

29. The tone of this passage is one of
   a. childish petulance
   b. cynical despair
   c. wistful condescension
   d. ironic wisdom
   e. unfathomable grief

30. The repetition of lines such as "not mine, not mine, not
   mine," and other expressions of denial illustrate which of
   the following emotions Rachel is experiencing?
   a. anger at being given a dirty sweater
   b. annoyance at people not believing her
   c. discomfort because unwanted attention is being drawn
      to her
   d. eagerness to be heard in any way possible
   e. awareness of the teacher's obliviousness

31. The image that best symbolizes Rachel is
   a. the sweater that smells like cottage cheese
   b. the tin Band-Aid box
   c. the little wooden dolls that fit inside one another
   d. the runaway balloon that is disappearing
   e. the birthday cake Mama is making

32. The "tiny *o* in the sky" represents Rachel's desire to
    I.   revert to infancy
    II. approach death
    III. become invisible
    a. I only
    b. II only
    c. I and II only
    d. I and III only
    e. I, II, and III

33. The statement in lines 5 and 6, "You open your eyes and everything's just like yesterday, only it's today," achieves all of the following EXCEPT
    a. it portrays Rachel's understanding of life
    b. it characterizes birthdays to be just another day
    c. it portrays the repetitiveness of life
    d. it characterizes Rachel as childish
    e. it characterizes Rachel as observant

34. In line 1, Rachel points out that there is something that "they" don't understand. Who is "they" referring to?
    a. other children who feel it is necessary to celebrate birthdays
    b. elders who celebrate the coming of a new age
    c. the general population
    d. mothers and fathers who feel that birthdays are simply a passage into a new year of life
    e. people who forget that a birthday is also a celebration of the years that a person has already experienced

35. The incident of the ugly red sweater symbolizes
    a. the teacher's dislike of Rachel
    b. Rachel's dislike of school
    c. Rachel's dislike of birthdays
    d. ironic cruelty
    e. adult justice

36. All of the following are effects produced by the imagery in the passage EXCEPT
    a. they add to the vividness of the passage
    b. they symbolize the youthful diction of an eleven-year-old
    c. they portray the intelligence of the speaker
    d. they portray the speaker's satisfaction at being eleven
    e. they link certain ages to certain actions

37. The irony in the short story does all of the following EXCEPT
    a. creates complexity in the character of Rachel
    b. illustrates the sadness of Rachel on a day that is usually joyful
    c. depicts Rachel as an intelligent eleven-year-old

    d. shows the contrast of Rachel's childish actions and mature thoughts

    e. gives the passage a sarcastic tone

38. The quotation "I wish I was one hundred and two" expresses all of the following EXCEPT

    a. expression of poignant hyperbole

    b. desire for the wisdom of adults

    c. a cry for external help

    d. example of juvenile exaggeration

    e. dissatisfaction with her birthday

39. How could Rachel be characterized?

    a. immature and childish

    b. extroverted but dignified

    c. intelligent but juvenile

    d. wise but youthful

    e. insightful but insensitive

40. The simile "kind of like an onion or the rings inside a tree" (lines 15–16) is used to depict

    a. a distorted perspective

    b. naïve thought

    c. an appreciation of nature

    d. an unexpected comprehension

    e. a complex and refined imagination

41. What is the author's intent in repeating numbers throughout the piece?

    a. to prove that Rachel is immature and bases life experiences on mere numbers

    b. to show that Rachel is mature in understanding that age is only a number

    c. to exemplify that throughout one's life, experiences build upon each other

    d. to depict Rachel's desperate wish to rid herself of childhood memories

    e. a means of escaping her present situation

QUESTIONS 42–50. Below is a short poem by Richard Wilbur. Read it carefully and then answer the questions that follow.

Museum Piece

> The good gray guardians of art
> Patrol the halls on spongy shoes,
> Impartially protective, though
> Perhaps suspicious of Toulouse.

> 5   Here dozes one against the wall,
> Disposed upon a funeral chair.

A Degas dancer pirouettes
Upon the parting of his hair

       See how she spins! The grace is there,
10   But strain as well is plain to see.
       Degas loved the two together:
       Beauty joined to energy.

       Edgar Degas purchased once
       A fine El Greco, which he kept
15   Against the wall beside his bed
       To hang his pants on while he slept.

42. Which of the following best describes the effect produced by the phrase, "patrol the halls on spongy shoes, impartially protective, though"?
    a. creates an atmosphere of tranquility
    b. is a metaphor for a parent watching over a child
    c. portrays the indifference of the guard's attitude
    d. contrasts the pirouettes of the ballerina
    e. corresponds to Degas' attitude toward El Greco's painting

43. The tone of the last stanza is one of
    a. detached amusement
    b. mild surprise
    c. critical cynicism
    d. respectful irreverence
    e. mock anger

44. The scansion of the second stanza reflects
    a. anapestic dimeter
    b. iambic tetrameter
    c. iambic pentameter
    d. trochaic octameter
    e. dactylic pentameter

45. What is the significance of Degas' hanging his pants over the El Greco painting?
    a. It shows his respect for El Greco's work.
    b. It shows his contempt for El Greco's work.
    c. It shows his indifference toward El Greco's work.
    d. It shows rivalry between El Greco and Degas.
    e. It shows his comfortable familiarity with El Greco's work.

46. The image of the dancer suggests all of the following EXCEPT
    a. grace
    b. bathos
    c. beauty
    d. strength
    e. fragility

47. It can be inferred from the phrase "impartially protective" (line 3) that the "good gray guardians of art" (line 1)
   a. have a deep respect for art
   b. have no interest in the art, but do their job
   c. are uninterested in and have no respect for the work
   d. do not express their opinions
   e. are suspicious of the museum visitors

48. The word "his" (line 8) is used to refer to
   a. good grey guardians
   b. Toulouse
   c. A Degas dancer
   d. El Greco
   e. "one" (line 5)

49. The lines "A Degas dancer pirouettes / upon the parting of his hair" (lines 7–8) emphasize
   a. the guard's obliviousness to the beauty around him
   b. the beauty and energy of the painting
   c. the lack of harmony between the guard's attitude and the painting's perfection
   d. that one should not take art too seriously
   e. that the dancer is frozen in a permanent position

50. In line 2, "spongy" could symbolize
   a. the importance of the guardians
   b. people in the museum absorbed in art
   c. the silence in the room
   d. guardians absorbing but not understanding art
   e. funereal atmosphere of the museum

QUESTIONS 51–54. Read carefully Governor Stevenson's veto letter to the state legislature and answer the questions that follow.

To the Honorable, the members of the Senate of the Sixty-sixth General Assembly:

I herewith return, without my approval, Senate Bill No. 93 entitled "an Act to Provide Protection to Insectivorous Birds by Restraining Cats." This is the so-called "Cat Bill." I veto and withhold my approval from this bill for the following reasons:

5   It would impose fines on owners or keepers who permitted their cats to run at large off their premises. It would permit any person to capture, or call upon the police to pick up and imprison, cats at large. It would permit the use of traps. The bill would have statewide application—on farms, in villages, and in metropolitan centers.

10   This legislation has been introduced in the past several sessions of the Legislature, and it has, over the years, been the source of much comment—not all of which has been in a serious vein. It may be that the General Assembly has now seen fit to refer it to one who can view

it with a fresh outlook. Whatever the reason for passage at this
15   session, I cannot believe there is a widespread public demand for this
law or that it could, as a practical matter, be enforced.

Furthermore, I cannot agree that it should be the declared public
policy of Illinois that a cat visiting a neighbor's yard or crossing the
highway is a public nuisance. It is in the nature of cats to do a certain
20   amount of unescorted roaming. Many live with their owners in
apartments or other restricted premise, and I doubt if we want to
make their every brief foray an opportunity for a small game hunt by
zealous citizens—with traps or otherwise. I am afraid this bill could
only create discord, recrimination and enmity. Also consider the
25   owner's dilemma: To escort a cat abroad on a leash is against the
nature of the cat, and to permit it to venture forth for exercise
unattended into a night of new dangers is against the nature of the
owner. Moreover, cats perform useful service, particularly in rural
areas, in combating rodents—work they necessarily perform alone
30   and without regard for property lines.

We are all interested in protecting certain varieties of birds. That
cats destroy some birds, I well know, but I believe this legislation
would further but little the worthy cause to which its proponents give
such unselfish effort. The problem of the cat versus bird is as old as
35   time. If we attempt to resolve it by legislation who knows but what
we may be called upon to take sides as well in the age-old problems
of dog versus cat, bird versus bird, or even bird versus worm. In my
opinion, the State of Illinois and its local governing bodies already
have enough to do without trying to consider feline delinquency.
40   For these reasons, and not because I love birds the less or cats
the more, I veto and withhold my approval from Senate Bill No. 93.

Respectfully,

Adlai E. Stevenson, Governor

51. The tone of Governor Stevenson's letter is
    a. broadly comical
    b. formally cynical
    c. hopefully supportive
    d. humorously mocking
    e. subtly serious

52. Stevenson uses all of the following EXCEPT
    a. *ad hominem*
    b. allusion
    c. anthropomorphism
    d. *reductio ad absurdum*
    e. use of detail

53. It can be inferred that Stevenson
    a. opposes this bill because he detests cats
    b. believes that the bill will protect "insectivorous birds,"
       but refuse to pass it because he loves cats
    c. opposes the bill because he feels it is an absurd request

    d. opposes the bill because it will be harmful to cat owners and the environment

    e. opposes the bill in order to protect the rights of cats

54. What is the purpose of "Also consider . . . nature of the owner" (lines 24–28)?

    a. clearly states both the opposing views of the owner and the feline in question

    b. demonstrates the cat as an anthropomorphic symbol

    c. juxtaposes the feelings of human and cat in an attempt to show their closeness

    d. offers the opposing view by demonstrating support for the piece of legislation offered

    e. relates the problems caused by the bill directly to the lives of all those affected by it

Practice Test 1

Section Two
120 minutes

Part Two: Essay Questions

QUESTION 1

(Suggested time—40 minutes) **This question counts as one-third of the total essay section score.**

The following passage from Shakespeare's *The Merchant of Venice* traces Bassanio's thought process as he selects from among three caskets* (a conventional "crucial test" in literature). Read the passage carefully and in a well-constructed essay, explain what we learn about Bassanio and how he arrives at his choice. Consider such techniques as allusion, comparison and contrast, and diction. Do not merely summarize the passage.

*treasure chests

Bassanio

So may the outward shows be least themselves:
The world is still deceived with ornament.
In law, what plea so tainted and corrupt,
But, being seasoned with a gracious voice,
5   Obscures the show of evil? In religion,
What damned error, but some sober brow
Will bless it and approve it with a text,
Hiding the grossness with fair ornament?
There is no vice so simple but assumes
10   Some mark of virtue on his outward parts:
How many cowards, whose hearts are all as false
As stairs of sand, wear yet upon their chins
The beards of Hercules and frowning Mars;
Who, inward search'd, have livers white as milk?
15   And these assume but valour's excrement
To render them redoubted! Look on beauty,
And you shall see 'tis purchased by the weight;
Which therein works a miracle in nature,
Making them lightest that wear most of it:
20   So are those crisped snaky golden locks
Which make such wanton gambols with the wind,
Upon supposed fairness, often known
To be the dowry of a second head,
The skull that bred them in the sepulchre.
25   Thus ornament is but the guiled shore
To a most dangerous sea; the beauteous scarf
Veiling an Indian beauty; in a word
The seeming truth which cunning times put on

To entrap the wisest. Therefore, thou gaudy gold,
30 Hard food for Midas, I will none of thee;
Nor none of thee, thou pale and common drudge
'Tween man and man: but thou, thou meagre lead,
Which rather threatenest than dost promise aught,
Thy paleness moves me more than eloquence;
35 And here choose I; joy be the consequence!

QUESTION 2

(Suggested time—40 minutes.) **This question counts as one-third of the total essay section score.**

The passage below is from Charles Dickens' *Bleak House.* Read it carefully. Then write a well-organized essay in which you describe the narrator's attitude toward Sir Leicester and Lady Dedlock and explain how he conveys his view of them through such literary devices as diction, tone, syntax, and humor. Do not summarize.

Sir Leicester Dedlock is only a baronet,[1] but there is no mightier baronet than he. His family is as old as the hills, and infinitely more respectable. He has a general opinion that the world might get on without hills, but would be done up without Dedlocks. He would on the whole admit Nature to be a good idea (a little low, perhaps, when not enclosed with a park-fence), but an idea dependent for its execution on your great county families. He is a gentleman of strict conscience, disdainful of all littleness and meanness, and ready, on the shortest notice, to die any death you may please to mention
10 rather than give occasion for the least impeachment of his integrity. He is an honourable, obstinate, truthful, high-spirited, intensely prejudiced, perfectly unreasonable man.

Sir Leicester is twenty years, full measure, older than my Lady. He will never see sixty-five again, nor perhaps sixty-six, nor yet sixty-seven. He has a twist of the gout now and then, and walks a little stiffly. He is of a worthy presence, with his light grey hair and whiskers, his fine shirt-frill, his pure white waistcoat, and his blue coat with bright buttons always buttoned. He is ceremonious, stately, most polite on every occasion to my Lady, and holds her personal
20 attractions in the highest estimation. His gallantry to my Lady, which has never changed since he courted her, is the one little touch of romantic fancy in him.

Indeed, he married her for love. A whisper still goes about, that she had not even family; howbeit, Sir Leicester had so much family that perhaps he had enough, and could dispense with any more. But she had beauty, pride, ambition, insolent resolve, and sense enough to portion out a legion of fine ladies. Wealth and station, added to these, soon floated her upward; and for years, now, my Lady Dedlock has been at the centre of the fashionable intelligence, and at

30 the top of the fashionable tree.

How Alexander[2] wept when he had no more worlds to conquer, everybody knows—or has some reason to know by this time, the matter having been rather frequently mentioned. My Lady Dedlock, having conquered *her* world, fell, not into the melting, but rather into the freezing mood. An exhausted composure, a worn-out placidity, an equanimity of fatigue not to be ruffled by interest or satisfaction, are the trophies of her victory. She is perfectly well-bred. If she could be translated to heaven to-morrow, she might be expected to ascend without any rapture.

40 She has beauty still, and, if it be not in its heyday, it is not yet in its autumn. She has a fine face—originally of a character that would be rather called very pretty than handsome, but improved into classicality by the acquired expression of her fashionable state. Her figure is elegant, and has the effect of being tall. Not that she is so, but that "the most is made," as the Honourable Bob Stables has frequently asserted upon oath, "of all her points." The same authority observes that she is perfectly got up; and remarks, in commendation of her hair especially, that she is the best-groomed woman in the whole stud.

(1) A knight whose title is hereditary; not a member of the House of Lords
(2) According to Plutarch, Alexander the Great wept when he was told of the existence of an infinite number of worlds because "where there is such a vast multitude of them we have not yet conquered one."

QUESTION 3

(Suggested time—40 minutes.) **This question counts as one-third of the total essay section score.**

"What I like in a good author is not what he says, but what he whispers."

—Logan Pearsall Smith

Oftentimes the most powerful literary works are those that do not state their meanings blatantly. Think of a work of literary merit you have read that has not "[said] . . . but whispered." In a well-developed essay, explain how the writer has hinted at, not stated, the meaning of the work. Consider such devices as metaphors, symbols, allusions, and tone.

You may write your essay on the work of one of the following authors, or on a work by another author of comparable merit.

Albee, Edward
Beckett, Samuel
Chopin, Kate
Golding, William
Hemingway, Ernest
Joyce, James
Kafka, Franz
O'Brien, Tim
Morrison, Toni
Shakespeare, William
Smiley, Jane
Williams, Tennessee

Practice Test 1

Answers, Rubrics, and Student Responses

The answer sections for the multiple-choice items (Part One of each of the two practice tests) give you the correct answer and also explain why all of the other answers are incorrect. If you missed the same types of questions consistently, this may point you to areas you need to review.

Sample student essays are also provided in the answer section for this test and for the one which follows. Look over the scoring rubrics before you read the essays, read the teachers' comments on the essays, and do your best to honestly evaluate your own efforts. Once again, you may find a pattern. Maybe you need to be more vigilant about supporting your statements with evidence from the passage, or maybe it's something simple, like working on smoother transitions.

The practice tests and answers are provided as another way for you to learn how to improve your score. Study the answers carefully, and you will learn not only *how* you scored, but *why* you scored as you did.

Practice Test 1

Part One: Multiple Choice

Anwers and Explanations:
"Something About the Family"

1. The correct answer is B, "mocking criticism." A is incorrect because "cynicism" implies bitterness and a belief that people will behave only selfishly. C is wrong because the tone is definitely not one of dignified respect. The narrator may be scornful of the family, but definitely is not arrogant (overbearingly haughty or proud), so D is incorrect. E is obviously wrong.

2. The correct answer is C. The events related in the passage are only rumors, not factual history, so A is wrong. The passage is not about the narrator's family, so B is wrong. While D may be true, it is not the author's purpose to show this. E is an obviously wrong answer.

3. The correct answer is E. This type of question should be answered last for several reasons. It takes time to check for all of the techniques. As you answer other questions, you might spot some of the techniques and be able to eliminate them. The passage contains all of the techniques listed except metaphors. The sentences are short and interrupted frequently by the narrator's own views. Parenthetical interruption (qualifying or explanatory information) means interspersing personal commentary or thoughts, not necessarily using parentheses, so this technique is present. The passage does contain modified sentences, exaggeration, and dramatization, but metaphors are absent.

4. The correct answer is C. The sarcastic tone of "too much attached" implies scandalous involvement, knowledge for- bidden the general public and the reader. This leaves out the other choices of scorn, disdain, friendship, and political alliance.

5. The correct answer is B. The biography is about a family during the Victorian Age, but not about the history of that time. Answer A is mentioned in the fifth paragraph: "its system of morality." Answers C and D are true—the entire passage is filled with irony and biting sarcasm aimed at high society. E is also true because the passage refers to the problems the family has encountered.

6. The correct answer is C. The narrator has neither admiration nor sympathy for the Pattle family. He downplays their experiences and makes fun of them. Thus we can eliminate A and B. Scorn is too strong a word for the narrator, so D is wrong. "Regretful" (E) implies sorrow; the passage does not reflect this.

7. The correct answer is D. The narrator does not address any people, objects, or entities. There is understatement ("rather eccentric"), hyperbole ("greatest liar in the world"), allitera- tion ("worldly woman") and humor ("too much attached").

8. The correct answer is B. "Heinous" means "grossly wicked or reprehensible." The narrator uses "very heinous crime" to describe a situation that is much less serious. While "happily ever after" (A) may be a stretch, it is not hyperbole. The other choices do not exaggerate; they simply state facts.

9. The correct answer is E. "group" is the dictionary definition of "bevy." "Plethora" and "abundance" mean the same thing,

so A and D can be eliminated. "Pack" is reminiscent of wolves or animalistic behavior. "Gang" is too casual.

10. The correct answer is B. The events listed are horrible, yet the narrator rattles them off as he would a grocery list. This contributes to the overall surreal tone. This narrator's purpose is not to create any particular feelings in the reader, so A and D are wrong. Nor is he trying to relate historical fact, so C and E can be eliminated.

11. The correct answer is B. Remember the EXCEPT. The narrator ridicules society for its reaction to the scandal, mentions that Lord Henry lived happily ever after, exaggerates the scandal by calling it a "heinous crime," and tells us what Isabel did after the scandal. While he mentions the admiration of the women Isabel helped, he does not express his own admiration for her.

12. The correct answer is C. Here the narrator uses a series of parallel actions which are unequal in gravity. The exploding cask is as important as a woman losing her mind in this sentence, which trivializes the latter. The narrator's casual tone allows you to eliminate A, D, and E. B is a distracter: while James Pattle's weaknesses are described, he is not the subject of this passage.

13. The correct answer is E. "Cask" is the tool of the pun. It can mean either a barrel for holding liquor or a casket for a corpse. In James Pattle's case, it was both. The other choices are not plays on words.

14. The correct answer is D. This sentence emphasizes how Henry's deeds caused problems for Isabel, while Henry escaped unscathed. We certainly do not feel sympathy for Lord Henry, so A is wrong. The narrator does not mock Isabel's method of coping with the scandal or question her motives, so B and E are incorrect. C is obviously wrong since Lord Henry simply walked away.

15. The correct answer is E. The narrator is obviously not Fisher because he says, "according to H.A.L. Fisher . . ." He neither participated in the situation nor observed it, so B and D are wrong. He is removed from the situation, so C is wrong. Since the narrator seems to have a good knowledge of history, we can conclude that he must be a well-informed historian.

"Punishment"

16. The correct answer is A. B is incorrect; there is no irony. C is wrong; the speaker does not participate, although he does indicate he might have. (Also, "participant" is not a word describing tone.) D is wrong, since the poet was obviously

intensely interested if he wrote this poem. There is no indication that the speaker's tone is authoritative or elevated (E).

17. The correct answer is A, since nothing in the poem suggests B, C, or D, and "unfortunate transgression" is not a quality.

18. The correct answer is D. The only choice the poem does **not** contain is a statement of a moral or principle. There is enjambment (A) throughout the poem. There are metpahors (B) in lines 14, 19, and 20. There is assonance (lines 10 and 16). Alliteration occurs throughout the poem, for example, lines 2/3, 10, 16, and 18.

19. The correct answer is D. The very first line shows the speaker feels great sympathy for the woman. A is wrong because there is no indication that the narrator feels actual physical pain. B is incorrect; the poem does not discuss hypocrisy. The poem's tone is not informal, so C is wrong. E is wrong because the poem brings us in rather than shutting us out.

20. The correct answer is C. Historically, shaving a woman's head was seen as a humiliating form of punishment. Corn is used as a simile, but there is no actual corn in the scene, so A is wrong. A woman's having short hair has nothing to do with punishment (the title), so B is wrong. D and E are obviously incorrect.

21. The correct answer is E. By agreeing silently, one is as guilty as the participants. A and B are literal stones and these "stones of silence" are metaphorical. C is wrong because a scapegoat is a person who takes the sins of a group upon him/herself. D is wrong because in the context of the line, the speaker is not being deceptive.

22. The correct answer is C. The weighing stone, rods, and boughs all relate to punishment by drowning. A is wrong because the stanza does not deal with the woman's appearance. B and E are irrelevant. D is wrong because "ascetic" means self-denying and austere, and this is not the stanza's mood.

23. The correct answer is A. the speaker views the woman as a victim of a tribal ritual. B is incorrect because the last two stanzas do not support Heaney's viewing of the woman's punishment as a barbaric act. C is incorrect since the poem focuses on the woman, not the masses. D is wrong because "tribal" does not mean "society" in this context. E is wrong because there is no indication of strife in the community.

24. The correct answer is D because earlier the poet has concentrated on the physical act of the punishment; now he switches to his feelings about the woman. A and B are

incorrect; he has been neither critical nor objective. C is irrelevant. E is incorrect because the poet switches from past to present.

25. The correct answer is D. "Undernourished" is simply a fact about the woman. A, B, C, and E relate to her punishment.

26. The correct answer is E. There is no evidence that the speaker is either a brother (A) or lover (C). There is no indication that the poet is experiencing pleasure from his observation, so B is wrong. D would indicate lack of feeling, and the poet is obviously expressing and feeling emotion.

27. The correct answer is A because an oxymoron is two contradictory words placed side by side. A simile (B) compares two things using "like" or "as." Synecdoche (C) uses a part for the whole. Apostrophe (D) is a direct address to an absent person or an inanimate object. Personification (E) gives human qualities to inanimate objects.

28. The correct answer is A. A bog is composed of partially carbonized matter. The woman's remains have blackened with time. "Flaxen-haired" (line 25) indicates the woman was not African, so B is wrong. C, D, and E can be eliminated because Heaney does not comment on the evil of this woman's act or on the nature of women, and the woman was not burned, but drowned.

"Eleven"

29. The correct answer is D. The reader can easily recognize the irony of the situation: Rachel, even as she wishes to be 102, is wise beyond her years. A is incorrect because although she often responds as a child would, she does not demonstrate petulance. B is wrong because Rachel has no contempt for others or disbelief in their virtues (cynicism). C is wrong because Rachel does not behave in a superior manner. E is wrong because her grief is understandable.

30. The correct answer is C. Rachel is timid, and doesn't know how to respond to this unwanted attention. She repeats what she is thinking, but doesn't explain or justify. She is frustrated, but there is nothing to indicate anger (A) or annoyance (B). D is wrong because she is thinking these words, not saying them. The point of the passage has nothing to do with the teacher, so E is wrong.

31. The correct answer is C. The layers of dolls represent the idea of the accumulation of years and experiences, as well as growth in stature. A is not the best answer because the red sweater does not symbolize Rachel at all. B is a distracter but is not as good an answer as C. D is wrong because Rachel does not escape her situation like the balloon does. E is not relevant.

32. The correct answer is D, both I and III are correct. There is no indication that Rachel wants to die, so II is incorrect. "I'm eleven, ten, nine, eight . . ." indicates she wishes she were an infant at that moment. III applies because Rachel does want to be invisible. If she was, she would not have to worry about crying like a three-year-old.

33. The correct answer is D. Rather than characterizing Rachel as childish, the statement shows her wisdom. It also does all of the things to which the other choices refer.

34. The correct answer is E. A is incorrect because Rachel is referring to adults, not children. B is incorrect because "elders" is too limiting a term. C is too broad a statement. D is wrong because the statement is not limited to mothers and fathers.

35. The correct answer is D because the scene with the sweater displays irony, everyone's random cruelty toward Rachel even though it is her birthday. A is incorrect because the teacher may very well like Rachel but is simply trying to maintain order and get the sweater out of the cloakroom. B is incorrect; this is never mentioned in the passage. C is incorrect because Rachel never says she doesn't like birthdays; she'd just like to forget this one because of how she was treated at school. E is incorrect because there is no justice in this situation.

36. The correct answer is D, because the speaker is dissatisfied with being eleven. The other choices are all true. Imagery always adds vividness (A), and in this story, the imagery is unsophisticated and appropriate for an eleven-year-old (B). Rachel's observations about the onion, the dolls, the tree, and the Band-Aid box all show her intelligence (C). Images like "cry like if you're three" link ages and actions (E).

37. The correct answer is E. Irony does not always correspond with a sarcastic tone; in this passage, the tone is not at all sarcastic. Because irony itself is a complex technique, its use to show Rachel's complexity is appropriate (A). It is ironic that Rachel wishes for her birthday to be over when most children enjoy birthdays (B). It is ironic that Rachel wishes she were 102 so she would be intelligent enough to know what to say—because it is obvious to the reader that she is very wise for her years (C). Finally, there is irony in the fact that Rachel's thoughts are adult-like, yet she behaves childishly over the sweater.

38. The correct answer is C. The other choices are all true. Rachel does not ask for help from anyone. She does overstate the age she wishes to be (A), and wishes for the wisdom of adults (B). Like many children, she is exaggerating (D). It is also true that she is dissatisfied with her birthday, which has been a disaster (E).

39. The correct answer is D because Rachel is both wise, shown by such things as her acknowledgment of the "layers" of years, and she is also youthful in that she experiences and expresses a child's tender emotions. A is incorrect because Rachel shows mature thinking and cannot really be classified as childish because of one incident. B is incorrect because nowhere in the passage is it displayed that Rachel is outgoing, thus eliminating the word "extroverted." "Dignified" would also eliminate this choice since she cries in a most undignified manner. C is incorrect: Rachel is intelligent but she cannot be considered juvenile, which has a negative connotation. E is incorrect because even though Rachel is very insightful the passage certainly does not portray her as insensitive.

40. The correct answer is D. It displays insight not usually found in a child. A is incorrect because the line displays clear thought. B is incorrect because the comparison is sophisticated. C is irrelevant and obviously wrong. E is wrong because "refined" suggests a polish or style that Rachel does not yet have.

41. The correct answer is E. Cisneros repeats numbers throughout the piece to symbolize Rachel's desire to escape her present situation. Counting is almost a mantra, something Rachel can do to combat the frustration of her helplessness. A is incorrect because Rachel is not basing her life experiences on numbers but merely using them as symbols. B is incorrect because although Rachel is beyond her years in maturity, it is not because age is only a number. C is incorrect. This is true for going forward in time, but not for going backward. When Rachel wishes to revert to infancy, it is for the purpose of behaving as an infant. D is incorrect. There is no indication that Rachel is a victim of an unhappy childhood.

"Museum Piece"

42. The correct answer is C. The key word here is "impartially," which choices A, D, and E don't encompass. B is a distracter; the correspondence is there, but the answer doesn't best describe the effect of the phrase.

43. The correct answer is A. Wilbur does not express any negative feelings about Degas' use of the El Greco painting, so C and E are wrong. He uses this stanza to report a fact—with neither irreverence nor surprise, so B and D are wrong.

44. The correct answer is B. This is the only possible answer because there are four beats to each line, and "tetra" means "four." The other choices are wrong because dimeter is two beats, pentameter is five beats, and octameter is eight beats.

45. The correct answer is C. Like the guardians, Degas showed indifference to great art. This stanza does not say that Degas bought the El Greco specifically for a pants hanger, so contempt (B) and rivalry (D) are out. Answer A can obviously be eliminated. E is a distracter, but can be eliminated because we have know way of knowing if it was true.

46. The correct answer is B. The key word is EXCEPT. The dancer's image does suggest grace, beauty, strength and fragility, but not bathos, which means "false pathos."

47. The correct answer is B. The guardians do not understand art well enough to deeply respect it, so A is incorrect. There is no indication that they are uninterested in their actual work (patrolling), that they don't express their opinions, or that they are suspicious of the museum's visitors.

48. The correct answer is E. A is incorrect; please note that "guardians" is plural and does not agree with the pronoun "one." B refers to Toulouse-Lautrec, another artist. C is incorrect. It would be a real contortionist who could pirouette upon his own hair. D is incorrect as well—El Greco is another artist.

49. The correct answer is A. C, D, and E are incorrect since they misinterpret the poem's meaning. While B is a true statement, it is irrelevant.

50. The correct answer is D. The guardians, like sponges, absorb without understanding. Answers A and C are incorrect. Silence and importance are not symbols. B is wrong because the phrase refers to the guardians' shoes. E is incorrect because the atmosphere is not gloomy like a funeral, just quiet.

Adlai Stevenson's Letter

51. The correct answer is D. With subtle humor, Stevenson gently mocks a bill he considers frivolous. A is incorrect since the governor is being humorous, but is not writing about a serious subject in an undignified style, which "broadly comical" means. B is incorrect because while the letter is somewhat formal, it is not cynical. C is incorrect since he is against the bill. E is incorrect since he is not serious.

52. The correct answer is A. Once again, the EXCEPT needs to be noted. Stevenson is not attacking any individuals. Allusion (B) is present in "Not that I love birds the less or cats the more." (It is an allusion to Antony's speech over Caesar's body in *Julius Caesar.*) Stevenson does give the cat some human qualities, so C is OK. He uses *reductio ad absurdum* in lines 31–34, so D exists in the passage. There are many details in the piece, so E also exists.

53. The correct answer is C. Stevenson notes several times that this bill does not make sense. A and B are incorrect because nowhere does Stevenson imply that he either dislikes cats or loves them. This is not the issue. D is incorrect since the environment is not part of his argument. E is incorrect because the choice is a non sequitur.

54. The correct answer is A. This is the purpose of the letter. B, C, and E are methods Stevenson uses. D makes no sense.

Practice Test 1

Essay Section

Sample Student Essays
with Scoring Rubrics and Teachers' Comments

Question 1, excerpt from *The Merchant of Venice*

Before you read the student essays below, study the rubric. Then, as you read each essay, keep the requirements of the rubric in mind and think about the scores you would give the essays. See if you had any of the same comments as the teachers who evaluated the essays.

Sample Scoring Rubric: *Merchant of Venice*	
9–8	Writers of these eloquent essays clearly understand Bassanio's speech. They also thoroughly respond to all parts of the prompt (question). These essays will accurately analyze the text and the methods (for example: allusions, diction, comparison and contrast) by which the author achieves his purpose. Writers of these essays demonstrate a sophisticated mastery of sentence structure, word choice, and organization. While the writing need not be flawless, it reveals the writer's ability to address the prompt with flair and efficiency.
7–6	These essays also accurately discuss the text, but they do so with less insight than do the essays in the 9–8 range. They may slightly misinterpret a minor part of the speech. Their discussion of the "how" (the techniques employed) will be less well-developed. While these essays are well written with a strong sense of audience, they are less sophisticated than the top-range essays. Lucid and insightful, these essays fulfill the task, although less completely than writers of the 9–8 essays.
5	These essays are adequately written, yet superficial. They do not demonstrate stylistic maturity or confident control over the elements of composition. These essays discuss the text vaguely, or they inadequately analyze Shakepeare's techniques. They may cite stylistic techniques without sufficiently supporting how they work in developing the playwright's purpose.

4–3	These essays are adequately written but either summarize or misinterpret the work. Even a well-written summary of Bassanio's speech will receive no higher than a 4. These essays may simply list stylistic techniques, providing little or no discussion, evidence, or support. The writing also may be significantly flawed with syntactical errors and a lack of organization.
2–1	These essays are poorly written and replete with errors in diction, spelling, or syntax. They may use the passage merely as a springboard for an essay on a general topic. There may also be serious misinterpretation of the text. They are often too short.
0	These essays are no more than a restatement of the prompt.
–	This is used for a response that has nothing to do with the question.

Essay Written by Christine   Score: 8

"The world is still deceived with ornament," begins Bassanio in a soliloquy from <u>The Merchant of Venice,</u> by William Shakespeare and it is this ornament that is used "to entrap the wise." The passage reveals Bassanio's philosophy on the meaning of a show of beauty or eloquence; the worst of humanity's faults can be glossed over with the veneer of falsehood. Bassanio's mythological allusions and effective use of diction and contrast make the choice between caskets clear—he will pick the one that glitters least because its luster is not illusion.

Bassanio is a learned man that has seen much of human nature. He is aware of the inherent tendency of man to depict himself as something else to gain acceptance. A coward may be the one with the most bombastic bravado; a true man of valour would not find it necessary to assume the "beards of Hercules" and swagger with the might of a "frowning Mars." Many times those who frown upon others do so because they see themselves reflected. Bassanio will choose the humble and unassuming casket. He will not make the mistake of King Midas, who was so blinded by the gold of the gift that he failed to see it for what it really was a curse. Bassanio refuses to be moved by such wealth.

The diction used by Bassanio reveals the intrinsic nature of deception in the show of life. It is the "crisped" and "snaky" locks of hair of supposed beauty that fight against the wind. Ornament is the "guiled shore" that leads to a "dangerous" sea. "Gaudy gold" and other precious things are sought but the "pale and common drudge" that come "'tween man and man." The pseudo-brave wear but the "excrements" of valour, and beauty is but a "beauteous scarf veiling" the truth from the world.

The contrast present in the passage is reflective of the contrast that exists in the world. That which is tangible, seen and heard, obscures the elusive truth. Religion is guilty of "damned errors"; pardon allowed for "grossness" which is blessed by a "sober brow." A "gracious voice" can concoct a plea to excuse the most obvious "show of evil." Beauty would be valuable enough to purchase "by the weight" but when it is piled on artificially by someone it makes them the lighter and the more devoid of substance. Beauty, to Bassanio, can be bred in the sepulchre.

Bassanio is a man that has learned that appearances mean nothing. The most golden lock of hair can spiral and entwine like a snake. That which is simple and open to man moves Bassanio "more than eloquence." He has learned that the only consequence of such a choice can be joy.

Teacher Comment on Christine's Essay

This essay focuses immediately on the question, beginning with an appropriate quote from the passage. The first paragraph addresses both the "what" and the "how" accurately and perceptively. The sophisticated tone and vocabulary—"bombastic bravado," "true man of valour," "inherent tendency of man"—propel the essay with confidence. The writer's breadth of knowledge enables her to discuss the mythological allusions accurately.

She obviously understands Bassanio's position and, without summarizing, analyzes it insightfully. The fourth paragraph exemplifies this. Quotes are blended with panache and her thoughts are expressed clearly and concisely. The syntactical variety of her sentences makes this essay a pleasure to read.

The ending, though short, ties up a polished piece of writing. We believe that this is a 7 essay that we would reward for its beauty of expression with an 8.

Essay Written by Nate   Score: 7

Man is often faced with hard choices, from which there is no turning back. Bassanio of Shakespeare's "The Merchant of Venice" finds himself facing a choice of this design. In order to arrive at a choice he must look inside himself and his surroundings in order to best understand the trial the mind undergoes in choosing.

"The world is still deceived with ornament"; we as people see beauty and assume perfection. Bassanio is a true believer in the guise everything assumes in order to hide the truth. Bassanio believes that the Bible even hides the grossness within fair ornament. Just as the devil was contained in the body of an angel. So what can he trust if not the Bible but himself, the only thing he truly can trust.

What the eyes deceive, the mind understands. Bassanio sees his three choices before him and ponders his conclusion ". . . many cowards . . . are all as false as stairs of sand"; the people afraid of trusting themselves have wills as weak as that of an impossible staircase. He knows he must not be weak in his choice for then his stone stairs may crumble to those of sand. However, even "seeming truth" may "entrap the wisest"; he must be careful in his choice.

With knowledge and trust Bassanio continues to choose; reflecting upon past blunders experienced by others. ". . . those crisped snaky golden locks"; he sees Medusa's seemingly harmless hair turn to snakes and her gaze turns men to stone; Bassanio will triumph where others have failed. Those who walk the stairs of sand would see Medusa as beauty, and not evil. Bassanio would look upon "supposed fairness" and move on, ". . . ornament is but the guiled shore to a most dangerous sea."

Bassanio's eyes and mind work as one, a machine designed to use the deceivedness that "obscures the show of evil" for his purpose. He recalls King Midas and his foolish heart, consumed by greed. His rash thinking and "sandy stairs" only gave him "hard food," nothing more. Bassanio will have "none of thee." Even the greatest fall prey to their own deceiving eyes; a disturbing fact Bassanio can only learn from.

Two caskets adorned; what to choose. The choice is simple to most, but then, those are the ones who stare longingly into Medusa's eyes. After his careful and seemingly long analysis of his dilemma, Bassanio has come to his conclusion. The chest "which rather threatenest than . . . promise" is his choice. Bassanio has no need for frivolous ornament and "thy paleness moves me more than eloquence"; Bassanio feels no remorse for his choice because he has outsmarted even a King.

One must always choose one way or another; how and why is left to us. Bassanio, never once believing he should accept what he sees, chooses not foolishly but more wisely than anyone could. If even the Bible, the "purest" of pages, hides an evil in the white cloak of an angel, then who *is he to believe in three ornate boxes: if ornateness and outward beauty bring evil, falsehood and grief, then plainness must be reserved for the elite enough to choose; and "joy be the consequence." We all choose, we can never not, for "nothing will come of nothing."*

Teacher Comment on Nate's Essay

While this essay is well-supported, it does not flow as smoothly as it should. This is most obvious in the beginning of the second paragraph. A quote from the passage is juxtaposed with a jarring commentary from the writer. There is an overuse of semicolons where it would be better to write new sentences, and this interferes with the flow of the essay.

On the positive side, not only does the writer use apt quotations, but he comments and analyzes them succinctly as well. As with the previous essay, his mythological background enhances the analysis. This is evident in his comments on Medusa, alluded to in the passage by "crisped snaky golden locks." Furthermore, he accomplishes his task without authorial intrusion, such as "I noticed that . . ." or "I think . . ."

The organization is good. It is not a summary, nor does it dwell too long on any one point. The ideas move along steadily. The ending is powerful, incorporating allusions to the Bible and to Lear's "nothing will come of nothing."

Question 2: *Bleak House*

Once again, read the rubric first. Then keep it in mind as you read the essays and the teacher's comments.

Sample Scoring Rubric: *Bleak House*

9–8 Writers of these eloquent essays clearly understand the text. They also thoroughly respond to all parts of the prompt (question). These essays will accurately analyze Dickens' attitude toward the Dedlocks. Writers note his syntax, diction, and tone, and they understand and can explain Dickens' humor. Writers of these essays demonstrate a sophisticated mastery of sentence structure, word choice, and organization. While the writing need not be flawless, it reveals the writer's ability to address the prompt with flair and efficiency.

7–6 These essays also accurately discuss the text, but they do so with less insight than do the essays in the 9–8 range. They may slightly misinterpret a minor part of the speech. They may not "get" the humor. Their discussion of the "how" (the techniques employed) will be less well-developed. While these essays are well written with a strong sense of audience, they are less sophisticated than the top-range essays. Lucid and insightful, these essays fulfill the task, although less completely than writers of the 9–8 essays.

5	These essays are adequately written, yet superficial. They do not demonstrate stylistic maturity or confident control over the elements of composition. These essays discuss the text vaguely, or they inadequately analyze Dickens' techniques. They may cite stylistic techniques without sufficiently supporting how they work in developing the author's purpose.
4–3	These essays are adequately written but either summarize or misinterpret the work. Even a well-written summary of the excerpt will receive no higher than a 4. These essays may simply list stylistic techniques, providing little or no discussion, evidence, or support. The writing also may be significantly flawed with syntactical errors and a lack of organization.
2–1	These essays are poorly written and replete with errors in diction, spelling, or syntax. They may use the passage merely as a springboard for an essay on a general topic. There may also be serious misinterpretation of the text. They are often too short.
0	These essays are no more than a restatement of the prompt.
–	This is for a response that has nothing to do with the question.

Essay Written by Erika   Score: 7

He has prestigious family ancestry, a respectable role in society. Dressed in "fine shirt frill" (line 17) and entirely polite, he epitomizes a fine, wealthy gentleman. She, fashionable and rumored to be "the best-groomed woman" (48) is a necessary and proper accessory to him. Yet, as dignified and wealthy as they appear, the speaker ridicules and derides Sir Leicester Dedlock and Lady Dedlock, revealing this attitude through a sarcastic, mocking tone, humor, and juxtaposition of their outer and inner qualities.

The narrator thoroughly expresses his discontent for the couple with a mocking tone. Coupled with hyperbole, his bombastic rhetoric deliberately scorns the couple. As he initially describes Sir Dedlock, ticking off a list of family credentials, the narrator does not applaud or agree with his esteemed accomplishments. Instead, he ridicules him for his bloated egotism, having a "family as old as the hills, and infinitely more respectable." The following line, "he has a general opinion that the world might get on without hills . . . but would be done up without Dedlocks," (lines 3-4) reaffirm this idea and further mocks Sir Dedlock for his self-driven perspective. The treatment of the subject of his family, having "so much that perhaps he had enough," (24-25) continues the narrator's mockery and contributes to his disapproval towards them.

Additionally, the narrator expresses a sense of disgust toward "the centre of the fashionable tree"– Lady Dedlock. This character, so "perfect" and "ideal," "could be translated to Heaven tomorrow . . . to ascend without any rapture." This example and contributing descriptions establish the narrator's disparaging view toward this "fine woman."

The narrator furthers his discontent with the reputable couple with use of humor and undercurrents of irony. Particularly, he emphasizes this through anaphora. While listing Sir Dedlock's many "respectable" qualities in lines 11 and 12, the narrator slips in several negative, mocking qualifiers. He describes him as "intensely prejudiced" (11) and "perfectly unreasonable" (12), using inflated diction to humor the idea of Sir Dedlock. Again, the narrator utilizes a similar descriptive technique while noting "his gallantry to my Lady" (20), "is the one little touch of romantic fancy in him" (21-22). This deliberately patronizing comment humors the romantic efforts of Sir Dedlock. Furthermore, by alluding to Alexander's journeys and triumphs, the narrator further scorns Lady Dedlock with humor and disbelief. For, as she finally "having conquered <u>her</u> world" (34) "fell . . . into the freezing mood." (35) This example suggests "how could she?" and ridicules her as well.

Finally, the narrator cleverly juxtaposes the couple's outer appearance and inner qualities to epitomize their superficial composures. By listing and contrasting their looks and personality traits, the narrator furthers his disapproval of the couple and promotes the idea of their "fakeness" and insincere motives.

Thus, by using a deliberately mocking tone, humor, anaphora, and juxtaposition, the narrator is able to express his disgust toward the "fine" Sir and Lady Dedlock. He portrays them as insincere, superficial, and <u>actually</u> having faults—not as a flawless, wonderful pair.

Teacher Comment on Erika's Essay

This writer understood a daunting passage and answers the questions asked in the prompt without summarizing the piece. She capably describes Dickens' derisive attitude toward the couple and notes his list of inane details to describe Leicester's shallowness. The writer uses active verbs—"deriding," "ridiculing"—and sophisticated vocabulary ("juxtaposition," "reputable," "disparaging," "patronizing"). The quotes to which she refers are smoothly woven into the essay and explained clearly and with appropriate reference to the thesis. This writer has a mature style and a good command of the language and its mechanics.

On the negative side, some of her assertions needed specific examples (anaphora, hyperbole). The transitions are adequate but somewhat uninspired.

Essay Written by Amy   Score: 4

Charles Dickens mocks the attitudes of Sir Leicester and Lady Dedlock in this piece from <u>Bleak House.</u> The two are looked upon in a similar light—as haughty and pretentious. Dickens sees Sir Leicester as pompous. This attitude shines through humor in the first line of the passage. He is continuously described through his ideas of self-grandeur and personality traits: "obstinate, truthful . . . intensely prejudiced, perfectly unreasonable man." The use of the word "perfectly" suggests that Leicester has made these qualities an art.

The physical description of Leicester only adds to the mocking tone—his "whiskers," "fine shirt frill," pure white waistcoat," and the coat that always haughtily remains unbuttoned.

Humor is found in the diction of this piece. Words such as "indeed," "my Lady Dedlock," "equanimity" inflate the language to add to the sarcasm and disapproval of Leicester and Dedlock. In fact, Dickens sarcastically notes that Dedlock is perfectly "well-bred" for being depressed after only conquering "her world." She is compared to Alexander the Great, who history tells us was never satisfied with what he had—it is a great parallelism. Dedlock strives to be "fashionable"—the word is mentioned twice, both times with sarcasm and subtle disdain. Everything about her is qualified—her beauty is not perfect, but well enough; she is not tall, but makes the most of what she has. Apparently, she has enough "beauty, pride, ambition, insolent resolve, and sense . . . to portion out to a legion of fine ladies."

Sir Leicester and Lady Dedlock try to obtain a stature that they do not rightly have. Dickens sees this and uses mocking humor to convey his critical and ironic view of the Dedlocks.

Teacher Comment on Amy's Essay

On the positive side, the writer understood the piece and tried to answer the question posed in the prompt. She used details and examples, but perhaps too many examples in relation to what the student wrote.

Word choices "pretentious" and "pompous" show appropriate and so-phisticated vocabulary.

On the negative side, this essay is incomplete. The writer probably ran out of time. The writer lists details, but more development is needed regarding how they affect the reader's view of the Dedlocks.

Question 3, Open response

We have not supplied a scoring rubric for this question, since there is a wide choice of novels and plays. As you read the student responses below, keep in mind that the prompt calls for the student to discuss how an author hints at the meaning of a work. As a logical extension of that task, the student should discuss devices such as metaphor, symbol, tone, and allusion.

The rubrics provided for the first two questions should give you a good idea of the kind of writing the readers are looking for here as well.

Essay Written by Samantha   Score: 9

A plane crashes, boys of varying ages are stranded, no rules, no adults. For them it is a paradise, and for the reader, the beginning of an adventure tale. But in his novel, <u>Lord of the Flies,</u> William Golding not only tells of an adventure, he whispers, through tones of chaos and tragedy, of the major human defect: the ultimate need for power and the atrocious consequences that follow. Using devices such as symbols, metaphor, and tone, Golding channels the whispered meaning to his audience.

Superficially, <u>Lord of the Flies</u> is a tangled tropical story—containing a romantic setting, mystery, drama, and a semi-"happy ending," but at the moment that the protagonist Ralph utilizes the conch to obtain control of the young population, it is clear that Golding intended the conch to represent more than its physique. It symbolizes power, control, even oppression. Once the conch becomes a need, a necessary tool for mass security, metaphors become evident and another of Golding's major themes emerges . . . the loss of innocence.

The boys are metaphors to Golding's society, perhaps our own, so the boys, in an inhumane rage, attack a sow, a giver of life, chanting the haunting phrase, "Kill the pig, cut its throat, drink its blood." Golding is reflecting his own disgusted views on the character of society—how ruthless and unforgiving man is in its form of greed. The tone of the phrase is shocking to the readers, raising awareness to the utter corruption of innocence through power.

But perhaps the loudest of Golding's whispered words is heard when these innocent boys (as people immediately label what is young as innocent) would go as far as to perform acts of murder on their own kind in the ages-long struggle for power.

In _Lord of the Flies,_ William Golding presents a whimsical adventure about golden boys surrounded by deep turquoise waters who, corrupted by power, ironically end up as hungry, murderous savages. Like a cool breeze, Golding's recurring themes of human fallacies caress the paradise, stirring its defects to a layer just below the surface. Through an undertone of symbols and metaphors he manages to whisper what society chooses not to hear.

Teacher Comment on Samantha's Essay

Although an interesting or provocative opening is not required, it certainly helps when an essay contains one: "A plane crashes, boys of varying ages are stranded, no rules, no adults." The risk-taking pays off, because it is apparent from the entire essay that the writer is in command of the English language. Thus a deliberate fragment works. Quickly addressing the prompt, the writer describes how Golding whispers "through tones of chaos and tragedy," and lets us know which devices she will discuss.

Note that there is no plot summary, no meandering along highways and byways. The writer is clear, concise, and focused. She includes striking details from the novel (the conch, Simon's murder, and the chant) and blends these poetically. The insightful analysis responds to the prompt. The fluency of her sophisticated language makes this a joy to read.

The writer herself is whispering. Can there be a better way to display understanding?

Essay Written by Julie   Score: 4

In Kate Chopin's <u>The Awakening,</u> Edna Pontillier is first presented in the form of a parrot, caged and suppressed from flying free. Often in literature the meanings of well written books are "whispered." Chopin uses many devices to show Edna's feelings of individuality and sexual desires.

Symbols are constantly used throughout the work to convey these themes. The shade as well as the parrot is used to show her past conformity. The tone at this time is passive and controlled. All of the women sit under the tree away from the light of truth while the children unknowingly play in the sun. It is not long before the women tell the children to sit in the shade with them. The parrot is a possession and like Edna, it is caged. Edna must break free of these bars if she is to ever be happy. The sea is a symbol for the beginning of Edna's awakening and the end as well.

When Edna finally gets the courage to go in the water, she immediately feels an awakening and tries to swim out as far as possible away from her life and the conformity. It is then that the music is introduced. The music gives Edna the strength to pursue her awakening. On numerous occasions Edna seeks to find Madame Reisz for her musical inspirations. The episode where Edna throws down the ring and steps on it shows the change in her tone from passiveness to anger. Edna realizes that the ring symbolizes a never-ending suppressed life and she is being choked by it. However, another awakening begins to develop. Sexual awakening is whispered by the author. Edna is kissed on the hand by a man other than her husband which symbolizes her first act of infidelity. The heat from the kiss sparks new feelings of sexual desires. This desire is met when she finally has intercourse with Arobin.

However, Edna soon falls from this beautiful time in her life when Robert leaves her because "he loves her." As if in a trance, Edna walks to the sea to submerge herself in the water that awakened her. This allusion is very powerful because the water which at first seems so dangerous and restricting, becomes an ironic savior. While the author's tone ends in sadness, she finally realizes that she will always be misunderstood but at last she understands herself.

Teacher Comment on Julie's Essay

By now, you can probably easily recognize an essay which simply summarizes or is off-topic. For this reason, we are including one which seems to answer the question, but does not really do so adequately. She lists; she does not develop. She does not analyze. The major problem, however, is choppy writing, the lack of fluency, the summary of various events without really tying them together or showing how each one relates to the meaning. She has read and understood the book and its themes and symbols, yet the essay lacks finesse. The last sentence almost redeems it, but that is not enough. It's a high 4, but not more than that.

Practice Test 2

Section One
60 minutes

Part One: Multiple-Choice Questions

QUESTIONS 1–11. The following passage is taken from a letter Mark Twain wrote replying to a request to use his name in advertising a play based on *Tom Sawyer*. **Read the selection carefully. Then answer the questions that follow.**

Now as I understand it, dear and magnanimous 1365, you are going to re-create Tom Sawyer dramatically, and then do me the compliment to put me in the bills as father of this shady offspring. Sir, do you know that this kind of compliment has destroyed people
5 before now? Listen.

Twenty-four years ago, I was strangely handsome. The remains of it are still visible through the rifts of time. I was so handsome that human activities ceased as if spellbound when I came in view, and even inanimate things stopped to look—like locomotives, and district
10 messenger boys and so on. In San Francisco, in rainy season I was often mistaken for fair weather. Upon one occasion I was traveling in the Sonora region, and stopped for an hour's nooning, to rest my horse and myself. All the town came out to look. A Piute squaw named her baby for me—a voluntary compliment which pleased me
15 greatly.

Other attentions were paid me. Last of all arrived the president and faculty of Sonora University and offered me the post of Professor of Moral Culture and Dogmatic Humanities; which I accepted gratefully, and entered at once upon my duties. But my name had
20 pleased the Indians, and in the deadly kindness of their hearts they went on naming their babies after me. I tried to stop it, but the Indians could not understand why I should object to so manifest a compliment. The thing grew and grew and spread and spread and became exceedingly embarrassing. The University stood it a couple of
25 years; but then for the sake of the college they felt obliged to call a halt, although I had the sympathy of the whole faculty.

The president himself said to me, "I am as sorry as I can be for you, and would still hold out if there were any hope ahead; but you see how it is: there are a hundred and thirty-two of them already, and
30 fourteen precincts to hear from. The circumstance has brought your name into most wide and unfortunate renown. It causes much comment—I believe that that is not an overstatement. Some of this comment is palliative, but some of it—by patrons at a distance, who only know the statistics without the explanation—is offensive, and in
35 some cases even violent. Nine students have been called home. The trustees of the college have been growing more and more uneasy all these last months—steadily along with the implacable increase in your census—and I will not conceal from you that more than once they have touched upon the expediency of a change in the
40 Professorship of Moral Culture. The coarsely sarcastic editorial in

45 yesterday's Alta—headed Give the Moral Acrobat a Rest—has brought
things to a crisis, and I am charged with the unpleasant duty of
receiving your resignation."

I know you only mean me a kindness, my dear 1365, but it is a
most deadly Mistake. Please do not name your Injun for me.

1. It can be inferred from the first paragraph that
   a. Twain is concerned that the compliment will ruin him
   b. Twain is ecstatic about this request
   c. Twain is indifferent about this request
   d. Twain is insulted by this request
   e. Twain thinks that it is a great compliment

2. By categorizing the district messenger boys as "inanimate
   things" (line 9), the author suggests that the boys are
   a. aesthetically pleasing
   b. dim-witted and slow
   c. exceedingly boring
   d. physically strong
   e. socially inept

3. The line "I was so handsome that human activities ceased"
   is an example of
   a. allusion
   b. anecdote
   c. hyperbole
   d. metaphor
   e. simile

4. In line 21, "it" refers to
   a. the "deadly kindness of their hearts"
   b. the locomotives in line 9
   c. the naming of the Indian babies after Twain
   d. the request to use Twain's name
   e. the unwanted recognition of his popularity

5. The pronoun "them" in line 29 most likely refers to
   a. complaints about the absurd naming
   b. Indians named after him
   c. major problems this naming has caused
   d. other precincts to hear from
   e. other letters requesting the use of his name

6. The president's quotation (lines 27–47) is used effectively to
   a. emphasize how important Twain's professorial position is
   b. explain that Twain is too busy to be featured on the
      playbill
   c. make 1365 feel sorry for Twain's dismissal
   d. metaphorically compare 1365's request with the naming
      of the babies
   e. show Twain's reluctance to openly reject 1365

7. In the fourth paragraph, the syntactic element most prevalent is
  a. cumulative sentences
  b. long, complex sentences
  c. fragmentary sentences
  d. short, simple sentences
  e. subject-verb inversion

8. In the last paragraph, Twain uses the word "Injun" to mean
  a. a play on the word *engine*, 1365's invention
  b. a slang term for *Native American*
  c. Mark Twain's *Tom Sawyer*
  d. the child that 1365 is having with a Piute squaw
  e. the play that 1365 is producing

9. Which of the following best describes the organizational structure of the letter?
  a. description of a problem followed by an exception to the problem
  b. forceful argumentation followed by a concession to opposing views
  c. general statement followed by illustrative anecdotes
  d. presentation of a problem followed by a possible solution
  e. statement of a fact followed by a series of assumptions

10. The tone of this passage is
  a. caustic and biting
  b. humorous and condescending
  c. humorous and sardonic
  d. melancholic and bleak
  e. sardonic and condescending

11. "1365" refers to the
  a. address of the person requesting Twain's consent
  b. number of Indians who named their children after Twain
  c. number of the acting troupe
  d. person asking Twain to lend his name to a playbill
  e. pun on medieval morality plays

QUESTIONS 12–26. The setting of Robert Browning's "The Laboratory" is pre-Revolutionary France—probably the court of Louis XIV (1643–1715). It should be noted that the court was rocked in the 1670s by numerous poisonings. Carefully read the poem and then answer the questions that follow.

The Laboratory

Now that I, tying thy glass mask[1] tightly,
May gaze thro' these faint smokes curling whitely,
As thou pliest thy trade in this devil's-smithy—
Which is the poison to poison her, prithee?

5   He is with her, and they know that I know
        Where they are, what they do: they believe my tears flow
        While they laugh, laugh at me, at me fled to the drear
        Empty church, to pray God in, for them!—I am here.

        Grind away, moisten and mash up thy paste,
10   Pound at thy powder,—I am not in haste!
        Better sit thus, and observe thy strange things,
        Than go where men wait me and dance at the King's.

        That in the mortar—you call it a gum(2)?
        Ah, the brave tree whence such gold oozings come!
15   And yonder soft phial, the exquisite blue(3),
        Sure to taste sweetly,—is that poison too?

        Had I but all of them, thee and thy treasures,
        What a wild crowd of invisible pleasures!
        To carry pure death in an earring, a casket,
20   A signet, a fan-mount, a filigree basket!

        Soon, at the King's, a mere lozenge to give,
        And Pauline should have just thirty minutes to live!
        But to light a pastille(4), and Elise, with her head
        And her breast and her arms and her hands, should drop dead!

25   Quick—is it finished? The colour's too grim!
        Why not soft like the phial's, enticing and dim?
        Let it brighten her drink, let her turn it and stir,
        And try it and taste, ere she fix(5) and prefer!

        What a drop! She's not little, no minion(6) like me!
30   That's why she ensnared him: this never will free
        The soul from those masculine eyes,—say, "no!"
        To that pulse's magnificent come-and-go.

        For only last night, as they whispered, I brought
        My own eyes to bear on her so, that I thought
35   Could I keep them one half minute fixed, she would fall
        Shrivelled; she fell not; yet this does it all!

        Not that I bid you spare her the pain;
        Let death be felt and the proof remain;
        Brand, burn up, bite into its grace—
40   He is sure to remember her dying face!

        Is it done? Take my mask off! Nay, be not morose;
        It kills her, and this prevents my seeing it close:
        The delicate droplet, my whole fortune's fee!
        If it hurts her, beside, can it ever hurt me?

45   Now, take all my jewels, gorge gold to your fill,
You may kiss me, old man, on my mouth if you will!
But brush this dust off me, lest horror it brings
Ere I know it—next moment I dance at the King's!

(1) chemist's protective mask
(2) used in preparing pills
(3) blue vitriol (copper sulfate), a poisonous compound
(4) tablet burned to deodorize the air
(5) make up one's mind
(6) archaic use meaning *small and delicate*

12. The image of "faint smokes curling" (line 2) conveys a
  a. sense of duplicity
  b. sense of fear
  c. sense of jealousy
  d. sense of sorcery
  e. sense of suffocation

13. The first stanza of the passage is characterized by all of the following EXCEPT
  a. alliteration
  b. assonance
  c. metaphor
  d. onomatopoeia
  e. meter

14. In line 12, "the King's" is a
  a. mews
  b. palace
  c. park
  d. tavern
  e. theater

15. In context, "treasures," (line 17) can best be interpreted as
  a. children
  b. gold
  c. poisons
  d. possessions
  e. wealth

16. "What a wild crowd of invisible pleasures" (line 18) is an example of
  a. consonance
  b. metaphor
  c. onomatopoeia
  d. oxymoron
  e. synecdoche

17. The speaker's vindictive nature is revealed best in the following words:
  a. "Which is the poison to poison her, prithee?" (line 4)
  b. "they believe my tears flow while they laugh, laugh at me" (lines 6–7)

   c. "Quick—is it finished? The colour's too grim!" (line 25)
   d. "That's why she ensnared him" (line 30)
   e. "But brush this dust off me, lest horror it brings" (line 47)

18. The phrase "to carry pure death in an earring, a casket, a signet, a fan-mount, a filigree basket" (lines 19–20) illustrates the speaker's
   a. felicity
   b. jubilation
   c. melancholy
   d. remorse
   e. trepidation

19. It can be inferred that the poet believes that humans often act in all of the following ways EXCEPT
   a. altruistically
   b. amorally
   c. irrationally
   d. seductively
   e. vindictively

20. The grammatical pauses reveal the speaker's
   a. apprehension regarding the ball
   b. guilt-ridden insecurity
   c. hasty and vehement state
   d. intermittent hesitation
   e. methodical and reasonable plan

21. Which of the following indicates a major shift in the speaker's words?
   a. "I am not in haste" (line 10)
   b. "Quick—is it finished?" (line 25)
   c. "Let death be felt" (line 38)
   d. "yet this does it all" (line 36)
   e. "Is it done? Take my mask off!" (line 41)

22. The phrase "on my mouth if you will" (line 46) symbolizes the speaker's
   a. unbridled seductiveness
   b. venomous greed
   c. sincere gratitude
   d. unadulterated evil
   e. uninhibited passion

23. All of the following adjectives characterize the speaker EXCEPT
   a. calculating
   b. jealous
   c. quixotic
   d. vain
   e. wealthy

24. In line 44, the pronoun "it" refers to
   a. "death" (line 38)
   b. "mask" (line 41)

    c. "delicate droplet" (line 43)
    d. the speaker's enemy
    e. the speaker's lover

25. The speaker's attitude in the last stanza is best described as
    a. excited
    b. fastidious
    c. flirtatious
    d. greedy
    e. regretful

26. The effect of the setting on the meaning of the poem is to develop the
    a. chemist's greed
    b. criticism of science
    c. experimental labor
    d. lover's quarrel
    e. mysterious atmosphere

QUESTIONS 27–34. Read carefully the following passage from Joy Kogawa's *Obasan*, a novel about the relocation of Japanese-Canadians to internment camps during the Second World War. Then answer the questions that follow.

1942.

    We are leaving the B.C. coast—rain, cloud, mist—an air overladen with weeping. Behind us lies a salty sea within which swim our drowning specks of memory—our small waterlogged eulogies. We
5   are going down to the middle of the earth with pickax eyes, tunneling by train to the interior, carried along by the momentum of the expulsion into the waiting wilderness.

    We are hammers and chisels in the hands of would-be sculptors, battering the spirit of the sleeping mountain. We are the chips and
10 sand, the fragments of fragments that fly like arrows from the heart to the rock. We are the silences that speak from stone. We are the despised rendered voiceless, stripped of car, radio, camera, and every means of communication, a trainload of eyes covered with mud and spittle. We are the man in the Gospel of John, born into the world for
15 the sake of the light. We are sent to Siloam, the pool called "Sent." We are sent to the sending, that we may bring sight. We are the scholarly and the illiterate, the envied and the ugly, the fierce and the docile. We are those pioneers who cleared the bush and the forest with our hands, the gardeners tending and attending the soil with our
20 tenderness, the fishermen who are flung from the sea to flounder in the dust of the prairies.

    We are the Issei and the Nisei and the Sansei, the Japanese Canadians. We disappear into the future undemanding as a dew.

    The memories are dream images. A pile of luggage in a large
25 hall. Missionaries at the railway station handing out packages of

toys. Stephen being carried on board the train, a white cast up to his thigh.

It is three decades ago and I am a small child resting my head in Obasan's lap. I am wearing a wine-colored dirndl skirt with straps
30 that crisscross at the back. My white silk blouse has a Peter Pan collar dotted with tiny red flowers. I have a wine-colored sweater with ivory duck buttons.

Stephen sits sideways on a seat by himself opposite us, his huge white leg like a cocoon.
35 The train is full of strangers. But even strangers are addressed as "Ojisan" or "Obasan," meaning Uncle or Aunt. Not one Uncle or Aunt, grandfather or grandmother, brother or sister, not one of us on this journey returns home again.

The train smells of oil and soot and orange peels and lurches
40 groggily as we rock our way inland. Along the window ledge, the black soot leaps and settles like insects. Underfoot and in the aisles and beside us on the seats we are surrounded by odd bits of luggage —bags, lunch baskets, blankets, pillows. My red umbrella with its knobby clear red handle sticks out of a box like the head of an exotic
45 bird. In the seat behind us is a boy in short gray pants and jacket carrying a wooden slatted box with a tabby kitten inside. He is trying to distract the kitten with his finger but the kitten mews and mews, its mouth opening and closing. I can barely hear its high steady cry in the clackity-clack and steamy hiss of the train.
50 A few seats in front, one young woman is sitting with her narrow shoulders hunched over a tiny red-faced baby. Her short black hair falls into her birdlike face. She is so young. I would call her "Onesan," older sister.

The woman in the aisle seat opposite us leans over and whispers to Obasan with a solemn nodding of her head and a flicker of her
55 eyes indicating the young woman.

Obasan moves her head slowly and gravely in a nod as she listens. "Kawaiso," she says under her breath. The word is used whenever there is hurt and a need for tenderness.

The young mother, Kuniko-san, came from Saltspring Island, the
60 woman says. Kuniko-san was rushed onto the train from Hastings Park, a few days after giving birth prematurely to her baby.

"She has nothing," the woman whispers. "Not even diapers."

Aya Obasan does not respond as she looks steadily at the dirt-covered floor. I lean out to the aisle and I can see the baby's tiny fist
65 curled tight against its wrinkled face. Its eyes are closed and its mouth is squinched small as a button. Kuniko-san does not lift her eyes at all.

"Kawai," I whisper to Obasan, meaning that the baby is cute.

Obasan hands me an orange from a wicker basket and gestures toward
70 Kuniko-san, indicating that I should take her the gift. But I pull back.

"For the baby," Obasan says urging me.

I withdraw farther into my seat. She shakes open a furoshiki—a square cloth that is used to carry things by tying the corners together—and places a towel and some apples and oranges in it. I
75 watch her lurching from side to side as she walks toward Kuniko-san.

Clutching the top of Kuniko-san's seat with one hand, Obasan bows and holds the furoshiki out to her. Kuniko-san clutches the baby against her breast and bows forward twice while accepting Obasan's gift without looking up.

27. The narrator's attitude toward internment can best be described as
    a. feeling betrayed and resentful
    b. feeling prideful and strong
    c. feeling excited and curious
    d. confused and mournful
    e. angry and enthralled

28. The speaker(s) of the passage is (or are)
    a. a mother sympathizing with her child's pain
    b. a young victim of the Japanese internment
    c. a young girl and her aunt
    d. the aunt of the little girl
    e. a detached bystander

29. The major shift in the text (line 22) has the following effect
    a. illustrates the difference between pity for herself and pity for the group
    b. shifts from concentration on herself to concentration on the woman with the baby
    c. it separates the events that happened in the past from the present
    d. it contrasts the difference between the Issei, Nisei, and Sansei, and modern Japanese Canadians
    e. portrays a change between the collective struggle of Japanese Canadians and the experience of one girl

30. The use of the words "a trainload of eyes" (line 13) is an example of
    a. anecdote
    b. hyperbole
    c. synecdoche
    d. alliteration
    e. litote

31. The style of the passage as a whole is that of
    a. reflective narration
    b. objective recollection
    c. nostalgic yearning
    d. explicit description
    e. rambling nostalgia

32. The primary effect of switching pronoun usage from first person plural to first person singular is to display the narrator's change between
    a. sophisticated adult to innocent child
    b. passive observer to active participant

c. loyalty to Canada to loyalty to Japan
d. a realization of Japanese individualism
e. a sense of compassion for Kogawa herself

33. The description of the mother with her baby has the primary effect of
    a. creating a feeling of remorse for the plight of the Japanese Canadians
    b. humanizing victims of the internment
    c. providing imagery for the passage
    d. demonstrating the narrator's maternal instincts
    e. demonstrating the narrator's feeling of betrayal

34. The use of the term "obasan" has the primary effect of
    a. showing respect in addressing an adult
    b. showing that they are Japanese
    c. showing how adversity can result in unity
    d. showing their previous knowledge of one another
    e. showing a familial relationship among the Japanese

QUESTIONS 35–42. Although author Louise Erdrich is most widely known as a novelist, she has also won a reputation as a poet. Read her poem entitled "Dear John Wayne" and then answer the questions that follow.

Dear John Wayne

August and the drive-in picture is packed.
We lounge on the hood of the Pontiac
surrounded by the slow-burning spirals they sell
at the window, to vanquish the hordes of mosquitoes.
5   Nothing works. They break through the smoke screen for blood.

Always the lookout spots the Indians first,
spread north to south, barring progress.
The Sioux or some other Plains bunch
in spectacular columns, ICBM missiles,
10   feathers bristling in the meaningful sunset.

The drum breaks. There will be no parlance.
Only the arrows whining, a death-cloud of nerves
swarming down on the settlers
who die beautifully, tumbling like dust weeds
15   into the history that brought us all here
together: this wide screen beneath the sign of the bear.

The sky fills, acres of blue squint and eye
that the crowd cheers. His face moves over us,
a thick cloud of vengeance, pitted

20   like the land that was once flesh. Each rut,
each scar makes a promise: *It is*
not over, this fight, not as long as you resist.

Everything we see belongs to us.

A few laughing Indians fall over the hood
25   slipping in the hot spilled butter.
The eye sees a lot, John, but the heart is so blind.
Death makes us owners of nothing.
He smiles, a horizon of teeth
the credits reel over, and then the white fields
30   again blowing in the true-to-life dark.
The dark films over everything.
We get into the car
scratching our mosquito bites, speechless and small
as people are when a movie is done.
35   We are back in our skins.
How can we help but keep hearing his voice,
the flip side of the sound track, still playing
Come on, boys, we got them
where we want them, drunk, running.

40   *They'll give us what we want, what we need.*
Even his disease was the idea of taking everything,
Those cells, burning, doubling, splitting out of their skins.

35. The speaker's attitude toward John Wayne can best be
    described as
    a. bitter resentment
    b. disillusioned frustration
    c. obvious disgust
    d. reluctant acceptance
    e. sardonic accusation

36. The phrase "slipping in the hot spilled butter" (line 25)
    emphasizes that
    a. much blood has been shed
    b. killing has been trivialized
    c. the Indians are hopeless and careless about their lives
    d. the Indians are becoming more inebriated, a symbol of a
        major problem
    e. the Indians are subconsciously denying the slaughter of
        their people

37. How do the italicized phrases change the tone of the poem?
    a. They add to the complexity of the poem.
    b. They contradict the adventurous tone of the poem to
        illustrate reality.

c. They emphasize the power struggle between the Indians and their predators.

d. They contradict the regretful tone of the poem to illustrate the Indians' acceptance of their lives.

e. They show the lack of power the Indians have to allow the predators to intercede in the first place.

38. The words "feathers bristling" in line 10 are used for all of the following EXCEPT
   a. to mock the Indians
   b. to illustrate the Indians' heritage
   c. to emphasize the Indians' pride
   d. to provide a contrast with the actual harsh setting
   e. to show ironic imagery during a life-threatening battle

39. John Wayne's disease, mentioned in lines 41–42, symbolizes all of the following EXCEPT
   a. destruction is often out of control
   b. death makes us the owner of nothing
   c. ironically, life does matter to the destroyer
   d. parallelism between the disease and Wayne's roles on the screen
   e. how the Indians were forced off their lands as the white man "took everything"

40. Why does the poet use a drive-in movie for the setting?
   a. to intensify irony
   b. to emphasize the popular culture's dependence
   c. to contrast the idea of history and modernism
   d. to further the stereotype of a "cowboys and Indians" movie
   e. to emphasize that the viewers are experiencing this now

41. What do the mosquitoes symbolize?
   a. carriers of disease
   b. the everyday troubles of society
   c. the savagery the Indians endured
   d. the Furies prodding the Indians to action
   e. the greedy men who want the Indians' blood

42. The overall tone of the poem can best be described as
   a. cynical
   b. nostalgic
   c. regretful
   d. somber
   e. vengeful

QUESTIONS 43–56. The passage below is by Richard Steele. Read it carefully and then answer the questions that follow.

Christmas Greens

January 14, 1712

Mr. Spectator,

I am a young woman and have my fortune to make, for which reason I come constantly to church to hear divine service and make conquests; but one great hindrance in this my design is that our clerk,
5   who was once a gardener, has this

Christmas so over-decked the church with greens that he has quite spoiled my prospect, insomuch that I have scarce seen the young baronet I dress at these three weeks, though we have both been very constant at our devotions, and don't sit above three pews off.
10   The church, as it is now equipped, looks more like a greenhouse than a

place of worship: the middle aisle is a very pretty shady walk, and the pews look like so many arbours on each side of it. The pulpit itself has such clusters of ivy, holly and rosemary about it, that a light
15   fellow in our pew took occasion to say that the congregation heard the word out of a bush, like Moses. Sir Anthony Love's pew in particular is so well hedged that all my batteries have no effect. I am obliged to shoot at random among the boughs, without taking any manner of aim. Mr. Spectator, unless you'll give orders for removing
20   these greens, I shall grow a very awkward creature at church, and soon have little else to do there but say my prayers. I am in haste,
Dear sir, Your most obedient servant
JENNY SIMPER

43. The tone of the piece is
  a. didactic indignation
  b. cheerful glee
  c. gentle irony
  d. ironic seriousness
  e. somber melancholy

44. The passage's speaker is a(n)
  a. altruistic congregant
  b. despondent romantic
  c. hypocritical Christian
  d. religious reformer
  e. self-absorbed woman

45. It can be inferred from the phrase, ". . . our clerk, who was once a gardener . . . I dress at these three weeks" (lines 4–8), that
  a. Jenny Simper is disappointed with the church's decorations
  b. Jenny Simper enjoys the clerk's talents as a gardener

    c. Jenny Simper does not embody the Christmas spirit
    d. the clerk intended to thwart Jenny Simper's plan
    e. the ornate decoration hinders Miss Simper's attempts at flirting

46. The pronoun "we" in line 8 refers to
    a. Jenny and the baronet
    b. Jenny and the clerk
    c. Jenny and the gardener
    d. Jenny and the priest
    e. Jenny and Mr. Spectator

47. A principal purpose of the word "greenhouse" (line 10) is to
    a. demonstrate the letter writer's familiarity with the church
    b. depict the church greens as analogous to farmland vegetation
    c. emphasize the idea that there are too many greens within the church
    d. illustrate the beauty appropriate within a place of worship
    e. stress the spaciousness and sunlight of the church

48. The function of the sentence beginning "The church, as it is now equipped . . ." (lines 10–13) is to
    a. describe the church's lavish interior
    b. emphasize the writer's feelings about the clerk
    c. express Jenny Simper's disapproval of the mass of greenery in the church
    d. show the handiwork of the gardener
    e. show the connection between God and nature

49. Jenny attends church to
    a. admire the beautiful scenery
    b. better her status in society
    c. find a husband
    d. socialize with congregants
    e. worship God

50. The word "light" in line 14 most nearly means
    a. amusing
    b. enlightened
    c. even-tempered
    d. pale in color
    e. slender

51. The primary rhetorical purpose of this passage is to
    a. candidly express the speaker's annoyance over an obstacle
    b. describe the lush atmosphere in the speaker's church
    c. disparage the overzealous botanical vicar
    d. reflect the annoyance of a devout Christian
    e. satirize the materialism of some churchgoers

52. The effect of the last two lines of the second paragraph is to
    a. emphasize Jenny Simper's self-absorption
    b. evoke pity for the speaker
    c. instill faith in Mr. Spectator's authority
    d. stress the irony of the situation
    e. stress the need for immediate action

53. Jenny Simper's attitude is best described as one of
    a. altruistic concern
    b. concerned activism
    c. selfish opportunism
    d. social consciousness
    e. trendy materialism

54. One prominent characteristic of the writer's style is the
    a. application of the first person to provide a sense of intimacy
    b. carefully balanced compound sentences
    c. relative paucity of qualifying adjectives
    d. stringing together several adjectives and adverbs
    e. use of long, complex sentences

55. The pattern of the author's discussion is best described as
    a. description of a problem followed by an exception to the problem
    b. forceful argument followed by concessions to opponents
    c. general statement followed by illustrative material
    d. presentation of a problem followed by resolution of the problem
    e. statement of fact followed by tentative assumptions

56. Jenny's last name contributes to the tone of the piece because *simper* means to
    a. be class conscious
    b. be simple
    c. cut hedges
    d. flirt openly
    e. smile in a silly fashion

Practice Test 2

Section Two
120 minutes

Part Two: Essay Questions

QUESTION 1

(Suggested time—40 minutes.) **This question counts as one-third of the total essay section score.**

> In William Shakespeare's *Henry V,* the King of England addresses the governor and townspeople of Harfleur, a French town under siege. In a well-developed essay explain how Henry's language reflects his intent.

ACT III, Scene iii.—*The same. Before the Gates of Harfleur*

The Governor *and some* Citizens *on the walls; the* English *forces below. Enter* KING HENRY, *and his Train.*

K. HEN. How yet resolves the governor of the town?
This is the latest parle we will admit:
Therefore, to our best mercy give yourselves,
Or, like men proud of destruction,
5   Defy us to our worst: for, as I am a soldier,
(A name, that, in my thoughts, becomes me best,)
If I begun the battery once again,
I will not leave the half-achieved Harfleur,
Till in her ashes she lie buried.
10   The gates of mercy shall be all shut up,
And the flesh'd soldier, rough and hard of heart,
In liberty of bloody hand, shall range
With conscience wide as hell; mowing like grass
Your fresh-fair virgins, and your flowering infants.
15   What is it then to me, if impious war,
Array'd in flames like to the prince of fiends,
Do, with his smirch'd complexion, all fell feats
Enlink'd to waste and desolation?
What is't to me, when you yourselves are cause,
20   If your pure maidens fall into the hand
Of hot and forcing violation?
What rein can hold licentious wickedness,
When down the hill he holds his fierce career?
We may as bootless spend our vain command;
25   Upon the enraged soldiers in their spoil,
As send precepts to the Leviathan
To come ashore. Therefore, you men of Harfleur,
Take pity of your town, and of your people,
Whiles yet my soldiers are in my command;

30   Whiles yet the cool and temperate wind of grace
      O'erblows the filthy and contagious clouds
      Of deadly murder, spoil, and villainy.
      If not, why, in a moment, look to see
      The blind and bloody soldier, with foul hand,
35   Defile the locks of your shrill-shrieking daughters;
      Your fathers taken by the silver beards,
      And their most reverend heads dash'd to the walls;
      Your naked infants spitted upon pikes,
      Whiles the mad mothers with their howls confus'd
40   Do break the clouds, as did the wives of Jewry,
      At Herod's bloody-hunting slaughtermen.
      What say you? Will you yield, and this avoid?
      Or, guilty in defence, be thus destroy'd?

QUESTION 2

(Suggested time—40 minutes.) **This question counts as one-third of the total essay section score.**

> In this passage from Toni Morrison's *Beloved,* the speaker conveys her views concerning the struggle between whites and blacks.
>
> Read the passage carefully. Then, in a well-organized essay, analyze how the author's stylistic devices contribute to our understanding of the passage.

The day Stamp Paid saw the two backs through the window and then hurried down the steps, he believed the undecipherable language clamoring around the house was the mumbling of the black and angry dead. Very few had died in bed, like Baby Suggs, and none that

5   he knew of, including Baby, had lived a livable life. Even the educated colored: the long-school people, the doctors, the teachers, the paper-writers and businessmen had a hard row to hoe. In addition to having to use their heads to get ahead, they had the weight of the whole race sitting there. You needed two heads for that. Whitepeople believed

10 that whatever the manners, under every dark skin was a jungle. Swift unnavigable waters, swinging screaming baboons, sleeping snakes, red gums ready for their sweet white blood. In a way, he thought, they were right. The more coloredpeople spent their strength trying to convince them how gentle they were, how clever and loving, how

15 human, the more they used themselves up to persuade whites of something Negroes believed could not be questioned, the deeper and more tangled the jungle grew inside. But it wasn't the jungle blacks

20

brought with them to this place from the other (livable) place. It was the jungle whitefolks planted in them. And it grew. It spread. In, through and after life, it spread, until it invaded the whites who had made it. Touched them every one. Changed and altered them. Made them bloody, silly, worse than they had ever wanted to be, so scared were they of the jungle they had made. The screaming baboon lived under their own white skin; the red gums were their own.

25

Meantime, the secret spread of this new kind of whitefolks' jungle was hidden, silent, except once in a while when you could hear its mumbling in places like 124.

30

Stamp Paid abandoned his efforts to see about Sethe, after the pain of knocking and not gaining entrance, and when he did, 124 was left to its own devices. When Sethe locked the door, the women inside were free at last to be what they liked, see whatever they saw and say whatever was on their minds.

35

Almost. Mixed in with the voices surrounding the house, recognizable but undecipherable to Stamp Paid, were the thoughts of the women of 124, unspeakable thoughts, unspoken.

QUESTION 3

(Suggested time—40 minutes.) **This question counts as one-third of the total essay section score.**

"Irony is the whisky of the mind."

—J. B. Priestley

Irony is one of the most frequently used techniques in literature. Think of an author who has successfully woven irony into his/her novel or play. In a well-constructed essay discuss how irony and other literary techniques are employed throughout the piece to develop the meaning of the work.

You may choose a work from the list below, or you may select a work of comparable merit.

A Thousand Acres
The Awakening
Beloved
Billy Budd
Black Like Me
Brave New World
Candide
The Catcher in the Rye

Death of a Salesman
Hamlet
In the Lake of the Woods
King Lear
Les Misérables
Lord of the ~~Flies~~ Riougth
Snow Falling on Cedars
Slaughterhouse Five
Their Eyes Were Watching God
Twelfth Night
Wuthering Heights

Practice Test 2

Answers, Rubrics, and Student Responses

Practice Test 2

Part One: Multiple Choice

Answers and Explanations
Mark Twain's Letter to 1365

1. The correct answer is D. To insult is to cause resentment by callous or rude behavior. Twain considers the request to be an effrontery (a presumption). A is incorrect because he is exaggerating and being ironic when he says "this kind of compliment has destroyed people." B, C, and E are incorrect since he is not at all happy with the request.

2. The correct answer is B. Inanimate, by definition, means "without life" and usually refers to objects such as pencils and telephone poles, not to people. Therefore, A and D can be eliminated. C and E are irrelevant and have nothing to do with the piece.

3. The correct answer is C. This is when knowing your literary terms is invaluable. Hyperbole means "exaggeration."

4. The correct answer is C. There is almost always one pronoun-antecedent question; if you take your time and try substituting the words in the answer choices for the pronoun, you can hardly go wrong.

5. The correct answer is B. Here is another antecedent question; this one is more challenging. You have to go all the way back to the middle of the preceding paragraph ("in the deadly kindness of their hearts . . .") to find the antecedent. "Them" refers to Indians named after Twain.

6. The correct answer is D because one child's being named after Twain led to the crisis described by the president. This explains how one play could lead to a similar crisis. A is incorrect because the president's quotation indicates that Twain was not important enough to overcome the problem and keep his position (had this actually been his position and had he wanted to keep it). B is incorrect because 1365 wants only Twain's name, not his time. C is incorrect because Twain is not asking for sympathy. E is incorrect because Twain does openly reject 1365's request in the last two sentences.

7. The correct answer is B. The paragraph is full of long, complex sentences. Choice E can be ruled out because none of the sentences contain subject-verb inversion. D can be eliminated because the sentences in this paragraph are certainly not short. A is incorrect because the paragraph does not build (cumulative). There are no fragments, so C is incorrect.

8. The correct answer is E, the play that 1365 is producing. We have already seen that Twain has used the story of the Indian baby-naming as a metaphor for the potential disaster. This is his wit at work, saying please do not do him the "favor" of crediting him with what he perceives as inferior work.

9. The correct answer is C; Twain makes the general statement that "that kind of compliment has destroyed people." He then follows this up with the anecdote about the squaw. A is incorrect because Twain does not mention an exception. B is incorrect because Twain does not introduce any opposing views. D is incorrect because he does not offer a solution. E is incorrect because he does not assume. He explains with anecdotes.

10. The correct answer is B. You can eliminate choice D right away; the piece is lighthearted and funny, not sad. You can also eliminate A because humor is prevalent in the letter, and "caustic and biting" does not indicate humor. "Sardonic" (bitter) is too strong a word to describe Twain's tone, so you can eliminate C and E.

11. The correct answer is D. Twain addresses the recipient of the letter as "dear and magnanimous 1365."

"The Laboratory"

12. The correct answer is D because it conjures up the image of a medieval magician. A is incorrect; the smoke does not convey a sense of chicanery or deceit (duplicity). Nor is there any fear (B). While the poem is about jealousy, this image is really part of the setting and does not contribute to

the feeling of jealousy. The speaker puts on the mask to protect her from the fumes, so E is incorrect.

13. The correct answer is D. This is one of the easy questions if you know your terminology and you remember the EXCEPT in the question. The stanza has alliteration, assonance, metaphor, and meter, but does not contain onomatopoeia.

14. The correct answer is B. The dance is a ball at "the King's," which is understood to mean "the palace." A is incorrect because mews are stables. The park, tavern, and theater have no particular association with the king, so C, D, and E are wrong.

15. The correct answer is C. Substitute the word you think is correct for the word in the question ("treasures") and this should help you see what makes sense. The speaker is talking to the apothecary and coveting all his poisons, thinking of all the enemies she could kill if she had them. The other choices are irrelevant and incorrect.

16. The correct answer is B. Once again, knowing your literary terms will help you. A metaphor says that one thing is something else. In this case, the apothecary's many poisons are "a wild crowd of invisible pleasures."

17. The correct answer is A. She repeats the word "poison" twice, emphasizing her desire, and beseeches the chemist ("I prithee") to choose the best one. B and D are incorrect because she is giving her reasons for wanting revenge, but they do not reveal her vindictive (vengeful) nature. C is incorrect since the line's emphasis is on her haste, not her nature. E simply indicates that she doesn't want to give herself away, or be accidentally poisoned herself.

18. The correct answer is B. The speaker is exultant, almost delirious with joy. While felicity (A) means happiness, her joy is stronger than that. C, D, and E, which mean sadness, regret, and fear respectively, are wrong since they are negative feelings and the speaker is obviously feeling very positive about what she is going to do.

19. The correct answer is A. Here is another question with EXCEPT. The question deals with universal, not specific, issues. Certainly these are people who behave amorally; they are willing to poison other people for revenge. Murder may be seen as irrational. The imagined or real affairs to which the speaker alludes show a belief that people are seductive. And they are obviously vindictive. This leaves only altruism, unselfish concern for others without expectation of reward.

20. The correct answer is C. The dashes ("Quick—is it finished?") indicate her vehemence and haste. A is incorrect since the speaker is filled with anticipatory glee rather than

fear or apprehension. B and D are wrong since she exhibits no guilt, insecurity, or hesitation. While she has a plan, it is hardly reasonable, so E is wrong.

21. The correct answer is E. It indicates that the apothecary's labors are over. She has the poison and is ready to go off and kill her rival. Until this point in the poem, she has been anticipating this completion, so the other answers are wrong.

22. The correct answer is D. Browning has certainly painted a portrait of pure evil. Remember that both words in the answer must apply. You can eliminate A and E since she is not trying to seduce the chemist. B is wrong because while the woman's jealousy and desire for revenge have been emphasized, she is not greedy. C is also wrong—she might see the kiss as a way of staying in good with the chemist or rewarding him, but she is not grateful.

23. The correct answer is C. "Quixotic" means ridiculously chivalrous and romantic, and she is certainly neither of these. She does exhibit the other traits listed in answers A, B, D, and E: she is calculating, jealous, vain, and apparently wealthy since she can pay for the poison and she associates with royalty.

24. The correct answer is C, "delicate droplet." This is the speaker's whole focus. If you substitute the other choices for the pronoun, it is easy to see that this is the best choice.

25. The correct answer is A because, having fulfilled her mission, the overriding emotion is one of excitement as she anticipates her triumph at the ball. B is a distracter. Nowhere in the poem does she appear especially fastidious (meticulous). She is simply brushing off the dust to remove any poisonous residue. C is incorrect; she is not flirting with the old man. D is incorrect as well because she tells the chemist to take all her gold and jewels—she wants her revenge. E is obviously wrong; she has no regret.

26. The correct answer is E. The atmosphere is definitely mysterious. A is incorrect: Although the chemist is being paid, he is not necessarily greedy. While the use of a laboratory to produce poison is not laudable, that is not the effect of the setting, so B is wrong. C is incorrect because the chemist seems to know just what he is doing. D is wrong because there is no indication of a lover's quarrel.

From *Obasan*

27. The correct answer is A because she feels betrayed by a society that has shunned her and resentful because she has to go to the internment camp. B is incorrect because she's prideful of her culture, not of the internment. C is incorrect

because she is not excited about going to the internment camp, but rather saddened. D is wrong because she's not confused, but seems to know what's going on. E is wrong because "angry" and "enthralled" are contradictory.

28. The correct answer is B—she was the little girl on the train to the camp. A is wrong because she is a grown woman looking back on her own childhood experience. There is only one speaker, so C is wrong. D is wrong because she is the little girl, not the aunt. E is wrong because she is not a bystander but a participant.

29. The correct answer is E because the first part is collective, centering on group experience, while the next section does focus on the individual experience. A is wrong because the tone is not one of pity. B is wrong because the first section focuses on the "we." C is incorrect because *events* in this passage happened only in the past. D is not the subject of the passage.

30. The correct answer is C; the eyes stand for people on the train. It cannot be A, anecdote, which means a very short story. While B might seem correct, it is no exaggeration that the train is crowded. There are no repeated letter sounds (alliteration) in the phrase, so you can eliminate D. The phrase is not an understatement (litote), so E is incorrect.

31. The correct answer is A. She is looking back (reflecting) and telling a story the way she saw it through her young eyes. She is not objective (B) because we can readily infer her feelings. Nostalgia (C, E) is the opposite of what she is feeling about this painful experience. D is also incorrect because it does not apply to the passage as a whole, even though description is there.

32. The correct answer is A. The author begins the story as an adult, then switches to the perspective of herself as a child. B may seem at first glance like a good answer, but she is not a passive observer in the beginning. C and D are incorrect as there is no mention of loyalty or individuality. E is incorrect because Kogawa does not ask for sympathy.

33. The correct answer is B. A is incorrect since remorse is self-reproach and guilt over one's deeds, and the reader is not responsible for the scene she describes. C is incorrect because imagery is the means to an end but not the end (or effect) itself. D is irrelevant and untrue. E is irrelevant. Although the Japanese certainly felt betrayed, that is not the effect of this particular anecdote.

34. The correct answer is C. Strangers meet on a train and call each other familial names. They feel a sense of unity in a time of distress. A is incorrect. While it does show respect, this is only part of the effect of the term. B is incorrect. They are all

Japanese. They do not need to use this term to show their ethnicity. D and E are incorrect. The train is full of strangers.

"Dear John Wayne"

35. The correct answer is E. "Sardonic" means cynical. In his movie roles, Wayne helped perpetuate negative myths about Indians. The speaker is well aware of this. A is incorrect because the speaker is not resentful. Her tone is "cooler" than that. B is incorrect. In order to be disillusioned, one must first have illusions. Nowhere does the speaker indicate she has had any illusions. The word "obvious" gives away C as being incorrect. This poem implies subtly. D is incorrect since there is no acceptance.

36. The correct answer is E. Laughing and clowning around while images of the slaughter of their people flash on the screen is an unusual response indicating psychological denial. A, while true, is too simplistic and not the best answer. B is irrelevant to the specific line in the poem. The poem doesn't indicate that the Indians are hopeless or careless, so C is wrong. D is incorrect. The poem doesn't focus on increased drunkenness.

37. The correct answer is D. Note especially "death makes us owners of nothing" (line 27). A is incorrect because although it is true, it is too superficial an answer. B is incorrect because the tone of the poem is not adventurous. C is incorrect. Remember that TONE refers to the *author's attitude* toward the subject. The italicized words emphasize the irony of the soldiers' attitude that theirs was a fair manifest destiny. The speaker does not share this view. E is incorrect because the italicized words are not said only by the soldiers. Lines 26–27 are said by the speaker. This choice does not take that into account.

38. The correct answer is A. The poem salutes the Indians. It does not mock them. The phrase does relate to their proud heritage, and the imagery provides contrast and irony.

39. The correct answer is C. Note the word EXCEPT. All but C are correct. In this poem, life does not matter either to the soldiers who took Indian lives or to the cancer cells that stole John Wayne's life.

40. The correct answer is A. It is ironic that the Indians, who have lost everything, are now watching themselves lose again on "this wide screen beneath the sign of the bear," paying to be on land that once belonged to their ancestors. B is a good distracter but limits and trivializes the real meaning of the poem. C is incorrect. The poem does not deal with the contrast between history and modernism. D is incorrect because the setting itself does not further any stereotypes of either cowboys or Indians. E is irrelevant.

41. The correct answer is E. This is precisely what the poem is about. A is too literal and B is too general. The mosquitoes are annoying, but they are not a good symbol of savagery. D is incorrect because it brings in a mythological allusion, and this is irrelevant.

42. The correct answer is A. A cynic is a person who is scornful of the motives and virtues of others. The overall tone of the poem is scornful of the "heroism of the white cavalry" personified by John Wayne. B is incorrect since there is no fond remembrance. C is incorrect since regret is mild sorrow, and the poem is not expressing this. D is incorrect since although the subject is serious, the language denies a somber tone. E is incorrect because John Wayne's cancer and the speaker's words express an overall irony rather than vengeance.

"Christmas Greens"

43. The correct answer is C. Addison and Steele poke gentle fun at the foibles and follies of 18th-century society. In this particular piece, Steele ironically points out that Jenny is more worried about her dress and making eye contact with Sir Andrew Love than about any form of worship. The final sally indicating that she would have "little else to do there but say my prayers" reveals the purpose of the passage. The other answer choices are incorrect.

44. The correct answer is E. A is incorrect because Jenny is not altruistic (unselfish). In fact, she is very self-centered. B is incorrect, as the tone is practical, not hopeless (despondent). C is incorrect since a hypocrite says one thing and does another. Jenny is at least forthright. D is incorrect since a religious reformer is concerned with spiritual matters.

45. The correct answer is E because, in Jenny's words, "I have scarce seen the young baronet," the object of her affection. A is incorrect since Jenny Simper is expressing disapproval, not disappointment in the decoration. B is incorrect since the whole letter is a criticism of the clerk's talents as a gardener. C is incorrect since, while this may be true, the question refers to one phrase and not to the entire passage. D is incorrect since there is no evidence in the letter to support this statement.

46. The correct answer is A. This pronoun-antecedent question can be answered by substituting the nouns given in the answer choices for the pronoun, and working out which one makes the most sense.

47. The correct answer is C. Jenny is not at all happy with the superfluity of greens in the church, and compares the church to a greenhouse. There would be no purpose for her to demonstrate her familiarity with the church (A). She does

not compare them to farm crops (B). She finds the greens excessive, not appropriate (D). And she definitely does not feel that the greens create a feeling of spaciousness (E).

48. The correct answer is C. A and D are incorrect. While true, they are not the functions of the sentence. B is incorrect since these lines express Jenny's feelings about the greens, not the clerk. To further the irony, Jenny does not mention God in her letter, so E is wrong.

49. The correct answer is C. Jenny is looking for a husband. She might better her status by finding one, and she might find one by socializing, but finding one is her primary purpose. She is not there to admire the scenery or worship God.

50. The correct answer is A. The fellow who made the comment was joking. You can infer the meaning of the word "light" by using context clues and substituting the choices for the word in question.

51. The correct answer is E. This is a difficult question. When examiners ask about *rhetorical purpose*, they are asking about the *author's* intention. Steele is writing this as if he were Jenny Simper, but it is Steele's view of Jenny and others like her that is important. Steele is gently poking fun at Jenny's real reasons for attending church. The other choices all relate to the intentions Steele has Jenny express in her letter.

52. The correct answer is A. We are left bemused by Jenny's ingenuous last words. She is too self-absorbed to even realize what she is saying.

53. The correct answer is C. Here is an example of the importance of a well-developed vocabulary. Jenny's concern is certainly for herself, so we can eliminate A, altruism (selflessness) and B, activism (attempts to right societal ills). Social consciousness (D) is an awareness of the needs of those who are less fortunate, not a quality Jenny exhibits. There is no indication that she is being trendy (E), following the crowd.

54. The correct answer is E. A is incorrect because even though the letter is written in first person, there is no sense of intimacy with the reader. B, C, and D are not supported by the text.

55. The correct answer is C. A and B are incorrect. She cites neither exceptions nor concessions to the problem. D is incorrect since it is not a resolution which would satisfy anyone else. E is incorrect in that there is nothing tentative about her position.

56. The correct answer is E. This is an unusual vocabulary question. Usually, the AP test has words that are defined but not exemplified in context. The College Board usually selects words whose meaning is not simply the dictionary meaning.

Eighteenth-century satirists often used a telling name to further ridicule their subjects. This is simply a word whose definition you would have to know.

Practice Test 2

Essay Section

Sample Student Essays
with Scoring Rubrics and Teachers' Comments

First read the scoring rubric for *Henry V.* Keep the elements of the rubric in mind as you read the student essays which follow. What score would you award each essay? How do they compare to yours?

Scoring Rubric: *Henry V*	
9–8	These essays are well written and display the student's command of the elements of good composition. The students accurately interpret the intent of the king: surrender or die. Henry argues that the people should surrender in order to avoid a bloodbath. Students address some of the following issues: tone, irony, parallel structure, imagery, rhetorical questions, biblical allusions, and others.
7–6	While these essays are also well written and fluid, and they accurately analyze the king's intent, they do so less persuasively and with less precision. There may be minor errors, but the writing demonstrates a high degree of control and organization. Support and insight may be somewhat limited.
5	These essays are adequate, but thinner in support and content. They may be superficial, and the essay may not show a full grasp of the intent of the king's language. The writing may be unsophisticated, even plodding at times. The essays may be poorly organized. Analyses may be perfunctory. Minor errors in interpretation sometimes characterize a 5. Overall, these essays convey the meaning, but with very little conviction.
4–3	These essays merely summarize the king's speech, or they may misunderstand the intent of the speech. The analysis, if any, is sketchy, incomplete, and unconvincing. Supportive illustrations from the text are few and may be inaccurate. There may be blatant grammatical errors.
2–1	These essays may simply be too short and lack any breadth and depth. Some may merely restate the prompt while others may be off topic or misconstrue the speaker's intent. If there is a thesis, it refers to something other than the passage. These essays may have egregious grammatical errors.
0	This essay simply mentions the task or restates the prompt. May be a blank paper or response that is off topic.
–	This is used for a response that has nothing to do with the question.

Question 1, excerpt from *Henry V*
Essay Written by Jessica   Score: 9

In the collision between two worlds there will be inevitable casualties; only a wall separates the warring French and English, a wall that will crumble and buckle under the pressure of primal blood lust. King Henry, of <u>Henry V</u> by William Shakespeare, addresses this issue when he asks the French governor if it will be surrender or war. King Henry's language reflects that of a person who has seen the dark side of humanity and who knows that as time goes on, the line between the rational and irrational bleeds into the indistinguishable.

King Henry is not hungry for violence but acknowledges that if there is no surrender, and the French soldiers resist, a deluge of blood will leave no one unspared. He tries to convey this to the French Governor by using graphic and chilling imagery. The image of "naked infants spitted upon pikes" sears itself into the psyche while the haunting wails of "pure maidens" fallen into the hands of "hot and forcing violation" echo. Only men "proud of destruction" would defy Henry V and allow this to happen.

War is a force that releases the "licentious wickedness" of man—no "rein" can hold it in. The "rein" also refers to the reign of a King or Holy King. King Henry knows that the human soldier "in the liberty of bloody hand, shall range with conscience wide as hell." In the realm of humanity there is the uncontrollable, and sometimes violent duality of nature. Henry refers to King Herod who slaughtered the innocent "Jewry" to prevent the inevitable. Just as the light of God was being born unto the earth was the darkness a pall over it. Henry recognizes that in any reign there is blood and inescapable fate.

Henry uses metaphor to symbolize the opposing choices of life and death—mercy or slaughter. "The cool and temperate winds of grace" fight continuously with the "filthy and contagious clouds of deadly murder, spoil and villainy." Once again Henry reminds the Governor that there will be a storm, for one cannot halt nature's clouds, but it is up to him if it will be a tempest or a cooling rain.

"Impious war, arrayed in flames" is destined to overtake the town if peace is not sought. Henry is a king in the world of men and thus must know men. It is this knowledge that gives him the unbearable weight of having to order the clouds to break or to leave the city in waste and desolation.

Teacher Comment on Jessica's Essay

This essay is a solid 9. The student's approach is direct; the interpretation is accurate, insightful and sophisticated, and the writing is persuasive, engaging, and mature. Opening with a beautifully constructed and well-balanced sentence, the student addresses the heart of the matter: the tenuousness of the French position and its potential imminent destruction. The second sentence accurately states the dilemma and Henry's position, specifically: surrender or face horrible slaughter. Using effective verbs such as "crumble" and "buckle," and strong adjectives like "primal blood [lust]," "inevitable," and "indistinguishable," the student demonstrates a wide command of appropriate vocabulary and develops a compelling opening paragraph.

This essay continues with a clear and direct discussion of the diction, imagery, and allusion which express the King's intent and rationale. The language is dexterous, accurate, and specific; it flows to a persuasive closing. The essay successfully meets all the requirements of a top score of 9.

Essay Written by Luis   Score: 7

A monarch is thought to be elegant and proper in his behavior, as is exemplified by his ostentatious wealth and majestic castles. Although dappled with flair and pomp, one must remember that they still possess "filthy and contagious" currents of violent barbaric behavior from the European Dark Ages. King Henry shows his controlled wrath towards an occupied French town in the passage by carefully manipulating contrasts in diction and an invective tone to stir fear in the helpless residents of Harfleur—knowing that the threats will bring tacit submission to his arbitrary whims.

This witty speaker knows his audience—the townspeople—are alert and interested in what he has to say. As if they were small but jarring knifes that cut through the "cool" composure of the town he peppers his dialogue with rhetorical questions; he repeats carefully thought-of threats to ask the residents if they want death and destruction. He supports his queries by verbally attacking them with foul diction that graphically portrays grotesque acts—"infants spitted on pikes," "heads dash'd to the walls" increasingly aware that such comments make the meek townspeople wince and cower in fear. Who wants their "fresh fair virgins" submitted to the "hot and forcing violation"? The look in the audience's faces drives his wicked, animalistic frenzy throughout his coercive argument.

Furthermore, by carefully placing references to highly-esteemed states of existence—"cool and temperate wind of graces," "silver beards under reverent heads"—he can easily crush their dreams with his bare hands. After all, he is "a soldier" and will do all in his power to make sure *"waste and desolation" prevail if the governor of the town doesn't succumb to his wishes. The King has effectively used contrasts in diction to shift the mood of his rhetoric—as quickly and deftly as if he were skillfully swordfighting against his French foe.*

King Henry V, "rough and hard of heart," kills all hope of rebellion or resistance through his carefully orchestrated rhetoric and supporting details. He wishes that the threads will work—and then the "pen" will truly be "mightier than the sword." Words, when used invectively, can "shut up" "the gates of mercy."

Teacher Comment on Luis' Essay

This fluent and insightful essay is replete with elegant vocabulary and clever commentary on the passage. The writer approaches the task at hand with flair, poise, and confidence, clearly demonstrating knowledge of history and the language of literature. The opening paragraph is strong, indicating that it will lead to an upper-level essay, in this case a 7.

The second paragraph continues with its perceptive comments regarding the "alert and interested townspeople," "the carefully thought-of threats," and the almost tongue-in-cheek, "Who wants their 'fresh fair virgins' submitted to the 'hot and forcing violation'?"

However, the interpretation is somewhat off in calling Henry's speech "wicked and animalistic." More could and should have been added to support the premise of rhetorical questions and "foul" diction. The support, therefore, is somewhat thinner than would be found in an 8 or 9 paper.

The writer continues his analysis with the contrast between King Henry's elegant prose and the reality of Henry's imminent threat as a fierce soldier, addressing shifts in mood and diction and linking both with the actual battle. The allusion to the pen and the sword exactly captures the essence of the King's intent. Thus the "what" of this essay is accurate and perceptive, but the "how" is underdeveloped. Irony and imagery could be addressed, as well as the biblical allusion to Herod's deeds. For these reasons this essay does not reach an 8 or a 9, but given the writer's intellect and skill with words, it can easily be seen as a 7.

Question 2, excerpt from *Beloved*

First read the scoring rubric. Then analyze the student essays keeping the rubric in mind. How do these students' essays compare to yours?

Scoring Rubric: *Beloved*

9–8	Writers of these outstanding essays clearly understand the nature of the struggle between blacks and whites at the time of the novel. They recognize Morrison's extraordinary use of language (e.g., vivid adjectives, strong and evocative verbs, contrast, oxymoron, the extended metaphor of the jungle) to convey the complexity of the relationship. They notice that, among other stylistic devices, varied sentence structure and brilliant poetic devices contribute to the impact of a powerful description of a difficult struggle. These essays need not be flawless, but they demonstrate a mastery of a broad range of the elements of good writing. They support their assertions with ample evidence from the text.
7–6	Writers of these very good essays understand the nature of the struggle depicted in the passage. They recognize Morrison's extraordinary use of language, but they do so with less perception than the top essays. These essays note at least two of the stylistic techniques used to create the passage, and they include the significance of the jungle metaphor. They are less inclusive than the best essays, but their assertions are insightful and well-supported. They demonstrate a competent command of the elements of effective writing.
5	These superficial essays interpret the passage adequately with possible lapses. They demonstrate less depth of understanding, analyze only one or two stylistic devices, and provide minimal support of their statements. They are fairly well written, but may be weak in some elements of effective writing.
4–3	These essays are merely summaries or they are inaccurate in substantial areas. They are thin, weak in support, and may be seriously flawed in syntax and organization.
2–1	These essays are poorly written and replete with errors in diction, spelling, or syntax. They may use the passage merely as a springboard for an essay on a general topic. There may also be serious misinterpretation of the text. They are often too short.
0	These essays are no more than a restatement of the prompt.
–	This is for a response that has nothing to do with the question.

Essay Written by Jamika   Score: 9

The nature of two hundred years of violence and injustice is elusive and volatile. The effects of bondage take root and even when the tree is cut down, the gnarled fingers of pain thrive and continue to invade like unseen cancer. The language of century old wrongs is an "undecipherable" clamor. <u>Beloved,</u> by Toni Morrison, conveys the struggle between hate, prejudice, and truth. She uses imagery and repetition to strengthen the parallels between the jungle of pain and hate.

The hidden effects of slavery fester and grow amid a climate of prejudice and resentment. The use of color to characterize things is used repeatedly in the passage. The jungle is black, white, and red—but the red stains everything. The violent red gums are ready for "their sweet white blood;" it is ironic that even the blood of white people is white. The denial of the white race is evident in that line—they do not even admit that everybody's blood is the same color. Both races harbor red rabid jungles in their being; the red gums of the dark man are reflected unto the white man.

However different the plantation owner and the slave may be they both live within a personal jungle. "Swift unnavigable waters, swinging screaming baboons," and "sleeping snakes" are said to reside under the skin of the negro. The jungle is a tangle of fear, anger and resentment within all who were mistreated; it did not thrive in the African sun that beat down upon the free black but under the beating of a society wrought with misconceptions it grows. It spreads until the whites are tangled in the vines of anger and hate that stem from their own hearts. The imagery of the "sleeping snake" characterizes the former slaves as vipers who are but waiting for a time to attack when in reality it is all humanity, regardless of color that nestles a snake within its breast—and has since it was born.

The jungle grows and cannot be stopped no matter how hard the oppressed try to change—not themselves but those around them. The din of voices from the past or the present and the ghosts of those not yet born all scream for change but their "undecipherable language" is feared and not understood. All those with willing hearts hurry down the steps away from the century-old screams of blame. Blacks who try to change use themselves and the fount of their being is dried. And so the years of tears feed the jungle and the souls of all humanity are twisted by the branches of hate.

Teacher Comment on Jamika's Essay

The reader is drawn into the essay immediately by the writer's first sentence: provocative and sophisticated. The original simile which follows, "tree is cut down, the gnarled fingers of pain thrive and continue to invade like unseen cancer," adds panache. Emulating Morrison's style shows the student's command of writing. Her philosophical generalization displays an understanding of the results of slavery and oppression and touches upon universal truths—lovely.

Insight is evident in the student's discussion of color imagery: "The jungle is black, white, and red—but the red stains everything." It takes considerable talent to conjure such vivid imagery in a timed essay. There is depth in the further explanation of the color imagery.

The analysis is subtle and implied. It is not always necessary to hit the reader over the head with explanations, and it certainly is not wise to define the terms one uses. This writer does neither, yet it is clear that the passage has been understood and responded to with eloquence and depth.

Note the memorable ending: "And so the years of tears feed the jungle and the souls of all humanity are twisted by the branches of hate."

Essay Written by Nick   Score: 6

Throughout time, the white man has suppressed the "educated" colored man. Through slavery and discrimination, the "whitepeople" have created, in their own minds, a race that could never reach the level they had already attained; whites had created a minority that they thought possessed the attributes of the "jungle" within.

Throughout Toni Morrison's Beloved, manifold examples of such discrimination are portrayed.

Through the use of extended metaphor, Toni Morrison proves the "obvious" differences between the races, as seen through the eyes of the "whitepeople." The "jungle," the "swift unnavigable waters [and] red gums ready for their sweet white blood" is utilized throughout the duration of the passage to present what the whites perceive to be the primitive and animalistic behavior of blacks, and to convey fear—a wariness—of a race they, the whites, have unknowingly created. This "jungle" encompasses all that the majority fears—all that the whites do not know. For it is the unknown that man fears most. The whites do not make an effort to know these Negroes with the jungle inside; they instead shun them and banish them to a place whereupon their "jungle" is allowed to grow "deeper and more tangled." And it is through "the jungle" that the audience is given a clearer understanding of the deep fear that these "whitefolks" encompass.

Yet, through this deft use of metaphor comes irony. For, as stated, "it wasn't the jungle blacks brought with them, [but] the jungle whitefolks planted in them." This irony, in turn, aids also in the understanding that the "jungle" is not a mere representation of shrubs and plants and baboons, but of man's cruelty, therefore creating a cyclical nature within the piece.

The irony continues. The "whitefolks," who created the "jungle" for the blacks, were also infected. "It grew [and] spread . . . until it invaded the whites who had made it." Their own perceptions enslaved the masters. The "screaming baboons lived under their own skins; the red gums were their own." Man's nature is portrayed as being corrupt.

Human beings discriminate—he has always found flaws within others. It is through this depiction that Toni Morrison projects her beliefs that although man creates, he does not necessarily understand—he is many times "scared of the jungle [he] has made"—and that this discrimination, although focused elsewhere, will eventually follow its cyclical path and invade him who has created it.

Teacher Comment on Nick's Essay

The writer has clearly understood and responded to the passage's prompt. The student has incisively analyzed the central dilemma: how enslavement enslaves. Pointing out the jungle metaphor as an apt and appropriate central device, the writer explores how this affects all involved.

Specific examples from the text are cited to support this thesis: "It wasn't the jungle the blacks brought with them, but the jungle white-folks planted in them." The student's understanding of the jungle metaphor is apparent since he sees a jungle "not of shrubs and plants, . . . but of man's cruelty." Taking this one step further, the writer then points out Morrison's use of irony, fully aware that we fear the unknown and give it attributes it does not possess.

Transitions are smooth and seamless and serve to unify the piece. More specificity would be necessary for a higher score. In addition, Morrison's other important stylistic devices such as tone, imagery, and repetition should be noted. While the student wrote well in the allotted time, there is lack of fluency and elegance. The essay is also a bit thin and avoids discussion of the last few paragraphs of the passage.

Question 3, Open Question on Irony

We have not provided a rubric for this prompt, but by now you probably know what kinds of things the readers would be looking for. When you read this prompt, your first task was to choose a novel or play you know well that *also* uses irony to develop meaning. To fully answer the prompt, you should also have cited some other techniques used by the author of your chosen novel or play.

Read the student essays and teacher comments below. What scores would you award these essays? How does your essay stack up?

Essay Written by Janelle   Score: 9

Woven into the structure of a literary work are values to be learned, meanings to be found, ideas to be communicated and themes to be discovered. However, some of the most important elements of effective literature are the elements of surprise, contrast, juxtaposition, and conflict, woven together tightly to form the intricate, powerful device called irony. Irony is the catalyst that amplifies theme, provokes insight, and bridges together the fibers of what may seem incompatible into a literary tree—blossoming on every branch with intense meaning and deeper purpose. In Zora Neale Hurston's <u>Their Eyes Were Watching God,</u> irony is used to create an entanglement of love and death, disappointment and self-fulfillment, and personal contentment amidst the criticism of a society bound by convention.

Janie's grandmother wished her the life of comparative luxury, and Logan, "a man with land," was who she felt best offered Janie that opportunity. However, Janie did not find the happiness her grandmother intended for her; Logan's emotions were embedded beneath a hardened exterior. Janie's defiance of her grandmother's wishes displays her as a stronger individual, and through leaving Logan, the theme of self-fulfillment is sought after in an unexpected light. Ironically, Janie leaves Logan, a man who cares but does not display his love, for Joe Sacks—a man who manipulates with power and money and rides among his town with not an ounce of modesty. He blindly leads his life, and Janie's without freedom or love. When he dies, Janie assumes the role of a sorrowful widow, a character cast in a production of superficial mourning and false grief.

Where wealth hides, Janie finds the love that will let her soul "come out of its hiding place." It is not where money, land, power, or even respect is that Janie finds love. Tea Cake is representative of the pinnacle of irony: the search for personal contentment finishes often where it is least expected. This concept perpetuates the theme of Hurston's book, reinforcing the importance of true happiness.

Tea Cake leads Janie to the swamps of the south, but despite their poor conditions, they live happily, and become the icon of unrequited love. In his life, he was her savior, rescuing her from a life entangled by tradition, and void of true love. But in this life, what seemed like perfection would be shattered like a "cracked plate" when a storm interrupts their life. A metaphor for fate and destiny, the hurricane strengthens the incorporation of irony; Motor Boat doubts himself and survives unharmed, while Tea Cake and Janie trust themselves, and God, and encounter what would prove to test their love. Ironically, Janie is forced to kill the one she loves, to end the life of the man who gave her hers. To further engrave the central theme of irony, Hurston gives Janie the will to mourn in total truth and honesty—in her clothes, the clothes indicative of their life together—of Tea Cake. She is "too sad to mourn."

The epitome of contrast exists within the juxtaposition of love unsettled by death, and sadness transcended by closure. Ironically, Janie is not destroyed by Tea Cake's death; she is strengthened, and learns to see him in everything that surrounds her. She "pulls the horizon" around her; Tea Cake blankets her, like a shield protecting her. Irony is central to the development of the characters in Hurston's tale of love and loss; its challenge lies in the trust of one's self, and the fulfillment of true happiness.

Teacher Comment on Janelle's Essay

This eloquently written essay displays an acute understanding of the concept of irony and its place in the literary realm. Fluent language and sophisticated vocabulary elevate the piece to a strong 8/9. The writer's opening paragraph includes a striking, original metaphor ("Irony is the catalyst . . ."). This also resonates with one of the book's major motifs, a tree. Immediately apparent, then, is her perspicacity and her absolute control of language.

The essay provides specificity as to characters, symbols, and literary techniques as well as to the meaning of the work. As we have stated before, irony is difficult to discuss fluently. Yet this writer unabashedly plunges right into the prompt. In her first paragraph she develops its relation to theme. In the second paragraph, she carefully selects appropriate evidence for her assertions: "Ironically, Janie leaves Logan, a man who cares but does not display his love . . ." Note the lack of summary, the avoidance of superfluous information.

She continues to discuss irony, and then carefully considers other literary techniques (as suggested in the prompt). These include contrast, metaphor, and simile. Even though she does not use the word "symbolism," this concept is implied throughout the paper. (English teachers appreciate subtlety.)

This is a paper which takes risks that pay off. The writing is poetic: "When he dies, Janie assumes the role of a sorrowful widow, a character cast in a production of superficial mourning and false grief." Moreover, she has obviously memorized quotes that are meaningful to her ("a man with land," "her soul come out of its hiding place," "cracked plate," "too sad to mourn," and "pulls in the horizon"). These are not simply thrown in at random, but are smoothly blended into the piece.

Essay Written by Raquel   Score: 4

We all wear a mask that shields our true selves from society. An image is presented of joy and perfection among the family unit. But under that deceitful mask lies a darkness full of lust, greed, and betrayal. These emotions date back to Adam and Eve and are carried on into today's literature. In *A Thousand Acres,* Jane Smiley incorporates the use of irony coupled with an allusion to the Garden of Eden to represent how pride can lead to a great downfall.

A thousand acres of beautiful and fruitful land—yet this land survived off the corruption, greed and pride. Larry Cook ran his land and household the way he wanted it run, with no suggestions or help. However his successful thousand acres was for him, his shield from society. Society only saw wealth and skill but were oblivious to the rage and manipulation. He had power and he used it to mold his children into his image of perfection. This control which he possessed for so long eventually permeated into the hearts of his daughters and with this came greed.

When it came time to test his daughters, they turned and failed him. The land was divided and ironically the only daughter who remained faithful was the one exiled from her home. The others' love was not true and their masks eventually fell to reveal their greed. The rage they felt towards their father unleashed, like the great storm, a flood of memories of their lost innocence and purity. The two which Larry surrendered his land to destroyed his kingdom and this "perfect" family was shattered. Larry's pride pushed him further from them, yet in the end, he was only left with false memories of little pink coats and childhood toys.

His plentiful and fruitful garden was once the image of perfection. However, once it was divided, it became the bitten apple, the doorway into all that is impure. All that is evil has been unveiled and Larry's utopia, diminished.

Teacher Comment on Raquel's Essay

Here is a lower-half paper. The excellent writing, the beautiful imagery, even the details from the novel cannot compensate for its almost complete disregard of the prompt. Irony, which is central to the question, is alluded to but once—and never developed. Nor are other literary techniques developed fully enough.

There is definite understanding of the book. However, this writer got off track and lost focus. She probably ran out of time, since most students write this essay last. (Our advice is to budget your time wisely. Perhaps some pre-planning would have helped her avoid the trap of digression.)

Because her writing is strong, it is possible that this essay would be bumped up to a 5 by the AP readers. But it clearly falls into the top of the lower half. It does not answer the prompt adequately.

Take from this essay one last reminder. We have said it before, but it bears repeating one more time: Make sure you understand the prompt, and make sure your essay addresses it.